Anthropology, Development and Modernities

While the diffusion of modernity and the spread of development schemes may bring prosperity, optimism and opportunity for some, for others it has brought poverty, a deterioration in quality of life and has given rise to violence. This collection brings an anthropological perspective to bear on understanding the diverse modernities we face in the contemporary world. It provides a critical review of interpretations of development and modernity, supported by rigorous case studies from regions as diverse as Guatemala, Sri Lanka, West Africa and contemporary Europe.

Together, the chapters in this volume demonstrate the crucial importance of looking to ethnography for guidance in shaping development policies. Ethnography can show how people's own agency transforms, recasts and complicates the modernities they experience. The contributors argue that explanations of change framed in terms of the dominant discourses and institutions of modernity are inadequate, and that we should give closer attention to discourses, images, beliefs and practices that run counter to these, yet play a part in shaping them and giving them meaning.

Anthropology, Development and Modernities deals with the realities of people's everyday lives and dilemmas. It is essential reading for students and scholars in anthropology, sociology and development studies. It should also be read by all those actively involved in development work.

Alberto Arce and **Norman Long** are both based in the Department of Sociology at Wageningen University in the Netherlands. Alberto Arce's research focuses on agricultural and environmental issues. Norman Long has developed an actor-oriented and interface approach to studying development and social change. Both have published widely.

Anthropology, Development and Modernities

Exploring discourses, counter-tendencies and violence

Edited by Alberto Arce and Norman Long

London and New York

First published 2000
by Routledge
11 New Fetter Lane, London EC4P 4EE

Simultaneously published in the USA and Canada
by Routledge
29 West 35th Street, New York, NY 10001

Selection and editorial matter © 2000 Alberto Arce and Norman Long
Individual contributions © 2000 the contributors

Typeset in Bembo by Taylor & Francis Books Ltd
Printed and bound in Great Britain by TJ International Ltd, Padstow,
Cornwall

British Library Cataloguing in Publication Data
A catalogue record for this book is available from the British Library

Library of Congress Cataloguing in Publication Data
Anthropology, development, and modernities: exploring discourses,
counter-tendencies, and violence/edited by Alberto Arce and Norman
Long.
Includes bibliographical references (p.) and index.
1. Applied anthropology–Developing countries. 2. Rural development–
Developing countries. 3. Economic development–Developing
countries. 4. Social change–Developing countries. 5. Violence–
Developing countries. 6. Developing countries–Social policy. 7.
Developing countries–Economic policy. I. Arce, Alberto, 1952– . II.
Long, Norman.
GN397.7.D44A47 1999
306'.091724–dc21   98–54357
                                                    CIP

ISBN 0–415–20499–2 (hbk)
ISBN 0–415–20500–X (pbk)

Contents

Contributors

Alberto Arce is Senior Lecturer in Development Sociology at Wageningen University, the Netherlands. His research interests focus upon the changing relationships between the state and rural producers, the globalisation of food, and environmental issues in Latin America and Africa. He is the author of *Negotiating Agricultural Development*, Wageningen Agricultural University, 1993, and has published a number of journal articles dealing with agrarian issues from an actor-oriented perspective. Until recently he was the managing editor of the *International Journal of Sociology of Agriculture and Food*.

Norman Long is Professor of Sociology of Development at Wageningen University, and has also held chairs at Durham and Bath Universities, UK. His work is best known for its actor-oriented and interface approach to the study of development processes. He has carried out anthropological research in Africa and Latin America. His most recent book publications are *Encounters at the Interface,* Wageningen Agricultural University, 1989, *Battlefields of Knowledge* (with Ann Long), Routledge, 1992, and (with Henk de Haan) *Images and Realities of Rural Life*, Van Gorcum, 1997.

Deniz Kandiyoti is Senior Lecturer in the Department of Development Studies at the School of Oriental and African Studies, London University. She has worked extensively on gender and development, feminist theory, nationalisms, Islam and the state in the Middle East and, more recently, on post-Soviet transformations in Central Asia. Her research is currently based in rural Uzbekistan. Recent publications include *Gendering the Middle East*, I.B. Tauris, 1996, and (in Turkish)*Concubines, Sisters and Citizens*, Metis, Istanbul, 1997.

Azza M. Karam is Senior Lecturer at the School of Politics and Centre of Ethnic Conflict, Queens University, Belfast, Northern Ireland. Until recently she managed the Middle East, Gender and Applied Research Programmes at the International Institute for Democracy and Electoral Assistance in Stockholm, Sweden, and prior to this was a research fellow at the University of Amsterdam. Her published books include *Women, Islamisms and the State,* Macmillan, 1997, and *Women in Parliaments: Beyond Numbers*, IDEA, Stockholm, 1998. She is currently co-editor of Critical Studies on Islam for Pluto Press.

Eleanor Fisher is a Research Officer at the Centre of Development Studies, University of Wales, Swansea. She is a social anthropologist specialising in poverty and environmental issues, natural resource management, rural livelihoods, and African development. She has carried out research on beekeeping and conservation issues in Western Tanzania, and has worked as the Fair Trade Co-ordinator for the Wiltshire Wildlife Trust. She has published on the global and fair trade aspects of beekeeping in *Beekeeping and Development*, 1996, and in the *International Journal of Sociology of Agriculture and Food,* 1997.

James Fairhead is Lecturer in Social Anthropology at the School of Oriental and African Studies, London University. His fieldwork, in former Zaire and the Republic of Guinea in West Africa, focuses on issues of fertility, productivity and health in crops and soils, on representations of environmental change, and on the formation of agricultural and environmental policy. His published books, *Misreading the African Landscape*, Cambridge, 1996, and *Reframing Deforestation*, Routledge, 1998, are both co-authored with Melissa Leach.

Pradeep Jeganathan is Assistant Professor of Anthropology and Global Studies at the University of Minnesota at Minneapolis/St Paul. He is co-editor with Quadri Ismail of *Unmaking the Nation: the Politics of Identity and History in Modern Sri Lanka*, Colombo, Social Scientists' Association, 1995, and with Partha Chatterjee of *Subaltern Studies XI: Writings on South Asian History and Society*, Delhi, Oxford University Press, forthcoming.

Finn Stepputat is a Senior Project Researcher at the Centre for Development Research, Copenhagen, Denmark. He is a geographer and cultural sociologist working on issues of armed conflict, mobility, and state formation. He has undertaken fieldwork in Mexico and Guatemala, and is currently developing research on processes of internal displacement in Peru, Colombia and Mozambique. His publications include *Beyond Relief: Life in a Guatemalan Refugee Settlement in Mexico,* Institute of Cultural Sociology, Copenhagen, 1992, and 'Politics of Displacement in Guatemala' in the *Journal of Historical Sociology*, 1999.

Ineke van Wetering is affiliated to the Amsterdam School for Social Science Research. She has conducted fieldwork among the Ndyuka Maroons in Surinam, and Creoles who form part of a European diaspora from Surinam. She has published on witchcraft and religious movements, and has co-authored (with H.U.E. Thoden van Velzen) *The Great Father and the Danger*, 1988.

Paul van Gelder is a sociologist/anthropologist from the University of Amsterdam affiliated to the Faculty of Political, Social and Cultural Studies. In 1984 he published a study of Paramaribo's informal sector called *Werken onder de Boom*. His current research interests cover the fields of drug abuse, ethnic minorities, irregular income activities, sexuality and prostitution.

Preface

The first seeds of this book were sown in December 1995, following a conference held by EIDOS (The European Inter-university Development Opportunities Study Group) at Wageningen in the Netherlands. The conference focused on the theme of 'globalisation and decivilisation'. The idea behind this topic was to depict the social paradoxes and counter-tendencies of the global diffusion of modernity in all its moments of promise, transgression and desire. We were looking for signposts that would not merely indicate the shortcomings and impossibilities of modernity but rather would reveal the ways in which locally-situated actors have appropriated and internalised the symbols, trappings and practices associated with modernity, in an attempt to reconstruct their own social worlds. In short, we wished to engage in a serious study of the dilemmas and refractions of contemporary 'modernising' processes. This, we hoped, would constitute the beginnings of a serious reflection on and criticism of the unattainable goals of 'progress' and its unforeseen and often uncontrollable implications and counter-tendencies.

We had envisaged that this theme would stimulate participants to offer observations and analysis on how it was that development and modernity could remain important conceptions in the vocabulary and practice of development and yet, at the same time, produce results of a highly ambiguous, contradictory and sometimes grotesque character. We provocatively portrayed these processes in terms of the interplay of globalisation and de-civilisation – a term which itself occasioned much heated debate and criticism, some polemical and some more reasoned and incisive.

Later, after much reflection, we decided to rethink some of the substantive issues raised in our conference discussions and to amplify the scope of our enquiry to embrace the larger concern of how precisely anthropology might contribute to an understanding of the 'multiple modernities' or so-called 'cultural hybrids' of contemporary global change and continuity. And of what might this anthropology consist? What exactly would be its epistemological, theoretical and methodological bearings? To address such questions, of course, is to enter a minefield of known but unresolved, or perhaps as yet insufficiently identified, dilemmas and complexities. These questions are not only confined to the field of development research but reach to the very heart of the anthropological endeavour itself. Mapping a path through such uncertain terrain clearly entails painstaking work and the dangers of falsely representing both intellectual positions and situated practices.

With this larger intellectual effort in mind, we decided to initiate the task by selecting a number of key papers drawn from the original EIDOS conference and to combine them with additional invited contributions to compose this book. On the basis of this we aimed to weave our way through the minefield and reposition ourselves vis-à-vis the worlds of development research and anthropology. In future publications we intend to explore and elaborate our points of view more fully. But here we adopt the more modest aim of arguing against those (mostly of a post-modernist persuasion) who are for the 'end of development' – as if the critical issues of social transformation and planned intervention are simply spirited away with the demise of developmentalism and the turn to neo-liberal thinking – and of elucidating how anthropological theory and methods can open up new and stimulating lines of enquiry that deal equally with the discursive, theoretical and pragmatic dimensions of our object of study.

Objectives, scope and thematic organisation of the volume

A first objective of this volume, therefore, is to provide some account of recent anthropological research on modernity and development. The general focus is to develop a comparative perspective on the constellations of people's beliefs and actions in their construction of diverse modernities.

The volume does not intend to offer a new and unified conceptual framework for the field of study. Rather, it presents new research findings and approaches that can serve to guide future studies and analysis. What is promising at this juncture is a new readiness to consider research across a range of topics and to question taken-for-granted assumptions. These concerns are at the forefront of many of the chapters of the book. The collective outcome is, we believe, an invigorating breath of fresh air on the relevance of people's experiences and predicaments, and an exploration of the question of reflexivity within the field of development studies.

The chapters of the book are interwoven around three central themes: 1) discourse and language representations of modernity; 2) disconnected constructions: state policy and people's counter-tendencies; and 3) violence and multiple modernities.

The book opens with a wide-ranging critical review of relevant literature on issues of development and modernity, with a view to delineating the contribution of anthropology and the value of ethnography in developing new perspectives and understandings in the field of development and social change. This is followed in Chapter 2 by an analysis of how languages of development acquire diverse meanings in different locales – in the institutions and practices of international development agencies, as well as at the level of local producers and the ways in which they operationalise information technology for accessing the market and consolidating their relations with 'global' actors.

In Chapter 3 the case of the Soviet East is analysed, where the coexistence of various facets of 'tradition' and 'modernity' provide a baseline for actors to construct a range of paradoxical discourses that deal, on the one hand, with political 'Russification', and on the other, with the demands of Islamic cultural practice. This situation has crystallised around struggles over issues of re-territorialisation and cultural self-preservation in relation to the constitution of new ethnic and national scenarios and identities. As a companion piece to this Russian example, Chapter 4 discusses the contrasting and sometimes violent discourses within Islam that are both transnational and global in scope. Such phenomena contribute to the time–space compression of Islamic socio-cultural idioms, offering relatively unhindered access to and interpretation of fundamentalist thinking. An important dimension relevant to both cases is the unpredictable potential for conflict, which arises from the crisis of legitimacy in Western development discourses.

Chapter 5 offers an interpretation of the interplay of idioms and practices associated with the outbreaks of sleeping sickness and the resettlement programmes in colonial Tanganyika. Although government justified resettlement in terms of the health concerns of the local population, the chapter highlights the issues of setting up territorial control and imposing procedures to 'purify' local environments. This process is contrasted with the ways in which the Muchape anti-witchcraft movement responded to the presence of the disease and to colonial intervention. Parallel anthropological observations have been made for present-day central Africa (Long 1998) where local counter-narratives have arisen in response to 'expert' knowledge and practice regarding the management of natural resources.

This discussion of how local people depict intervention and modernity and interpret change through the construction of local narratives is followed by Chapter 6 which explores how the elaboration of 'problems', 'solutions' and 'the path to development' in West Africa becomes disconnected – both discursively and pragmatically – from natural and social science, as well as from 'field realities'. This is illustrated by reference to the way in which the state bureaucracies have represented issues of 'nature' and 'the environment' through perpetuating a narrative linking deforestation, climatic desiccation and soil sterilisation with human impoverishment, which has constantly shaped and justified West African forest reservation and conservation policies.

A third theme of the book centres on violence as part of the increasingly diversified, volatile and global world. As a counter-tendency to modernity, violence sets loose a chain of critical events in which social, political and economic practices tend to escape institutional control. While our comprehension of violent events is, of course, significantly shaped by global media, still we do not agree on how to characterise these trends. Bodies, death and silence have persisted during the whole of the last decade in continents as far apart as Asia, Africa and Latin-America. The 'state of emergency' has become not the exception but the rule for the majority of people in the world. Issues of social order and governability give rise to new forms of communal violence and the re-construction of the 'internal boundaries' of the nation-state. Alongside this, we witness the emergence and development of new heterogeneous links between localities and centres of economic growth, authority, power and knowledge that go beyond the traditional mapping and social interactions of local, regional and national spaces. In several instances, individual and political violence is the condition or property of 'new' communal identities and religious revival.

In Chapter 7, violence surfaces explicitly as a property of multiple contemporary modernities in accounts of Sri Lankan ethnic strife, which produced both alliance and rupture between ethnicities, showing how particular identities were constructed around struggles over conceptions of political autonomy and modernity. This argument challenges dominant narratives of progress and development by creating a critical counter-representation to those narratives from within discourses of violence.

These excesses of modernity also reveal themselves in the management of the 'frontiers' and in the 'displacement of people' by the modern state of post-war Guatemala. Chapter 8 discusses the meaning of violence and the 'politics of space' in a territory where the modern nation-state was not able to establish and legitimise modern techniques of government and individual surveillance and control. The massacres in Guatemala transgressed the traditional limits of violence between the public and the private, and became a tactic aimed at achieving a spatial organisation that would facilitate the army's control over the population whilst containing violence in manageable spaces (areas of 'wilderness').

Chapter 9 pictures the plight of young Surinamese migrants who, in the face of the unfulfilled promises of modernity in their home country, arrived in Amsterdam where they were unable to become integrated into 'mainstream' life and opportunities. Instead, they developed orientations to the double *anomie* of cultural rejection by both their 'native' and 'host' societies. This induced their families to draw upon existing beliefs in a magical world inhabited by traditional/modern avenging spirits and zombies. Far from being a contradictory tendency to modernity, this counter-tendency emerged as a vital force in the lives of these international migrants in late twentieth century Europe.

In Chapter 10 modernity is seen as a tendency that populates all spheres and interstices of the globe. The analysis focuses upon the case of a globalised commodity – that of coca/cocaine – in the Chapare area of the Cochabamba region of Bolivia. The study of the cultivation and processing of this illegal crop provides the opportunity to argue that all societies contain within them a multiplicity of rationalities that may or may not run counter to dominant interests. The arguments stress the view that counter-tendencies of modernisation involve a constant rearrangement or re-assembling that takes precedent over so-called 'externalities' which involve a shift of knowledge and types of social ordering from 'without' to 'within'. These transformations, the authors suggest, can be described as social mutations that are self organising and transforming rather than hybrid entities of mixed ancestry.

The final chapter, Chapter 11, contributes to the problematisation of 'globalisation' and local/global relations and representations of modernity. It then identifies a way forward conceptually and methodologically for analysing these processes. The discussion ends with a brief account of how these concepts and insights can be applied to research on transnational migration.

Among the many questions posed by the authors are the following: how do dominant or hegemonic discourses of modernity or tradition underpin locally situated processes of social change, development, knowledge and practice? Are the social contradictions and transformations of multiple modernities conditioned by the same set of cultural factors that legitimise intervention? Is the faith in progress a taken-for-granted factor in the growing ignorance that depoliticises development, reifies the 'realities' and subjectivities of local people, and erases significant cultural and political difference? Are we to replace the historical and relative terms 'modernity' and 'tradition' with a more general distinction between 'global' and 'local'? Do Third World and other endogenous cases of modernity offer any alternatives for looking at policy options in a fresh way?

Alberto Arce and Norman Long
Teffont Magna and Bennekom
15 September 1998

Acknowledgements

Like similar collective ventures, this volume has been slow in coming but nonetheless worthwhile since it represents a critical reflection on development and anthropology – an idea that was at the heart of the very conception of the EIDOS group and its meetings, and also close to our own intellectual inclinations. In Wageningen we are sometimes seen as being intellectually too aggressive because we always take a strong stance against simplistic and reductionist diagnoses of the 'modern condition', as well as against theories that deny (even if implicitly) the force of people's own capacities and abilities to intervene and shape the contours of social life. Hence, we emphasise the centrality of self-organising processes, both for change and continuity. Fortunately, we are not anymore alone in this endeavour, as this book itself amply demonstrates.

The process of bringing this collection to fruition was certainly not an easy task. Soon after we committed ourselves to producing the book, we became aware of the necessity of engaging others – outside the original EIDOS 'club'- whose work bore directly on the central themes of anthropology, development and modernities. These new intellectual companions helped us to place the original papers that addressed issues of 'development' and 'decivilisation' into a new and refreshing framework of thinking based upon rich ethnographies of development discourses, counter-tendencies and violence. This revitalised and brought to blossom the theoretical potential of the original idea of the conference, whose various contributors at times verged on the brink of simply reinforcing postmodernist and sometimes nihilist assumptions and postures. Thus, by combining both selected conference and non-conference papers, it became possible to construct what we consider to be an interesting and challenging volume.

In this struggle to create something of value – which we ourselves could engage with and assemble – we received much encouragement from David Parkin of the Institute of Social Anthropology, Oxford University, and Terry Marsden of the Department of Urban and Regional Planning, the University of Wales, Cardiff. Though each originates from different spectrums of the field of social science, they enthusiastically supported our project from the very beginning. David is a committed anthropologist interested in the intertwining of processes of cultural continuity and transformation, and Terry, a social geographer who is as much at home among policy scientists and planners as among skeptical sociologists and nitty-gritty anthropologists. We thank them both for their insightful appreciation of what we were trying to achieve with this book.

In addition, we would like to acknowledge the support we had from the Routledge editors who were quick to realise that here was a good idea in the making, even if commonsense advised against backing the enterprise when it was still in a formative stage. We especially wish to thank Vicky Peters for perceiving the relevance of the issues we were debating for revitalising the anthropology of development – a field which must necessarily straddle both theories and practices of development, while at the same time avoiding the naiveties and perils of social engineering.

A further obstacle we had to overcome was that of finding enough time to gather together the various contributions, edit them and frame them analytically. The paradox of being workaday academics these days is that one hardly has time to devote oneself effectively to reading and writing: these vital activities often get sidelined by heavy teaching and administrative responsibilities. Yet, fortunately, we have been able to rely on the multifaceted skills of Ann Long, who combines an insider knowledge and empathy for anthropological work with an amazing dexterity for redrafting and editing texts so that they come to life in sometimes unexpected ways. She also made every effort to get us to meet deadlines. We thank her for her resilience in dealing with two well-meaning but stubborn characters.

Alberto Arce and Norman Long
Teffont Magna and Bennekom
15 September 1998

1 Reconfiguring modernity and development from an anthropological perspective

Alberto Arce and Norman Long

After a long period when development economics, normative policy debates and political science dominated the field of development studies, the 1990s have ushered in a more open intellectual climate which is more receptive to locating the analysis of development within theoretical frameworks that deal explicitly with the dynamics of cross-cultural practices, meanings and discourses. These new approaches to development and local/global relationships underline the importance of analysing how knowledge and power are constituted and reconfigured.[1]

From its inception, anthropology has struggled with the problem of how to engage with and represent other cultures whilst trying to understand and move away from its own historical roots in Western rationality and the commitment to 'progress' (Marcus & Fischer 1986). Though this dilemma remains with us, the present volume provides new anthropological perspectives on the encounter between Western visions of modernity and the *modi operandi* of other cultural repertoires. The various contributions also compel us to seek imaginative connections between the so-called 'good' and 'ugly' sides of development, and they help us to understand the complex intercultural and now increasingly global scales of contemporary change and development, and their counter-tendencies.

We build upon Hobart's (1993) contention that systematic modes of 'ignorance' arise out of the specialisation and thus fragmentation of development expertise, and from the inappropriateness of rationalistic assumptions in assessing the success or otherwise of economies and social systems. But, at the same time, our argument goes beyond the discussion of the nature of 'expert' knowledge and the power of science. It explores how the ideas and practices of modernity are themselves appropriated and re-embedded in locally-situated practices, thus accelerating the fragmentation and dispersal of modernity into constantly proliferating modernities. These 'multiple modernities' (Comaroff & Comaroff 1993: 1) generate powerful counter-tendencies to what is conceived of as Western modernisation, exhibiting so-called 'distorted' or 'divergent' patterns of development, and re-assembling what is often naively designated as 'tradition'. In this respect the book challenges existing interpretations of contemporary social change that emphasise either the 'end' or the 'incompleteness' of modernity, by replacing this line of reasoning with a careful analysis of localised practices that focuses on the ongoing reworkings of modernity from within. In this way we document and show the significance of processes of dismembering and reconfiguring Western ideology, discipline and techniques of modernity.

In pursuing this line of analysis we try, wherever possible, to differentiate clearly between 'modernity' as a metaphor for new or emerging 'here-and-now' materialities, meanings and cultural styles seen in relation to the notion of some past state of things (cf. Comaroff & Comaroff 1993: xiii) and 'modernisation' as a comprehensive package of technical and institutional measures aimed at widespread societal transformation and underpinned by neo-evolutionary theoretical narratives. Whereas modernity entails self-organising and transforming practices in different strata and sectors of society, modernisation is normally a policy initiative undertaken and implemented by cosmopolitan administrative and technological elites (national or international).

The above observations suggest that, as a field of enquiry and practical endeavour, development studies is clearly in need of a theoretical overhaul.[2] In order to achieve this, there is a desperate need for more ethnographically-informed research inputs, something that international development institutions have seldom been much interested in financing. Thus, it has fallen to anthropologists and other field-based researchers to fill the gap, and to bring their findings into public debate whenever they have wished to reshape or contest current policy measures that threaten the livelihoods or human rights of affected populations. At the same time, there is a need for researchers to rethink critically the nature of anthropological research in a global era, and the kinds of contribution that anthropology can make to issues of development and modernity.

As we have noted in the Preface, this book forms part of a larger intellectual project which in part has emerged out of the 1995 EIDOS conference on 'globalisation and de-civilisation'. A positive result of this meeting was an increased awareness of the urgency of defining new analytical approaches to the confrontation between Western trajectories of modernity and various 'localised' counter-representations, -discourses and -practices. For example, several of the cases presented at the conference exposed the contradictory character of Western discourses on modernity and globality, which give promise of access to new forms of knowledge and resources, but often end up denying that local people can in fact think, argue and act for themselves. On the other hand, other contributions were able to show, through detailed ethnography, how modernity was 'reworked from within' by local actors who appropriated the symbols, practices and trappings associated with it, thus combining 'modern' with so-called 'traditional' features, sometimes in grotesque hybrid forms.

What the conference was unable to achieve, however, was a systematic theoretical rethinking and reconceptualisation of how different discourses, values and practices associated with notions of 'modernity' and 'tradition' intersect and are intertwined in the everyday encounters and experiences of people from diverse socio-cultural backgrounds.

This issue is central to understanding the blending and juxtapositioning of elements of modernity and tradition in the creation of various modernities. Such a perspective requires the recognition of what Strathern (1991) calls 'partial connections', whereby people, ideas and representations of space and time are interconnected but are never totally symmetrical or fully integrated. From this point of view, modernity as a particular assemblage of social and discursive practices carries only traces of similitude with other instantiations, and is never entirely consistent and coherent. Instead it is characterised by a heterogeneous dynamism wherein ambivalence and ambiguity make it possible for differences of interests and knowledge to be contained within provisional arrangements that allow for the resolution of the practicalities of everyday life (Parkin 1995). Because problems arise from the uncertainties and fragilities of the connections, the constant re-positioning of actors vis-à-vis each other and critical events generates a series of social and epistemic interfaces in which discontinuities are managed through such practices as deferral, accommodation, negotiation, selective appropriation, and distantiation or absenteeism (Long 1989, 1997).

These notions are central to our characterisation of 'localised modernities', which we discuss later in the chapter in relation to the need for a reflexive anthropology of modernity and development. The task of getting to grips theoretically and methodologically with these processes amounts to nothing less than an appreciation and theorisation of the ways in which anthropology and ethnography can contribute to development research and practice. The present volume signals the need for a re-invigoration and re-orientation of development research, and for anthropologists to take stock of their possible roles in this. But its scope remains limited to identifying ways forward analytically, and to illustrating our argument by reference to a series of ethnographically rich and theoretically perceptive anthropological cases.

One of the more testing issues with which development researchers have to struggle concerns the significance and potency of 'official' discourses of development as compared to the strategies and language games of local people who face new and increasingly global social relations. This poses the following interrelated questions. Whose narratives and visions of the world can be considered more persuasive or 'valid' in terms of how they represent change, continuity and critical problems? How do the different discourses and discursive practices interrelate or interface? Are they simply mutually untranslatable and incommensurable, or is there some possible middle ground? While it is possible in an abstract philosophical sense to lay bare the epistemological bases of 'expert' versus 'lay' or 'indigenous' knowledge (as Hobart has eloquently done), does this help us to comprehend the ongoing processes of translation and mediation involving different actors and different knowledge domains? How can the anthropologist capture the dynamics of these situations and processes? How can one deal theoretically and pragmatically with the partial connections, ambiguities and incompatibilities in meanings and social practices? How can the researcher construct a convincing narrative of events and outcomes that does full, or at least adequate, justice to these complexities? And how can this be done in such a way that political decision-makers and practitioners of planning and policy implementation will take serious cognisance of the researcher's narrative and its implicit or explicit policy recommendations?

These questions are inevitably raised by any attempt to evaluate development processes, which present themselves incessantly and disturbingly in the beguiling faces of modernity, especially when ideas of modernity are internalised by local actors and appear in the assumptions that guide local practices, expectations and even conversations with researchers. This state of affairs has de-centred the once-assumed homogeneous Western modernisation path to development and has increased our awareness of the multiplicity of forms of modernity. Thus, it is important to re-analyse the issue of modernity, but this time through the lens of its counter-tendencies. That this is an increasingly important intellectual task is well captured in the words of Smart: '[I]t is one which, of necessity, must simultaneously embrace an analysis of existing institutional forms and developments, as well as an elaboration of potential alternative social futures immanent in the present' (1992: 27). In other words, focusing on the counter-tendencies of modernity enables us to incorporate reflexivity and something of the post-modern critical perspective into the field of development studies.

Modernity and development: models and myths

In the most general sense, the term 'modern' connotes a sense of belonging to the present and an awareness of a past to which people can link and at the same time distantiate themselves. In this way, historical or pseudo-historical continuities are constructed and justified. Thus, as Habermas (1983) has suggested, the linguistic term 'modern', from the Latin *modernus*, has since the latter part of the fifth century in Europe 'appeared and reappeared', each time re-emerging as Europeans underwent a process of representing a 'new epoch' by refurbishing their relationship to the ancients. To illustrate this point, Habermas gives the example of the uses of the term in the fifth century, when it was deployed by the new Roman converts to Christianity to differentiate themselves from two types of 'barbarians' – the heathens of antiquity and the Jews, and in the Renaissance to imply learning and a cultivated life style with links back to the classical Greek and Roman civilisations. Later, during the renaissance of the seventeenth and eighteenth centuries, 'modernity' was again reinvented to characterise science, rationalism and the pursuit of 'progress' – meanings that still have considerable currency at the end of the twentieth century. This history of the term is useful, since it is suggestive of how one might explore within development studies the unfolding of various theories and visions heralding a common (hegemonic?) picture of social change and temporality.

Development studies arose as a distinctive field of study only after 1945, when Western experts became concerned with the modernisation of the colonial territories and newly-emerging independent countries. At that time, the strategic idea of modernity was organised around attitudes and policies based on a sense of the superiority of those nations that had successfully modernised themselves. Thus, the emulation of 'civilisation' (or modernity) over designated 'barbarism' constituted the construction of a notion of 'time' (modern) which simultaneously posited the so-called 'backward' or 'underdeveloped' countries (later exalted as the 'Third World') as representing an earlier stage of technological inferiority and ignorance (due principally to their lack of scientific knowledge and modern legal-rational institutions). This had the implication that the 'modernisation project' could offer them the help they needed to 'catch up'. This representation expressed more than the desire for change in these countries. It implied the establishment of a new optic on the value and practical use of local traditions: thus aid policies and planning models of the industrialised countries, promoted by international organisations and underpinned by academic research, sought to identify and eradicate the various 'traditional' cultural and institutional obstacles that were assumed to block 'progress'. In this way, a 'developmentalist' relationship with Third World traditions was established and legitimised. Any idea of there having existed specific types of modernity linked to the past in these countries[3] before the arrival of colonial rule and development aid was denied. Yet, in a paradoxical twist, the transfer to the Third World of European and American fabricated modernities was even more abstracted and removed from local social and political realities than its parent varieties, and consequently, the policies and belief in the power of science and technology were seldom questioned. From this perspective, the prerequisites of social development could only be achieved through the replication of successful European and American experiences and models. This situation was the beginning of a modern regime of discipline in the development field constituted by its special relation with what were conceived of as ahistorical and reified 'traditional' societies, whose exoticism revealed to the West the need for these 'backward' societies to strive for development and cultural modernity.

This modernist disposition inspired a narrative concerning the way to achieve rapid economic development in Third World countries. The theory which best captures the spirit of the times is that of W.W. Rostow (1960) who put forward an evolutionary taxonomy of five stages through which countries had to pass in order to reach the modern condition, and his famous characterisation of the pre-conditions for 'take-off'. The latter marks the turning point at which new values and social institutions finally inject economic motives into people's lives, infecting tradition with modernism and establishing economic growth as a normal condition of progress. According to this narrative, the model for underdeveloped countries is the West, particularly the US. This denotes one of the origins for Western romanticism, as applied to the field of development.

Such optimistic evolutionism inherent to modernisation became the dominant theoretical narrative of the West from the 1950s into the early 1960s. Arthur Lewis (1954), one of the founders of development economics, argued that to achieve economic growth it was necessary to mobilise resources (capital and labour) out of the traditional sector into the incipient modern one. According to him, progress refers not only to the transcendence of tradition, but also to the use of the organisation of the economy's modern sector as a beacon for the successes of modernisation.

In modernisation theory, economic, technological and demographic conditions, and the organisation of appropriate social institutions and value frameworks, were located as functionally segmented orders, and treated by experts as separate from the multifarious, and at times contradictory, experiences and practices of everyday life. Such a segmented view of the social world could not allow for how viable social organisation might exist outside defined 'systems' in the form of multiplex relations that cross-cut several institutional domains, as anthropological studies had clearly demonstrated.

As a theoretical model of social change, modernisation theory has of course been assessed many times and is now widely recognised as seriously flawed,[4] but for the purposes of our argument one further observation is required. This concerns the fact that, whether or not one accepts the heuristic value of the model of segmented orders, a reworking of modernity values and practices takes place through the ways in which various social actors and groups process and act upon their experiences, thus re-constituting or transforming existing 'localised' situations, cultural boundaries and knowledge. This often results in the opposition or negation (not always directly) of the culture and knowledge of the expert or intervenor in favour of well-tried local ways and understandings, and through the appropriation and re-interpretation of modern idioms, technologies and organising practices. Hence, it becomes necessary to analyse the differentiated and uneven social patchwork that interconnects local with various modernising scenarios.

Yet, despite the above critical remarks directed at the excesses and short-comings of modernisation theory, it is unlikely in the foreseeable future that the problematic of modernity will disappear entirely from the field of development studies. It would be difficult, for example, to imagine that the language of post-modernism or a new futurology could easily dislodge modernity from its position in the lexicons of social change and political ideology. Indeed, the more closely one looks into this matter, the more evident it is that we must continue to grapple with the problems of how best to describe and analyse the plethora of modernities that now characterise change in the global era. At one time it was supposed that one might be able to construct some kind of genealogy of modernity, like the call for 'a genealogy of capitalism'. Today it would seem – given the enormous diversity and self-transforming nature of modern cultures – that a more urgent analytical issue is that of understanding better the processes by which highly heterogeneous social forms are constructed on the basis of an assemblage of diverse cultural elements, including the ideas and practices of modernity.

An ethnographic re-positioning of modernity

It is here that Latour's (1993) argument in *We have never been Modern* is highly pertinent. Latour contends that notions of modernity depend upon the dichotomisation of 'nature' and 'culture', and 'people' and 'things'. Such a conception fails to acknowledge the complex and heterogeneous mixing of nature-culture and human–nonhuman. This he attributes to the 'purification' principle of conventional science, which hides from view and sanitises certain critical activities and processes that are variously composed of human, cultural, material, and nonhuman elements. In this manner, specific domains of activity are artificially sealed off from each other – a procedure akin to what we have described as the segmented model of modernisation theory. Thus science, politics, economics, technology, the environment, religion, etc. acquire their own operating principles and explanatory 'laws', with the consequence that we are prevented from comprehending the manifold ways in which modernity in fact reproduces itself as a complex set of ideas and practices through the proliferation of hybrid forms.

In Latour's (1993: 7) opinion it is anthropology, with its stress on the 'seamless fabric' of lived experience, that has made it possible to construct narratives which weave 'together the way people regard the heavens and their ancestors, the way they build houses and the way they grow yams or manioc or rice, the way they construct their government and their cosmology'; and which therefore challenges us to adopt a new critical stance towards issues of modernity based upon a combination of the ethnographic method with insights from post-modernism.[5]

Post-modernist writings often stress the epistemological uncertainties of the ethnographic method by inflating the centrality of 'the ethnographer's own meditations on the self and on the destiny of the ethnographic work' (Parkin 1995: 145). But we should not react to this by replacing post-modernist critique with a naive neo-positivist reassertion of the value of ethnography. Rather, as Parkin (1995: 144) cogently puts it, the starting point for anthropological enquiry should be 'ethnographic ambiguities and initial untranslatability [of different cultures], as we seek to transcend existing comparative frameworks and assumptions. This renunciation of theorising from uncontextualised hypotheses removes initial security, but offers greater if more frustrating challenges'.

The defence of ethnography should not then simply depend upon the veneration of the founding father, Malinowski, and his disciples who are credited with its 'invention' and dissemination, but rather on the creativity and critical reflexivity of present-day researchers using and developing the ethnographic approach in an attempt to come to grips with the predicaments and struggles – theoretical and practical – of contemporary social life. Since the method is grounded in the detailed observation and interpretation of the ongoing lived experiences of particular individuals and groups, it necessarily confronts the complexities, uncertainties and ambiguities of actions, beliefs and values. It characteristically does this in 'real-life' situations in which the researcher himself or herself participates.

Good ethnography, therefore, must 'repudiate the idea of the detached and "objective" or "neutral" observer, the search for over-arching and systemic socio-cultural orders, and the denial of the importance of the experiential and subjective in social life' (Long & Long 1992: x). Indeed its strength lies in fully acknowledging the 'battlefields' of knowledge and power wherein a multiplicity of actors engage in struggles over the meanings and practicalities of livelihoods, values and organising processes. It thus implies detailed and systematic treatment of how the life-worlds of the researcher and other social actors intersect in the production of specific ethnographies and types of interpretation. Central to this is the attempt to theorise these processes through the elaboration of actor-grounded constructs that aim to reveal the variable, composite and provisional nature of social life, to explore the practical and discursive forms of consciousness and social action that compose it, and to expose the socially-constructed and continuously negotiated nature of knowledge and intervention processes.

Here, the concept of 'counterwork' introduced by Parkin (1995: 144) in his study of the intertwining of religious and medical knowledge and practice (Islamic and non-Islamic) acquires significance. He conceptualises 'counterwork' 'as the rebounding effects of knowledge in its diversity' which, he argues, sheds light on the complex ways in which specific knowledge practices (in this case relating to how to deal with particular 'ailments') are constructed and re-transposed or re-accentuated, both within and outside the patient/doctor consultations that take place. Unlike structural models of knowledge construction which see this process as an outcome of the interaction of culturally distinct knowledge categories or systems, Parkin (1995: 148) highlights the blending together and the 'relocation of the origins of beliefs and behaviour', as people engage in counterwork that involves the interplay of 'hegemonic' and 'non-hegemonic' discourses and values – irrespective of whether they emanate from global or local scenarios. Counterwork is also, of course, a feature of anthropological field-work since the ethnographer is part of the rebounding effects of knowledge and experience. Hence, we should look to ethnography for the inspiration to realise a more grounded and reflexive anthropology of development. We will return to this issue later in the chapter.

The notion of counterwork can also be applied more generally to rethink how one might understand how multiple modernities are generated. Counterwork against and within modernity is embedded in particular histories and situations that are part of the wider process of Western expansion. Studies of such counterwork can inform us about the tendencies of modernisation, of which they are of course an integral part. In other words, they help us to understand the re-organising processes that arise with the expansion of the West and the significance of counter-tendencies for those who experience these 'new realities'.

The spurts and counter-spurts of modernity

It is at this point useful to recall Elias's (1994, original German text of 1939) analysis of the emergence of the modern, bourgeois, Western world, whose roots he traces to the conduct and rationality of the royal and aristocratic courts of the Middle Ages. In depicting what he designates 'the civilising process', Elias emphasises how court society 'developed a civilising and cultural physiognomy which was taken over by professional-bourgeois society partly as a heritage and partly as an antithesis, and preserved in this way, was further developed' (The Court Society 1983 [1969]). Hence, we have the intricate manoeuvres of courtly life, which aimed at exhibiting one's position and status through various mannerisms and forms of ostentatious consumption, and which were later transformed into patterns of 'conspicuous consumption' and status competition among sectors of the professional bourgeoisie, even though the latter were at the same time committed to the pursuit of economic gain on the basis of legal-rational and bureaucratic types of rationality.

Related to this argument about the coexistence and interplay of contrasting courtly and bourgeois styles is Elias's more general insistence that social change takes place in 'a long sequence of spurts and counter-spurts' (1994: 469). Nor does it follow a straight line: it generates 'repeatedly greater or lesser counter-movements in which the contrasts in society and the fluctuations in the behaviour of individuals, their effective outbreaks, increase again' (Elias 1994: 462). This has constituted the form in which Western civilisation has spread and its institutions have developed. Here, the result of social change is seen as both reducing and amplifying the contrasts between the West and those places that are 'beyond the West'.

One critical outcome has been the fusion (through the diffusion of technology, education and cultural styles) of class patterns of conduct between, for example, 'the functionally upper classes with those of the rising classes' in order to establish the instruments of Occidental superiority and dominance. This process is dependent on the precise forms of dominance and the position that the group or region occupies within the large network of differentiated functions of the modern West. From our point of view, this notion of fusion permits one to focus on the new unique entities that constitute the spread of 'civilised conduct' (1994: 463). But, at the same time, modernity (or 'civilisation' as Elias terms it) increases the 'varieties or nuances' within itself, as clearly witnessed during the period of colonial rule. Colonisation epitomises the spread of 'civilised standards' of modernity and the way that local people blend the influence of modernity into their own 'traditional' idioms.[6] Yet, despite the pervasiveness of such processes of counterwork, the greater efficacy of the technology through which modernity manifests itself is seldom challenged. Rather, the key feature is that people reposition these elements within their own familiar contexts. In doing so, they de-essentialise them of their superior power, creating distinctive social spaces where contests for authority are fought out, often as a prelude to new power claims.

It becomes apparent, then, that within universalistic Western patterns of conduct, local contrasts emerge. The behaviour of actors and their capacity to re-position the modern within the familiar constitutes one of the facets of the rapid and constant transformation that Western modernity brings. Hand-in-hand with this local capacity to encompass Western society goes a critical attitude against what is seen as Western. This generates a dynamism which is represented through fusion, blending and counter-movements to modernity, entailing the disembedding of Western civilised standards and their re-embedding within various local (and sometimes distinctly 'non-Western') representations of modernity. In this way, the West has always been confronted by questions that challenge the existence of a singular and fully encompassing modernity or civilisation.

In this respect, we are compelled to reassess the concept of social change, especially now that older notions of Western development are in demise just at the point when they have reached their zenith of success. The study of the counterworks of modernisation opens up the possibility of analysing creative breaks within the premises and contours of orthodox concepts of economic development, and in the face of market expansion and the uncontested optimism of neo-liberal representations of development. The importance of Elias's vista is that it helps us to appreciate the relevance of the varieties of socio-cultural forms and repertoires inherent to the development of world modernities. Treating these as fundamentally endogenous to the processes of change is in certain respects more convincing than the presently fashionable use of 'cultural hybridity' (Werbner 1997), which evokes the image of the fabrication of new forms through the assembling and pasting together of discrete traits or fragments. We will explicate this point later when we propose an alternative interpretation in Chapter 12, based on the idea of the 'mutants of modernities'.

Heterogeneity as a counterpoint of values

Let us now consider how heterogeneity relates to social conflict and value discrepancies. In order to pursue this, we begin with a brief review of Wertheim's (1965) discussion of counterpoint processes.

He begins by sketching out the treatment of social conflict in certain classical anthropological works on tribal societies, from which he draws the conclusion that, by and large, they were committed to a strong social integrationist point of view that saw antagonisms between social categories and groups as functional or structurally necessary for the society as a whole. Thus, Radcliffe-Brown never allows for institutionalised aggression or bantering (such as that common in 'joking relationships') to spill over into actual strife that would permanently disrupt or destroy existing social arrangements. Similarly, Evans-Pritchard developed a model of conflict resolution based on the principle of the balanced opposition of structurally equivalent lineage segments that played down the existence of major internal and external power differentials.[7] Even Gluckman and Turner, who attempted to show how African societies were shaped by the encroachment of the market, Western values and colonial rule, could not in the end extract themselves from the seduction of the equilibrium model, and thus failed to provide a satisfactory analysis of social transformations and discrepancies in cultural values.

According to Wertheim (1965: 25–6), it was only with Leach's study of Kachin society in highland Burma that a clear shift in focus away from organic and institutional equilibrium models took place. Leach conceived of social change as a consequence of the interlocking and oscillation of conflicting value systems present in Kachin society, and not as driven primarily by external forces. Although Leach does not always make absolutely clear in his monograph when he is writing about ideal-typical representations and when about concrete political events and constellations, Wertheim nevertheless builds upon Leach's contribution to offer his own theorisation of society and social change. He starts with the observation that society is never a 'completely integrated entity' since in any community there exist forms of protest in conflict with the current hierarchical structure. These protests are based on sets of values 'which function as a kind of counterpoint to the leading melody' (Wertheim 1965: 26). He characterises counterpoint as composed of 'deviant' values that, in some way or other, are institutionally contained. They therefore do not directly threaten the integrity of society, although they remain potentially the locus for the development of new sets of practices that can seriously disrupt existing social hierarchies.

Wertheim's central point then is that '[t]he dynamic processes of change can never be understood if the opposing value systems within society are not taken into full account'(1965: 32). He develops his argument by reference to certain types of public performance in Bali[8] that caricature or ridicule the principle of status hierarchy and challenge the position and life style of the Hinduised aristocrats. Also, popular stories often focus on the feats of local heroes who successfully hoodwink their feudal lords. Given the right conditions, these counterpoint sentiments may lead to active resistance against ruling groups and eventually to changes in the social order.

What is required sociologically in understanding these processes is a careful analysis of the circumstances under which the amplification of counterpoint values leads to the challenging of existing institutional arrangements. Wertheim briefly discusses this in reference to Margaret Mead's (1956) restudy of Manus society undertaken some twenty-odd years after her original field-work, during which time the islanders had experienced extensive contact with the West. One striking change Mead noted during her first field-work was the discrepancy between the cultures of children and adults: 'the child's world formed a kind of counterpoint to the acquisitive adult world, a more or less separate subculture in the total fabric of Manus culture' (Wertheim 1965: 32). But by the 1950s, the relationship between these two worlds had shifted from 'a universal polarity between generations into a true conflict of generations' (Wertheim 1965: 32–3).

Although schematic and simple in argument, and lacking detailed empirical elaboration, Wertheim's discussion of counterpoint values is clearly relevant to the analysis of the social construction of modernities. In the first place, he criticises researchers for the tendency to assume that values in society always converge into some unitary and dominant hierarchical system. Such an assumption, he argues, over-estimates the homogeneity of social values and fails to address the contrasting subjectivities and perceptions of society and of status found among different segments of society. In contrast to hierarchical models of society, and '[i]nstead of searching exclusively for integrative expedients', he maintains that 'we should with equal intellectual force try to detect strains and conflicts in society, as possible agents in future change' (1965: 35). He is also concerned to research how members of the different segments of society come to perceive their positions vis-à-vis each other, and how they use specific value repertoires for managing these relations.

Wertheim's treatment of value differentiation and competition using the concept of counterpoint complements Parkin's notion of counterwork. Like the social practices associated with the latter, heterogeneous counterpoint values are present as emergent properties of people-acting-in-settings, and as such they also constitute the conditions in which further actions and value choices are embedded. Everyday life is inherently pregnant with a wide range of contrasting as well as overlapping values, and to a degree people steer their way through them. The analytical challenge is to identify the boundaries, conditions and implications of choice. We need to explain, for example, why certain notions of modernity are considered less efficacious than 'non-modern' beliefs and values in reference to specific problematic situations or action-contexts. And, on the other hand, we must explore the manner in which modernity discourses and institutions have contributed to the undermining of existing authorities and forms of political control and cultural legitimation.[9]

These issues of heterogeneity and value discrepancy are best explored through the study of specific life-situations or critical events in which certain modes of authority are constructed, contested and/or reconstructed by people struggling to give some order, goals and targets to their lives, and thus to legitimise their actions. In short, we should examine the formulation, negotiation and implementation of rules, procedures, laws, and timetables which aim to frame how people 'talk' and 'do things' in order to make effective particular regimes of discipline, whilst at the same time giving meaning to their own individual life-worlds made up of a host of fears and expectations.

As we have suggested in previous publications (Long 1989; Arce & Long 1993), a useful methodological approach for getting to grips with these different and entangled life-worlds is through the identification of fields of interface. Life-worlds exist as specific time, space and experiential configurations (Arce 1997: 180), where some coexist, some clash, some mix, and others separate or retreat into themselves. This generates different combinational patterns, which are variously described in the literature as 'syncretism', 'hybridisation', 'creolisation', and 'cyborgs', each being a specific form of synthesising material, cultural, organisational and human combinations.[10]

In the next section we take two illustrations - one concerning African witchcraft practices in relation to processes of modernisation and the distribution of power, and the other dealing with the dissolving of boundaries due to the expansion of agro-export production in the US and Mexico.

Syncretism, hybridity and transnational space

Geschiere's (1997, French edn 1995) book deals with the central significance of witchcraft in the local and national political economy of Cameroon. A brief account of witchcraft discourse is presented in the opening chapter. This deals with the testimony of a Baptist minister who is visited by an old woman – a practising Christian – who seeks religious support from him. She complains that she had been working all night. The minister then asks her to explain what she means exactly. The story she tells is that she has been 'driving' a plane all night to transport food, rain and other things from places of plenty to a place of scarcity. The old woman argues that whites were trying to take away the plane from us but that she was so skilful a pilot, with thirty years of experience, that she managed to avoid this. When the minister questions if she really is a pilot, she responds that, although she has never seen a plane in her life, she knows how to build one. Then she explains, without any sense of doubt or fatalism in the face of Western idioms of modernity, '[a]ll planes are in the world of witchcraft, and when the white man gets it from the black man, he then interprets it into real life. As it is with planes, so with televisions, radios, telephones etc.' (Geschiere 1997: 3).

Geschiere's brief commentary on this story stresses its syncretistic nature and concludes that in Africa the notions and images that compose this kind of narrative on modernity and witchcraft 'are the subject of constant reformulations and re-creations, which often express a determined effort for signifying politico-economic changes or even gaining control over them' (1997: 3). Hence, he asserts the power of witchcraft beliefs to appropriate elements of modernity and to ascribe them with new meanings. On one level, the story depicts the struggle that arises over who has control and capacity to organise the path to modernity – the old woman/witches, the whites or the minister? On another level, it indicates the origin of 'modern' things, namely that they essentially derive from the 'world of witchcraft' or the occult, but are materialised through the actions of whites who have the power of 're-presenting' them in 'real life'. Of course, in the account it is the old woman piloting the plane who re-distributes the goods and the rain from centres of affluence to places of shortage, thus demonstrating the imagined strategic 'agency' of witchcraft to intervene and affect the outcomes of modernisation. Paradoxically, too, it is the minister who, at the end of his testimony, calls for the development of a 'theology of witchcraft ... not dominated by foreign theological models' (1997: 225, note 3).

This line of analysis is interesting because it simultaneously points to the limitations of functional, cognitive, as well as rational choice explanations of such phenomena. It directs us, that is, towards giving due attention to the intensity and emotional commitment of everyday lived and imagined experiences – often associated with what people perceive as critical events – which set off a rapid transposition of images deriving from, and transgressing, different and seemingly contradictory cultural and social worlds. Also, it emphasises the need to recognise the ambiguity and indeterminateness of practices and representations manufactured out of the subtle combinations of past and present values, experiences, doubts, and people's fears and expectations that mould their visions of the future.

People, then, do not experience the 'arrival' of modernity as the disintegration of their 'old' worlds, marked by the establishment of an unproblematic new and 'pure' code of communication and rationality. Rather, they visualise reality as made up of 'living' ensembles of imagined and felt experiences that juxtapose and interrelate different materialities and types of agency, embracing notions associated with aspects of both modernity and tradition.

It is through illustrations, such as this witchcraft narrative of the old woman, that we come to appreciate that the modern monopoly of technical purification is not enough to frame and contain the dispersed and fragmented images of these seemingly incompatible worlds. Nor can they easily be depicted in binary categories, such as 'indigenous' versus 'universal' knowledge and beliefs, where communication between them is problematic, though, with the right 'instruments', not impossible. Witches and witchcraft exist (implicitly or explicitly) in many worlds, including those where so-called 'modernising' images and practices prevail, but they become temporarily visible through particular actors' semantic and pragmatic manoeuvres. Witches and witchcraft are not a momentary stage in social development, but rather enduring entities which, as Geschiere's study and Chapters 5 and 6 of the present volume illustrate, occupy the same space with ancestral spirits, living kinsmen, Christian missionaries, colonial administrators, and contemporary African politicians and bureaucrats.[11]

The social actions that dissolve boundaries[12] and allow actors to deal with different worlds often shake the foundations of Western universal logic and modes of representation and communication. However, as the above case demonstrates, people have no difficulties in adapting to these disparate worlds; and in this sense they do not engage in syncretistic practices that synthesise contrasting world views or shreds of culture. Neither can the homogenising practices of 'globality' ever obliterate 'locality' as a significant organising and experiential point of reference (cf. Appadurai 1995).

Some of these issues can be further explored by reviewing Kearney's (1996) argument concerning transnational migrants working in the US and Mexican border states. Central to his interpretation is the concept of 'hyperspace', which he borrows from Jameson (1984). Kearney uses the term to register the point at which activities 'become partially or completely cognitively detached from geographic space and are reconstituted in a hyperspace' (1996: 118). He gives as examples of this type of space, international airports, shopping malls, international hotels and fast-food chains. This is a socially constructed space and its main characteristics are that it is not 'anchored permanently in a specific locale', is 'inhabited mainly by strangers', and yet 'has a certain universal quality that is independent of any specific locale in which it might occur' (1996: 118).

The agroindustrial production system found throughout north-west Mexico and in California, Oregon, and Washington, is presented as another example. This 'continuous system [is] marked by a uniformity that is imposed onto and obliterates local landscapes and communities as distinct locales' (1996: 118), and thus acquires a certain sameness typified by the use of identical technologies: chemical fertilisers, pesticides, and genetically-engineered crops. Focusing on the migrant Mixtec workers involved in such agroindustrial production, Kearney points out that they ignore the particularities of the geographical area in which they are working in favour of identifying location with crop within the production hyperspace. One worker said he did not know where he had been working, only that he had been 'with tomatoes'. Another worker located his sons as having gone to 'the oranges'. So Kearney concludes that what we have here is a system of production, distribution, and consumption in which a number of internally differentiated persons, corporations, and agencies come together and articulate facets of their identities to produce and reproduce in a transnational hyperspace. It is in such hyperspace, detached from a bounded geographical place, that transnational communities are situated (Kearney 1996: 118–19).

But there is a paradox in Kearney's idea. While one might accept the point that in some senses there is an element of unbounded geographical and social sameness in hyperspace locations, and therefore conclude that there are 'no distinct centres that are primary reference points', this is clearly not the case from what we know of the life-worlds and social struggles of migrant workers, which Kearney himself has fully documented in his other writings.[13]

In depending upon the metaphor of hyperspace, Kearney portrays a form of space that is empty of actors' subjective experiences.[14] A Mexican migrant worker from Oaxaca, for example, continues to be identified by himself and others as Mixtec and a peasant. But, at the same time, he incorporates into his life-world many aspects of his Californian and other US experiences, including the social relations he forms with other workers, neighbours and relatives living there, as well as what he picks up from the media and from observing a wide range of life styles in the course of his daily routines. In other words, he exists in his entirety in any space that he inhabits. Nor are these elements simply discarded on his return to the village, since the village itself is a repository of members' accumulated experiences, relationships, and individual and collective memories.

Therefore, in this 'hyperspace', there are no properties that could challenge or undermine the authority of the agroindustrial system of production. In the 'sameness' of hyperspace we do not find the varieties and nuances of Elias, nor can we take account of the variety of value discrepancies and social conflicts founded upon status, gender, and ethnic divisions, both within and outside the workplace. The significance of such social differences and their transformations, as more global and flexible forms of production are put in place, impacts on workers' livelihoods and life-worlds in various ways. Nor does this concept of hyperspace allow us to take up Wertheim's suggestion to study counterpoint values: hyperspace ends up with hegemonic institutions which apparently subsume ordinary people's everyday practices and conceptions of self across the different production locations. The model does not acknowledge that the space of the transnational corporations does not always coincide with the space of migrant labourers. In this hyperspace, if persons, corporations and agencies articulate with each other, totally detached from geographic space, how do we understand the complex and strategic interactions that can take place between workers (often themselves divided in terms of social and cultural background), and the representatives (managers and the frontline staff) of the corporations they work for? As Torres (1994, 1997) shows, this can only be achieved through a major rethinking of processes of domination and resistance, and by means of reflexive ethnography. Torres' study of the everyday lives of tomato workers in an agroindustrial company operating in western Mexico brings out the paradoxical effects of power and local knowledge. He demonstrates how, even in the everyday work situation, workers are able to establish a social and epistemological space for their own interests, and in this way challenge the hegemonic strategies and expertise of the company.

To conclude this section, it appears then that neither syncretism, nor hybridity, nor the global uniformities of hyperspatial ordering, in themselves, provide a wholly satisfactory understanding of the ways in which diverse modernities and traditions are interwoven in contemporary societies.

Hybrids and mutants

We must, therefore, consider adding to the lexicon on social and cultural change. As illustrated in Chapter 12, we believe that it is useful to think through these issues using the notions of 'mutants' and 'mutation'. By common definition, hybrids (whether human, organic, material or cultural) are entities of a mixed ancestry, that is they result from the cross between different forms, and require a constant infusion of new stock or elements from some external sources if they are not to become depleted and eventually productively 'degenerated' to the point of extinction. Like the development of new hybrid maize varieties, some aesthetic or cultural hybrids are purpose-fully engineered by artists and intellectuals, while others may arise quite accidentally through 'playing around' with ideas and objects.

However, the use of the notion of hybrids (and by implication syncretism) to characterise the make up of certain newly emergent life styles and socio-cultural arrangements falls short, since what we are dealing with are dynamically generated changes that involve, often rapidly and unpredictably, the re-assembling of the recursive properties of entities and the redrawing of boundaries in such a way that new social forms emerge out of existing ones. These new forms possess the capacity to reproduce or transform themselves in various ways: that is, they can lose (deletion), gain (translocation) and exchange (transduction) specific characteristics or properties. The forms that result are never fully controllable and may be propelled, in certain circum-stances, by outside interventions, although internal rearrangements take precedence over externalities, because it is these that give the form its identity, qualities, organisational shape, capacities and meanings. This is what we mean by 'mutation' and 'mutants'. It goes well beyond the focus in discussions of hybridity on issues of mixed cultural ancestry and practice. One advantage of using mutants and mutation is that the terms take us out of the maze of dualisms, binary oppositions and simple amalgamations, which still plague most discussions on modernity, premodernity/tradition and post-modernity. As Haraway (1991: 181) declares, when writing of cyborgs – a close cousin of our mutants – '[t]his is a dream not of a common language, but of a powerful infidel heteroglossia'.

This mutant imagery assists us in developing an ethnography of multiple modernities which simultaneously embraces what one might call 'civilising' and 'decivilising' practices and processes. Of course, we wish to dissociate our use of the terms 'mutation' and 'mutants' from the perjorative connotations they sometimes carry in everyday parlance – the word mutants quickly conjures up images of weird, deformed human-like, outer-space creatures! Instead, what we wish to convey with these terms is the importance of recognising the intensity, rapidity and self-organising properties of much contemporary social change.

In order to understand and analyse these types of transformations, we need to develop a perspective on the 'counter-tendencies' implied in so-called 'dominant' or 'normal' patterns of development. We do this through exploring the ideas of 'counter-development', originally proposed by Galjart in his discussion of how to make development relevant to people's interests and to their time-bounded realities and expectations.

Counter-tendencies and counter-development

Social change and development need to be portrayed as multi-dimensional and contested realities. This holds whether the particular focus is on contrasting interpretations of modernity, transformations in development policy and practice, diverse forms of livelihood and experience, differentiated institutional and power domains, or local and regional spaces of production, distribution and consumption. Implicit in the notion of counter-tendencies to development is an approach which offers a useful vantage point for understanding the diversity of difference, and allows the ethnographer to engage with local people's images and discourses that give meaning to their actions.[15]

According to this line of analysis, the issue of how people transgress or cross social and cognitive boundaries or manage to generate changes based on the reorganisation of values, is important for assessing the significance of specific social activities. State officials and intervention experts work at bringing change in local practices. This usually implies changes in the use and control of territories, both spatial and social, and in self-organising processes. Such changes may entail the threat to or destruction of existing social arrangements and can result in violent confrontations. The latter is likely to occur when farmers or local groups appear to be growing too independent. In most cases this will not trigger revolution or even crisis, but simply represents the spurts and counter-spurts in the expansion of Western-led development. The participation of local people in decision-making processes usually generates the disembedding and re-embedding of existing political and economic factors, creating social forms that can only be conceptualised as processes of counter-development to modernity.

Galjart (1981) convincingly argues that focusing on counter-development (i.e. strategic actions that counter the dominant development trends and thinking) helps to avoid viewing development simply as a geographical and administrative process of incorporation. It also questions the image of the state as the only legitimate body for carrying out tasks relating to law and order maintenance, economic planning and the delivery of public services. Although it is often assumed that the state is stronger than sectional interests in society, Galjart argues that the state usually flexes its muscles at the point when protest threatens to undermine state practice or, one should add, when the territorial integrity of the nation-state is at stake. To restore political control the state applies measures aimed at neutralising political adversaries. Frequently, however, such political moves have the opposite effect of generating the de-centralisation of political decisions, thus creating room for the furthering of alternative or opposing policies. It is at this point that Galjart proposes that the main role of external donors should not be that of managing the uncertainties of development projects, but that of supporting these counter-tendencies through the exercise of political pressure on government.

One must conclude then that those who support this view, as do many contemporary NGOs, base their strategies on the necessary existence of societal antagonisms, which they can utilise in their search for political alliances with local groups and international bodies funding development co-operation. Galjart's view is that counter-development initiatives should be supported with resources and specialised knowledge, especially as they usually start in a low-key manner and do not immediately imply a major reversal of existing policies. Counter-development is thus a balancing act between introduced bureaucratic procedures and local practices. But unlike many heavy-handed state interventions, local actors and change agents have less difficulty in managing and appropriating new procedures, methods and rationalisations. In other words, counter-development is based on people's scope and power to blend and shape things emerging in the wake of the spread of 'the techniques' of modernity and in the re-positioning of local modes of organisation. The process is consistent with our argument that modernity assumes multifarious forms and practices in its contemporary diffusion and refractions as a global process.

The notion of counter-development is oriented therefore to understanding and acting upon the processes by which multiple modernities are established. It helps to identify the types of representations, practices, discourses, performances, organisational forms, institutions and forums of counter-tendency that emerge; and what modes of authority and power open up and are consolidated in the re-directing of social change. According to Galjart, the constant mobilisation of people's collective actions is linked to the significance of their numerous social commitments. Co-operation needs to be understood in relation to interaction of different spheres of life and in terms of how actors share and compete within common social spaces, wherein struggles take place over how people should work together in relation to labour, markets, technologies and so forth. And, in order to comprehend those practices by which people manage the uncertainties and risks of everyday life, we need to identify the formal and informal coalitions that act for or against certain strategic representations of development. Only by understanding how different actors go about their various tasks and livelihood concerns, can we avoid the homogeneous picture painted of 'community' solidarity. Differentiation entails allocations of responsibility, time and identity.

The degree and quality of organising processes are dependent upon the partial connections and the intensity of experiential configurations that reveal the ways in which actors tend to bridge gaps, juxtapose ideas and practices and engage in displays and performances (see Strathern 1991: 1–41). Actors' informal contacts, their use of existing institutions, how they diffuse information, exchange experiences, participate in discussions, meetings, celebrations and religious ceremonies, and share and counterpose their perceptions and ideologies about the world around them make up these bundles of experiential partial connections. In this way actors re-position themselves and their relationships vis-à-vis their own social and cultural standpoints of modernity. Commitment then is not a 'compulsory' moral social act (like some interpretations of class consciousness). It must be seen as part of the everyday choices of individuals (for example concerning labour, technology or the utilisation of natural resources) that replicate and proliferate notions of tradition and modernity in a variety of social forms. These social forms, while regularly, may not be similar and, if similar, they may not be regular. As Strathern has put it in a rather different context, here we are confronted by a paradox of contacts between surfaces. A related point is that '[c]omplexity is not a property just of the number of component parts or even the direction of their relationships, but of the variety of their interactions and thus the possibility to align into many different configurations' (Lee 1997: 20).

Counter-development means shaping and establishing the here-and-now of modernity. Viewed from above, this may result in the loss of the power of implementation and the minimisation of the role of expert knowledge. From below, it represents a series of opportunities for organising specific projects which, in turn, may help to promote and finance further projects. For people to have a voice and a share in the arrangement of such localised modernities, projects need to be run by those who are cognisant of both the implications of counter-development and how to support it. The use of surplus for financing other projects, the elaboration of contracts and the institution building of counter-development associations offer opportunities for individuals to create livelihoods for the project group, but they also promote additional sources of employment for other members of the group and possibly society at large.

Counter-development thus implies a decrease in the central profitability rule in favour of contradictory objectives, such as mobilisation or the commitment to collective action. Galjart conceptualises this element in counter-development as solidarity. But solidarity should be grounded in market prices and the spread of benefits according to procedures established beforehand. These could regulate 'wage' rates and differentials, as well as the use of profits. In order to avoid the possible paralysis that may arise because single interests do not take account of overall social costs and benefits, Galjart suggests the creation of 'second-order' organisations. 'A group which works profitably does not simply hand over its profits as if it were paying tax: it remains the owner, but the usufruct is decided on another level, where other interests can also make themselves heard' (1981: 95).

Thus, Galjart's notion of counter-development is based on successful market orientation, organisation building, sound financial strategies, and the combination of individual profit with a concern for social costs and benefits. As we hope we have shown, his account provides a useful perspective on the formation of new modernities 'from below', and on how small-scale intervention programmes can play a role in shaping counter-development processes. Although we tend to be somewhat sceptical of the broader benefits of externally-designed participatory development programmes, Galjart's theoretical and practical recommendations on counter-development clearly reinforce our argument for detailed actor-oriented ethnographic work on the production and transformation of social practices of development.

As with the concept of counterwork, ideas of counter-development and counter-tendencies again raise issues of ambiguity, ambivalence and the crossing of cultural boundaries in the constitution of newly assembled localised modernities. Counter-development evidently involves multiple processes of reworking old modes of organisation and meaning and experimenting with new ones. In order to counter or deploy successfully the authority and powers of existing state institutions and centrally-organised development bodies, it is necessary to play with not only the inevitable ambiguities of policy texts and domains of implementation, but also the ambivalences attached to various sets of social relations and value commitments (which become manifest in problematic situations where conflicts of loyalty arise), and finally, to be bold enough to cross preconceived cultural frontiers (for instance associating with government officials of different ethnic or class status). The viability of these manoeuvres – not unknown to the field anthropologist – will depend on the kinds of processes identified by Galjart, namely, mobilisation, commitment and solidarity, not only of relations but also of values and meanings. New social forms are inherently multivalent and allow for possible ambivalences that can transcend existing divisions, hierarchies and membership groupings.

A parallel line of argument has been developed by Barth (1992) in response to mainstream social anthropology and its misuse of the concept of society. He argues that in order to use the concept of society, 'we need to think of society as the context of actions and result of actions but not as a thing' (1992: 31). The basis of his critique lies in the need for anthropology to recognise social positioning and multiple voices, and to abandon its position that society is made up of a 'shared set of ideas enacted by a population' (Barth 1992: 32). Anthropologists need to adopt a perspective that allows us to 'model the resulting processes, the disordered systematic properties that are thereby generated, and the pervasive flux that ensues' (1992: 32). Looking at such processes through the study of everyday practices is complex, but essential if we are to develop new insights into social change and development.

New evolving agendas for development research: the contribution of anthropology

The creative destruction, or deconstruction, of the idea of a singular, Western modernity by people with different, localised values and knowledge underlines the fact that the spread of modernity has resulted in a plethora of modernities. This has transformed the geopolitical and social representation of the globe. Fifty years ago the world was transformed from a template made up of colonial powers and their colonies to one consisting of rich industrialised and poor emerging nations – or what eventually became labelled as the 'developed' and the 'lesser developed' countries or 'the Third World'. Nowadays, the idea of a world of development carries with it a more distinct global connotation, though many of the same wealth and power divides remain. This new global picture has become associated with the growth of information-based technologies and rapid means of transport and communications; dynamic and at times perverse flows of capital and commodities through global markets; complex and fragile political orders; and a variegated transnational cultural and symbolic life composed of both homogenising and diversifying processes.

This changed global scene has brought to the fore many new (and rediscovered) social and moral concerns which increasingly involve action by international bodies, including various institutions concerned with development aid and co-operation. These issues include new forms of colonialism, civil war and inter-state conflict, military aid, human rights, international terrorism, the drug trade, immigration and refugee movements, especially from the South to the North, health epidemics such as AIDS and food poisoning, and disaster prevention and relief. In each scenario, experts of various kinds are contracted to carry out diagnostic studies and to plan and implement remedial courses of action. Much of this work is still undertaken within a framework of thinking based upon mainstream development policy and planning that pays homage to the power of science and rational management.

According to Lynn (1996), this corresponds to 'a production of knowledge and identities' based on 'first world' representational practices. Hence, the reasons for certain so-called 'problems' in the South – such as the production and commercialisation of drugs or the 'mismanagement' of natural resources – remain outside the parameters of expert knowledge or they are excluded politically from the agenda of discussions and therefore seem to have no influence on the actions taken. For example, it was only when the American president declared a war on drugs and Bolivian troops finally invaded the Chapare region to stop farmers from cultivating coca, that a political problem emerged between local farmers and civil authorities around the question of anti-drug enforcement policy. While the expansion of the cultivation of coca was seen, principally by Americans, as the origin of the drug problem, the Chapare farmers argued that the growing of the plant was simply following age-old Bolivian custom and agricultural practice. These two positions were, at this point, incompatible. But as events moved on, it became possible to strike some form of compromise, though still somewhat shaky, since the issue hinged upon the dilemma of finding an alternative, equally commercially viable crop. Discussions and confrontations now involved the parties concerned on the basis of arguing their contrary opinions. This constructed partial connections between them, whether or not they were directly represented around the negotiating table. This situation would offer either a new beginning for reaching some agreements or would fan the escalation of violence. Chapters 8, 9 and 11 of this volume explore these and related issues.

According to Cooper & Packard (1997), since the 1980s two distinct sets of critics of developmentalist frameworks have emerged. The first is the ultramodernist who maintains the position that economic laws are universally valid, with the free market rather than state policy offering the best solution for stimulating investment and 'efficient' allocation of resources. The second is the post-modernist who argues that development is no more than a discourse justifying control and surveillance of people's practices by powerful institutions. Both positions share a concern with power. For the ultramodernist, power represents a distortion in self-regulated markets; for the post-modernist, power is associated with a Western-based 'power-knowledge regime' which has the capacity to manipulate social life and conditions everywhere.

In spite of some intellectual optimism, by the mid-1990s social development was still mapping out the extent of our own ideological orthodoxies and searching for a new coherence around theory and method. On the other hand, increasing awareness of global transformations motivated by technological advances in transport, the media, communications and new commodity trading networks, together with a critical awareness of modernity, had pushed us to focus on the issue of how to describe change and analyse contemporary living conditions in the world.

Although from time to time anthropologists have entered this debate, for the most part they have tried to avoid making any such generalised assertions. Instead, they have addressed the question of institutional control and the issue of market versus state through conducting empirical research on development practice and its outcomes. Here special attention is given to the analysis of the formulation and implementation of national policy programmes and projects and their differential local responses and transformations. For instance, planned intervention in the field of rural development became a central focus for research by Long and colleagues at Wageningen, the Netherlands, from the mid-1980s onwards.[16] Their studies portrayed the social life surrounding the implementation of projects and policies as complex and subject to modifications through the everyday actions of people, including not only the so-called beneficiaries but also frontline development personnel and other so-called stakeholders such as politicians and traders. Within these arenas of struggle two themes were of special significance: the strategic importance and re-constitution of bureaucratic practice and ideology, and the active engagement of local beneficiaries, not as the passive subjects of development institutions and ideology, but as 'knowing' agents in their own right. This actor-oriented approach presented the anthropology of development as concerning a field of contested realities in which struggles over values, resources, knowledge and images constitute the battlefield between different actors and their life-worlds.

Another trend to emerge in development studies (see works by Apthorpe & Gasper 1996; Escobar 1995; Ferguson 1990; and Crush 1995) was the emphasis placed on the production and reproduction of development discourse. According to Grillo & Stirrat (1997), this finally opened up the discussion concerning the significance of Western hegemonic views and practice in the representation of the Third World and its 'problems'. Both actor-oriented research and discourse studies demonstrate the importance of analysing localised power configurations and knowledge interfaces. But, whereas discourse scholars (Escobar, Ferguson, Crush & Hobart (1993) who take a broader philosophical stance) give priority to understanding how Western science and development models enrol, discipline and transform forms of knowledge rooted in other cultural traditions, actor-oriented research focuses upon the 'diverse and discontinuous configurations of knowledge' (Long & Long 1992: 26) that we encounter in specific development arenas. The latter actor perspective is congruent with Apthorpe's argument that development discourses not only often misrepresent the 'realities' faced by those for whom development is planned, but they differ greatly amongst themselves, both within and between the development institutions mandated to formulate and/or implement policy. In other words, rather than premise one's views of knowledge on a binary opposition between Western and non-Western epistemologies and practice, one should attempt to deal with the intricate interplay and joint appropriation and transformation of different bodies of knowledge.

Thus, while a host of interesting studies have been produced that explicate the contents of expert, lay and 'indigenous' types of knowledge ,[17] the critical task for the development anthropologist is to develop methodologies and theoretical interpretations of the different knowledge interfaces inherent in intervention processes and local/global change. Issues of knowledge have also provided a grounding for an analysis of contrasting perceptions and management of the environment (see Croll & Parkin 1992) – a field of increasing interest given the commitments made by national governments and international bodies to include ecological and conservation issues within development work. A recent contribution to this field is the work of Fisher (1997), who has analysed livelihoods and local resource use in a Tanzanian game reserve. A central part of her study is devoted to analysing the knowledge interfaces that take place between scientific experts who frame conservation policies, game reserve staff who put them into practice, and local people who are constantly creatively breaking or bending rules in order to exploit the natural resources of the game reserve for their own purposes. Fisher argues that, in dealing with the conservation programme, local people draw upon 'collective' memories of previous government interventions. In this case, the latter concern the local history of colonial resettlement programmes, which closed off parts of tribal territory and moved a large proportion of the population to new and unfamiliar areas where they had to devise new ways of surviving. Thus, local assessments of present events, concerning the game reserve and actions of conservation personnel, are always cast in relation to past critical situations, and provide the basis for creating space for the pursuit of their own livelihood options (particularly fishing, hunting and beekeeping) which run counter to the scientifically-designed management plan of government, although not necessarily the interests of local conservation officers. The case highlights, then, the need to examine these dimensions through the study of the pragmatics of value negotiation and claim-making, and not in terms of the assumed incompatibility of local people's livelihoods and the objectives of the conservation programme (for an interesting Dutch example see Röling & Wagenmakers 1998).

This line of analysis has been pursued systematically, using concepts drawn explicitly from an actor-oriented framework, to elucidate conflicts that arise over the interpretation of environmental change in African contexts (Fairhead & Leach 1995, Leach & Mearns 1996, and Leach, Mearns & Scoones 1997). The authors demonstrate how experts' 'received wisdom' on issues such as land degradation and deforestation is actively challenged by the historical and ecological experience of local actors, who devise counter-narratives and engage in counterwork pitched against the knowledge of the environmental specialist. In the present volume, Chapters 5, 6 and 7 are devoted to the further exploration of these issues.

We can extend this point about the practical implications of knowledge confrontations in policy implementation to mention briefly the efforts made by some anthropologists to introduce ethnographic methods into project planning and evaluation. A useful recent volume dealing with this problem is that by Pottier (1993) who brings together a number of interesting contributions on methodology.[18] One observation made by Pottier (1993: 11) is that development workers implementing policies 'must "listen and learn"' from local actors and be guided, not by 'inflexible methods', but by well-informed ethnographic practice that relates sensitively to the everyday problematics of project beneficiaries and frontline development personnel (see also Arce 1993).

Building upon Pottier's emphasis on the critical usefulness of anthropological field research, Gardner and Lewis (1996) make more explicit the importance of '[a]nthropology's contribution to positive post-developmental change'(1996: 167). They argue for a critical post-modern stance against the ethnocentric assumptions of the world of development, whilst also affirming the continuing role of the anthropologist 'in unpicking, analysing and changing development practice over time' (1996: 168). But it is not enough to proclaim, as they do at the very end their book, that '[we] can see important roles for the anthropologist in reconstructing ideas and practice in order to overcome poverty and improve the quality of life across the world' (1996: 168). We would argue that what we urgently need is a theoretically-grounded methodology that goes beyond this kind of Western romanticism. To achieve this we must exercise critical reflection to unpick and analyse precisely the representations, practices and taken-for-granted goals of development inherent in their statement. Only in this way can we tackle the larger problem of decontaminating the underlying ideological assumptions of prevailing approaches to development practice and its improvement.

According to Grillo & Stirrat (1997), a promising way forward is to build upon the work of Long & Long (1992) which centres on the issue of 'multiple realities' and diverse social practices and bodies of knowledge that make up the 'middleground' of development. Long & Long (1992: 5–6) stress the importance of more reflexive ethnography aimed at developing 'theoretically grounded methods of social research that allow for the elucidation of actors' interpretations and strategies, and of how these interlock through processes of negotiation and accommodation'. Futhermore, the study of partial connections between these different and 'often incompatible social worlds' of actors involved in struggles, and the different social interests and values that are embodied within them, especially in situations of contested boundaries and their re-definition, can provide us with a better understanding of how anthropology can capture the dynamics of the recursiveness of ideas and practices of development. Such an approach necessarily also requires a sensitivity towards the encounters that occur between the researched and the researcher, as well as giving attention to the counter-tendencies and counterwork of social change. Commenting on the work of Long & Long, Grillo suggests a link with Marcus & Fisher's 'multi-sited' anthropological perspective, which the Wageningen research group has, for some time, been working with in addressing the intellectual crisis of representation in ethnographic accounts.

As we mentioned earlier, the recent general upsurge of social science contributions to the field of development studies seems to have its roots in the problematisation of power (Cooper & Packard 1997), which is in part a legacy of Foucault's ideas on processes of 'micro-power' in everyday life. Yet, it is important to acknowledge that European researchers, by and large, have responded to this challenge somewhat differently from their American colleagues. As Grillo & Stirrat (1997) suggest, while the major figures of American discourse analysis as applied to development seek a 'politically correct anthropology' which requires a foundational rethinking of the nature of the discipline in order to put behind them the binary opposition of 'the West' versus 'the Rest', European researchers have been more inclined to continue with ethnographically-informed enquiries into the differential experiences of modernity and development practice, with emphasis on the social life of development. This has generated a self-criticism of Western development policy and practice that confronts the paradoxes and ugly sides of modernity as they manifest themselves in particular contexts, without abandoning the contributions of an established ethnographic orientation.

What one learns from ethnographic tradition as applied to development is that an anthropology of development must be multivocal (Grillo & Stirrat 1997), multi-sited (Marcus: 1995), but also increasingly concerned with people's counter-tendencies to modernity. The clash of localised cultures with varying modes of modernity provides the possibility of constructing ethnographies that may not refer to clearly defined social subjects, but instead are concerned with the depiction of the particular dynamics and actions for disembedding and re-embedding elements of multiple modernities and traditions.

A key point here – which is central to the actor-oriented perspective – is to capture how people experience the establishment of new and the transformation of old codes of communication and to understand how they re-order their myths, images and 'monsters' (i.e. their fears, as well as their hopes and expectations) in narratives and practices which are held together through partial relations. From an actor-oriented standpoint, people's self-organising practices can only effectively be grasped if we give close attention to the recursiveness and reflexivity of social life, though, unlike some writers, we insist that the latter processes are essential for analysing the generation of new social forms and practices and not simply the reproduction of existing arrangements. A sound anthropology of development, then, necessitates the building of a more reflexive ethnographic approach, which will allow us to analyse the dynamics of re-assembling practices and experiences by local actors, and not just their reactions to the so-called 'induced' changes and socially-engineered experiments identified with modernisation theory or strategies. This concern for reflexivity must be extended to include the researcher's own encounters and experiences with the life-worlds of actors in the development arena.

In the chapters that follow we focus on a number of critical events, viewed as refractions generated by the intersection of global/local processes, in which local people are both implicated and involved in the transformations that take place. In this making of 'new realities' actors differentially ascribe meanings to their experiences and re-position themselves vis-à-vis various intervening parties, old and new solidarities and divisions, and alternative visions of the world.

Notes

1 For recent anthropological and sociological contributions which stress these issues, one might mention Ferguson's (1990) *The Anti-Politics Machine*, Long & Long's (1992) *Battlefields of Knowledge*, Hobart's (1993) *An Anthropological Critique of Development*, Schuurman's (1993) *Beyond the Impasse*, Booth's (1994) *Rethinking Social Development*, Escobar's (1995) *Encountering Development*, Apthorpe & Gasper's (1996) *Arguing Development Policy*, Gardner & Lewis's (1996) *Anthropology, Development and the Post-modern Critique*, Grillo & Stirrat's (1997) *Discourses of Development*, and Abram & Waldren (1998) *Anthropological Perspectives on Local Development*.

2 Indeed some observers predict its total demise as the 'era of development' (by which they mean *planned* development) draws to a close. This viewpoint, however, is clearly too extreme since authoritative and powerful international bodies such as the IMF and World Bank, as well as national governments, continue to

play a major role in the planning and regulating of economic and social development, albeit from a neoliberal standpoint (see Chapter 2 of the present volume).

3 Making treaties with existing traditional leaders and shoring up existing structures
   and cultures of authority was of course essential to the setting up and maintenance of colonial rule, especially of the 'indirect' type. Hence, while allegiance to
   the colonial masters was demanded, ceremonialised deference was often shown to
   senior chiefs and certain local leaders who were expected to be the guardians of
   'indigenous' tradition.

4 This holds even if we consider some of the more elaborated and sophisticated
   versions of the general thesis (e.g. Parsons 1966; Eisenstadt 1966) and take account
   of the recent emergence of 'neofunctionalism' which has had a relatively big
   impact within social theory, especially in the US (see Alexander 1985; Colomy
   1990).

5 See note 13 for a short criticism of actor-network theory put forward by Latour
   and colleagues for analysing heterogeneous networks.

6 See, for instance, Mitchell's (1957) analysis of the Kalela Dance performed in the
   Copperbelt towns of what was then Northern Rhodesia, wherein tribal and
   modern-urban roles, dress and attitudes were interwoven to construct a cultural
   collage that mirrored the changing patterns of social difference based upon
   distinctions of ethnicity, class and occupational status.

7 While fully recognising the important theoretical and ethnographic contributions
   of Evans-Pritchard, Hutchinson (1996) has produced a fascinating historical
   anthropology of the major economic, political and religious transformations
   among the Nuer, which demonstrates the shortcomings of analyses rooted in
   notions of cultural 'boundedness', 'homogeneity' and 'order'. She argues (1996:
   28) that this dependence (in Evans-Pritchard's work) on 'a static structural model'
   makes invisible 'how conflicts of interest, perspective, and power among various
   age, gender, wealth and status groups are continuously being re-negotiated and
   worked out "on the ground". What earlier generations of anthropologists tended
   to view as "the logic" of a particular social system has thus often appeared, on
   closer inspection, to be merely the logic of some segment of it. As a result, our
   very notion of culture and society has begun to fracture and dissolve.'

8 Here we skate over the interesting issue of the prevalence of theatrical metaphors
   in anthropological interpretations of Balinese culture. For example, Geertz (1974)
   writes: 'Physically men come and go … of no importance even to themselves. But
   the masks they wear, the stage they occupy … and, most important, the spectacles
   they mount remain and comprise not the facade but the substance of things, not
   least the self' (1984 edn: 128–9). For an extended critique of this 'public culture'
   position, from the standpoint of interpreting the emotions and predicaments of
   everyday life, see Wikan 1990: especially xviii–xxi, 124–7.

9 Yet, as Heelas points out, 'people – whether "pre-modern"/"traditional",
   "modern" or even "post-modern"/"post-traditional" – *always* live in terms of
   those typically conflicting demands associated … with voices of authority emanating from realms transcending the self *qua* self, and … with those voices emanating from the desires, expectations, and competitive or idiosyncratic aspirations
   of the individual' (Heelas 1996: 7). This suggests that there is no totalising system
   based on 'tradition' (usually represented as 'the belief in pre-given or natural
   orders of things') or on modernity. So-called 'tradition' cannot subsume or govern
   individual actions, nor can so-called 'modern' or 'post-modern' actors act without
   some regard for collective norms and values.

10 Due to limits of space, we cannot here deal with the attributes of these different
   heterogenous entities, which we believe merit full heuristic treatment. Hence, we
   restrict ourselves to a brief comment on the excellent ethnography of Geschiere,
   which permits us to reflect upon the limitations and insights provided by the idea

of syncretism as applied to the mixing of traditional and modern values. Geschiere's text stands apart from Stewart & Shaw's (1994) volume on issues of syncretism and anti-syncreticism (which concentrates on the politics and discourses of the synthesis of religious forms) by offering a detailed analysis of the interpenetration of witchcraft beliefs and practices in relation to political life in Cameroon, tied to situated events rather than being presented as illustrating the merging or synthesis of religious or cultural traditions. In so doing, Geschiere's ethnography brings out the nuances and varieties of practice deployed by particular actors in the management of their everyday lives. For a discussion of hybridity, see Latour (1993), Garcia Canclini (1989), Werbner (1997), and Harvey (1996); for creolisation, see Hannerz (1992), and Richards (1996); for cyborgs, see Haraway (1991), and Gray (1995).

11 This coexistence of the spirit world and everyday life has frequently been documented in studies of African religious beliefs and practice, especially concerning ancestral and other types of spirits. These spirit kinsmen/women manifest themselves in a variety of forms, for example as animals or natural phenomena such as rocks, water, and trees. They often intervene in everyday critical situations, causing illness or generating bad relations between specific individuals and groups. Indeed, as Carin Vijfhuizen (1998) shows, for the Ndau-Shona of Zimbabwe, they play a significant role in the ordering of family, household and gender relations. But they show little or no respect for the status position or authority of those they encounter, and frequently, speaking through spirit mediums, they reveal the sources of misfortune and culpability of particular individuals. Thus it is impossible in documenting the everyday events of a Ndau-Shona village to ignore their influence, since they occupy the same spaces as do the living actors. This is illustrated in Vijfhuizen's study by the fact that village people argued that the increase in angry avenging spirits has resulted from the colonial government's law prohibiting witch hunting and the killing of witches (1998: 205).

12 It is beyond the scope of this chapter to fully examine how actors' practices mark out and rework cultural boundaries in situations of change and development. For interesting studies of this process see Barth (1969), Cohen (1985, 1986), Rosaldo (1989), Skar (1994), and Malkki (1992).

13 None of this fits well with the other strand of Kearney's argument where he stresses the 'polybian' characteristic of migrants, who 'move in and out of multiple niches', and 'back and forth from "peasant" to "proletarian" life spaces' during their working lives. Thus in one context an individual may appear 'as a peasant, in another as a plantation worker, and in others as a petty merchant or an urban slum dweller...[T]hese slippery creatures defy constructed social bounds; they cross out of their "proper" places and enter into marginal spaces. And by populating these border areas they threaten normal social categories that the state has a responsibility to maintain' (Kearney 1996: 141–2).

14 In a recent paper, Whatmore & Thorne (1997) have strongly criticised the spatial imagery of orthodox accounts of globalisation for 'the eradication of social agency and struggle from the compass of analysis by presenting global reach as a systemic and logical, rather than a partial and contested, process' (1997: 288). These accounts also magnify out of proportion the 'scale' and 'mass' of institutions such as transnationals and regulatory bureaucracies, to the detriment of exploring the 'intricate interweavings of *situated* people, artefacts, codes and living things and the maintenance of particular tapestries of connection across the world. Such processes and patterns of connection are not reducible to a single logic or determinant interest lying somewhere *outside* or *above* the social fray' (1997: 288).

In an attempt to rethink issues of space and social transformation, Whatmore & Thorne look to certain new analytical trends in geography and anthropology for 'the beginnings of an understanding of globalisation as partial, uneven and unstable' (1997: 289). In particular, they build upon actor-network theory (Latour 1993, Law 1994, and Callon & Law 1995), which they apply to the case of fair trade in coffee in the UK. However, while the approach breaks some new ground in agro-food studies, in the end it falls short for the very same reasons as do other actor-network studies. Their presentation is based on showing how actors *enact* certain 'modes of ordering' (Law 1994: 25) which allow them to construct narratives based on an encoding of existing representational or cognitive repertoires that become inscribed in the stories they tell and, like ritual, in the symbols that make performance practices routine. As Golinski's (1998: 37–43) balanced and incisive critique of actor-network theory demonstrates, the approach concentrates on constructing accounts of 'how the actants [humans and non-humans] they identify function as signifiers in a discursive field'(1998: 40). This tends to lay emphasis on semiotic dimensions rather than on the close-up study of situated social practice or what Golinski describes as 'incidents of practical engagement with the material world'. Thus, when confronted with actor-network studies, one continually asks how these textual signifiers relate to specific actions in 'real life' situations. This problem is confounded by ascribing an equal degree of agency to non-humans as to humans (cf. Lynch's 1996 critique). Discussing Latour's book on Pasteur, Golinski concludes that 'the conflation of semiotics with ontology seems like a failure to distinguish between reinscribing the accounts of scientists [or other social actors] themselves and giving a detached sociological analysis' (op.cit: 41). The same issues arise with Whatmore & Thorne's application of the theory.

15 We use the term 'counter-tendencies' to problematise the issues of globality and modernity 'from the centre', thus revealing how communicated messages, information, material resources, technologies, and various cultural repertoires and relations are received, translated and reworked by locally situated actors who assemble these various elements in order to re-position themselves in relation to so-called macro influences and frameworks. The idea of counter-tendencies does not imply binary oppositions such as centre-periphery or dominant-subordinate relations, since such tendencies can work in several directions. They may mediate global or hegemonic relations but they are not the direct effect of these assumed dominant relations, though they may in the end contribute to the reproduction of certain power relations. They are perhaps most significant for the ways in which they pose and promote alternative agendas for change and can, under certain circumstances, challenge the assumptions and authorities of so-called centres of representation and control.

In this essay we cannot possibly attempt to unravel all the complexities involved in the idea of counter-tendencies, of which one version is Galjart's counter-development proposal. But the approach is, we believe, useful for documenting and analysing how various social actors manage to create space for change (see Long 1984), in spite of being on the receiving ends of organised interventions that bring with them systematic models and packages designed to achieve development and modernity.

16 This body of work is extensive. Key works include Long 1984, Arce 1986 (1993), Arce & Long 1987, Long 1988, Long 1989, Long & van der Ploeg 1989, Arce 1989, Seur 1992, de Vries 1992 (1997), van der Zaag 1992, Long & Long 1992, Arce, Villarreal & de Vries 1994, Long & van der Ploeg 1994, and Mongbo 1995. In addition, one should mention here a recent useful contribution to the recognition of 'an anthropology of policy' by Shore & Wright (1997). It is somewhat odd, however, that there is not one reference to any of the above works in their call for 'a new field of anthropology'. Nor is there any acknowledgement of the important contributions by Schaffer (1984, 1985), Wood (1985), Handelman & Leyton (1978) and Grindle (1980, 1986), to name but a few, that laid the ground-

work for an anthropological interpretation of policy processes and planned interventions. In addition, there is no recognition of the volumes of Pottier (1993), and Hobart (1993) which make explicit the importance of ethnography and knowledge construction in the analysis of policy implementation processes at the level of projects.

17 Brokensha, Warren & Werner's (1980) *Indigenous Knowledge Systems and Development* and Richards' (1985) *Indigenous Agricultural Revolution* mark the beginnings of the growth of a large body of work dealing with local knowledge practices. Hobart's (1993) collection explicates the dynamics of knowledge processes between 'developers' and their clients, and Warren, Brokensha & Slikkerveer's (1995) volume provides an update on local knowledge issues. This work has been complemented by many empirical and theoretical studies exploring issues of discourse, knowledge and power. See for example Marglin & Marglin (1990), Long & Long (1992), Scoones & Thompson (1992) and Grillo & Stirrat (1997).

18 Elements of an actor-oriented perspective have been enthusiastically taken up in applied fields such as agricultural extension and communication studies (Röling 1994, Leeuwis 1993, Engel 1995), participatory rural appraisal (PRA) and stakeholder analysis (Salomon & Engel 1997), and used for framing research on environmental change and natural resource managment (Lockie 1996 on the Australian land-care movement, and Leach & Mearns 1996 on African environmental change and policy). In addition, a group of German, French and West African anthropologists working mostly in French West Africa on questions of development and social change has evolved a theoretical standpoint that is highly compatible with actor-oriented analysis at Wageningen (see Elwert & Bierschenk 1988, Olivier de Sardan 1995).

2 Creating or regulating development

Representing modernities through language and discourse

Alberto Arce[1]

Introduction

This chapter starts from the assumption that languages of development constitute an important representational field in which the meanings and intentionalities of development policies can be grasped and analysed. The social ordering of this field is the outcome of how cultural practices, ideas, concepts and distributions of meaning are enacted and experienced through human activity.[2] In other words, it is through actors' interactions and 'translations' of experience that institutions and the complexities of practice take shape. Embodied in these processes are the ways in which different actors' perceptions, views, desires and values are framed and defended, or challenged and contested. Hence, struggles over meanings, representations and images – what Bourdieu (1984: 479–84) calls 'classification struggles' – are central to understanding development institutions, policies and outcomes. In addition, it is important to explore the ways in which development practitioners/experts and local actors articulate their languages of development, and how far these resonate with each other or create a cacophony of divergent and discordant messages.

The discussion takes a broad view of what constitutes the articulation of languages of development. Here we need to consider three ways in which the term 'development' is located linguistically. First, it is seen as centrally linked to theoretical ways of talking about the manifestations and dilemmas of 'modernity'. Chapter 1 of this book amply illustrates the close affinity of development discourse to matters of modernity and modernisation. Second, it has been heavily influenced by the successive re-thinking of policy options from within international development agencies. Hence, its meaning has shifted in accordance with the different points of view of the global experts and bureaucrats involved. This process has tended to promote homogeneous models for Third World change from a Western optic. This modelling becomes significant because it entails a penmanship concerning how to describe and analyse processes of modernisation using language representations and strategies generated by these decision-makers themselves.

Third, it is used as a political/pragmatic term which serves to make people aware of the ambiguity of the processes of intervention. Recent studies have shown development processes to be far more complicated and fragmented events than earlier work unveiled. For example, for an engineer to bring modernity into a locality is not an easy task. It requires disciplining people, creating an exploitable labour force, and introducing Westernised life styles, a process that encounters resistance, struggles and many unintended consequences. Indeed, there is a rich vocabulary of political solutions and action programmes which attempt to shift the debate about development towards emancipatory goals, 'bottom-up' participation, and gender and local knowledge sensitive dimensions. This range of views and commitments suggests that development situations should be assessed for their ambiguities and in order to identify the space for change. From this practical perspective the language of development defines the sites of struggle and the supposed 'stakeholders' involved.

Both the intellectual and political representations of Western modernity outline not only a cartography of authority and power, but aim to show how it actually works, who shapes it, under what circumstances, and how it might be related to local cosmologies of progress or the composition of modernity. In this chapter I will argue that it is possible to see and understand locally-situated experiences of modernity as controversial and contested processes that are embedded in continuities and change. In this way, not only global decision-makers and development activists, but also local actors reposition themselves vis-à-vis the state, markets, international policies, nature and culture. Given the multivocality of the concept of development, which has not yet reached saturation point, it is unlikely that the concept will disappear from our vocabulary.

The language of development then is a combined set of linguistic representations and linguistic constructions of how to relate 'problems' to 'solutions'. It is a certain way of framing problems, attributing essences, and finding solutions based on the objectivisation of what constitutes development. This linguistic set operates against a background of human activities organised through policy actions, technologies and the deployment of specific language strategies. Hence, we need to study how people practise the language of development and experience its associated constructions.

The chapter argues that the language of development frames our understanding of contemporary 'problems'. This practice of framing issues is Janus faced: on the one hand it creates judgemental statements concerning how people ought to translate the language of institutional development; on the other, it broadens our capacity to visualise human activities beyond these judgemental statements (cf. Dilley 1992). The chapter also explores how different facets of development language are organised and governed by people's existing practices.

The language of development, representations and international institutions

In the language of development, the authoritative statements of international developmental organisations such as the IMF and the World Bank are extremely important in representing societies and development priorities. Furthermore, it is the habit of these international organisations to use the linguistic representations of development to construct a meaningful discourse in which experts can identify and isolate a quantifiable number of development issues.

Ideas such as the efficiency of free markets to allocate resources, or views that see market-oriented economic policies as a contribution to good government and political accountability, have the capacity to connect development indicators or variables to a physical description of development problems and failures. Consequently, their way of representing problems, options and solutions eventually results in a meeting point of a range of ordering influences whose intentionalities can only be observed in the way that policies are constructed. This linguistic activity corresponds to a political evaluation and judgement of the existing stock of knowledge and balance of power among diverse social and political interests shaping development agendas. In this manner, linguistic representations from international institutions can become a political instrument which contributes to the maintenance of an international political order and establishment, within a well defined administrative sphere of agency influences (see Corbridge 1992).

In short, linguistic representations are essentially formal and normative in character, and their sanctity usually culminates in the formulation of an authoritative document or a 'new policy'. Such policy does not fully describe the 'development realities', nor take account of people's experiences of change or their coping strategies, but instead reconstitutes fragmented representations into simulation models of 'progress' and economic growth. Wrapped up in a technological and detached universal vocabulary, these representations divert attention from the fact that a language of development should address actors' political, economic and social practices and knowledge construction processes.

The formulation of a global development language constitutes a field of representation where a diversity of actors who are politically and administratively co-ordinated by an authority, participate in identifying and presenting a problem. They represent people and issues in their institutional search for finding solutions. This pragmatic use of language tends to close or curtail political and cultural debates very effectively. It is the authority of these institutions which defines the form and content of the language of development. This becomes an international pattern of ordering, that is usually concerned with institutional actors who draw images from their development policy universe, and who share a common identity or interest with the international agencies. These international institutional actors 'transact' representations and images with each other, exchange resources and balance political games in order to enhance and optimise their mutual relationships (Wright 1988). Using linguistic devices and mapping their interactions, these expert actors build realities in which international agencies impose their presence. With time this distinctiveness of the institution and experts interacting with local actors comes to compose a 'policy community' (Arce & Mitra 1991) which is organised around the understandings that members of the community attach to the linguistic representations which flow within the network. This constructs the consistency and technical operationability of the specific language of development.

When considering these issues, one could not do better than refer to Franz von Benda-Beckmann's (1994) interesting paper on the linkages between good governance and economic development. Benda-Beckmann provides a detailed analysis of the genealogy of discussions on good governance tied to the human rights situation of recipient countries, which has led to the imposition of legal constraints under which the World Bank and the International Bank for Reconstruction and Development (IBRD) were expected to operate from the 1960s. Furthermore, loan applications for developing countries stipulated that they had to adhere to strict economic considerations. He illustrates how some of these debates created tension between the UN and the World Bank on development policy, particularly with respect to the cases of South Africa and Portugal. Here we see the importance of discontinuities in interests at the level of international institutions and we learn about the nature of these conflicts, their representations and interactions.

The question of conflict is close to the central problem of how to represent development issues. It was perhaps as a result of the different views on human rights and the conflicts that ensued, that the incorporation of the environmental factor was facilitated in the mid-1980s. According to Benda-Beckmann, it was only in 1990 that the World Bank finally recognised that 'internal or external political events' due to their 'economic nature, may properly be taken into consideration in the Bank's decisions' (1994: 4, see also Peet & Watts 1993: 231–2). Political considerations were no longer perceived as factors external to economics, implying that the spheres of economy and good governance were connected through law. Benda-Beckmann sees in this modification the new international guideline for legislative, administrative and judicial practices. From our point of view, this process represents a clear linguistic shift by the Bank to argue that these conditions could provide the perfect competitive environment required for economic development. Thus the linguistic strategies governing the language of economic development permeate and construct the intentional aims of development.

Benda-Beckmann suggests that this statement of principles – or linguistic shift – had wider political implications. The World Bank immediately tried to neutralise the practical implications of the linkage that was made between economics and politics. This institutional action to restore 'normality' was made by Vice-President Shihata who asserted that 'governance becomes an issue to the Bank only in its strict sense of the good order required for a positive investment climate and the efficient use of resources'. In effect, he himself posited an institutional discourse to mark out the complex map of linguistic rules and practices within which the World Bank would operate.

While accepting that some economic considerations may have political origins, the Vice-President saw his main task as that of closing off the process of interpretation and empathy with the political issues of Third World societies. Moreover, he provided a clear institutional meaning to the word 'politics' insofar as he understood politics to be a factor subject to prediction and control for economic investment. The representation of development was no longer in need of further political interpretation.

The sorts of linguistic shifts described above have been called by Peet & Watts (1993) the cartography of development discourses. That is, the way in which an international institution is able 'to rewrite history to suit the Bank's own ideological purpose, its unwillingness to assume accountability for past activities' (Peet & Watts 1993: 231). I wish to expand upon this interesting idea by suggesting that the power of the cartography of discourses rests not only in the ability to re-write history, but in the capacity to draw contemporary linguistic maps. The strength of development discourse lies in the way that institutional authorities speak of 'certainties', and effectively represent these certainties in linguistic reference maps of reality. Hence the question that arises here is, do we need to accept these linguistic maps as the only acceptable representation of knowledge and belief in navigating safely from A to B?

The significance of the language of development as a representational field

The meanings and intentionalities of policies are expressed through words, and words are located in the language of the institution, and become used to accomplish technical tasks. My concern here is with the process of intervening in the ordering of the use of knowledge. There is no knowledge outside language representations. The authority of representation from Vice-President Shihata's discourse was his 'new' notion of politics. This drew my attention to the specific value of studying linguistic constructions of development as a significant field for understanding phenomena arising from the contestation of different socio-political development discourses, and how these discourses are integrated within an institution such as the World Bank, whose international authority and credibility is clearly situated in relation to 'other' socio-political discourses. This is to suggest that the language of development provides a significant basis on which to map out political intervention, it gives depth to the organising make-up of international institutions and extends the domain of these 'institutional' cultures to the specific regulation of the globe.

The World Bank desk dealing with Africa gives particular meaning to the language of Vice-President Shihata and extends the domain of 'good governance' to 'the field' in a direction that will not be entirely dominated by the forces of capital and financial control, but also by the network of individuals operating in the specific geographical area. What does demand further discussion is whether these 'new' languages of development simply reflect the existing geo-representational divisions and their cultural spheres of influence. Do the interests of the University of Chicago, Cambridge or Wageningen and their graduates necessarily collude with the hegemonic role of the West as a power bloc? Is the language of the World Bank merely another device to construct representations of Third World countries – a device that reinforces its own organising practices and uses of knowledge? It is here that the cartography of discourses can help us to identify forms of linguistic representation and the extent to which they produce rather than reflect their objects of intervention. In our example, the discourse constructed jointly by Vice-President Shihata and the international institution becomes an important part of the interpretive framework of normative development used to tame political factors. As Benda-Beckmann argues for the World Bank, 'economic, political and legal factors are not of equal value', therefore, through the discourse of good governance, politics and law have been made the subjects of economics (see Stirrat 1992).

The normative form through which the representations and constructions of the international language of development are organised reveals the pre-eminent use of abstract representations for enquiry and explanation. But then, what is the point of using these abstract representations? Abstract representations are used to remove 'local' institutional or political distortions from the language of development. The entire exercise is to construct an objectifying optic, that comes to resemble nothing more than a 'neutral' engineer's tool-kit in which reality is presented as predictable and subject to control. These abstract representations construct development issues as universals. In so doing development issues are presented as 'material', 'real' and with an 'objective' consistency that exists externally and independent from people or their construction of localities. Since these abstract representations do not take into consideration people's experiences, any institutional use of the language of development will run into trouble because in practice these abstract representations have to operate against a background of local human activities. It is not surprising then that international experts always encounter difficulties in controlling the meanings that local people attribute to the global distribution of development idioms.

Unlike other ways of ordering,[3] these abstract representations of develop-ment meticulously attribute a version of agency that removes the debate away from substantial issues – 'matters of good governance as accountability, rule of law, participation, human rights or democratisation. Their primary concern is with the reconstruction of the economy, in which legal and administrative elements become subordinated to economics' (Benda–Beckmann 1994: 2). We cannot make heard our voices on issues, such as 'corruption, legal insecurity, or violation of human rights'. Thus Benda-Beckmann suggests that 'in development then our focus of attention should be on bad rather than good governance' (1994: 2). But our representations of development should also include counter-tendencies of development. By implication policy formulation should be part of the images and representations that constitute the social world of development as well as the nature of how and who is selecting the issues of international development policy. So far, the exclusion (censorship) of development counter-tendencies and their risks is made a part of a normative condition in the language of development. This systematically generates ignorance through the attribution of authority and power to the performance of international experts as centres of representation.

World Bank officials are skilled language users and their skills are directed towards creating 'a wider berth for pragmatic manoeuvring within the legally constrained sphere of its activities' (Benda-Beckmann 1994: 6). Their language usually seeks to overcome differences within the complex field of policy formulation. The abstract representational use of concepts like economics, objectivity and neutrality, underlines an image of development as something concerned with technical considerations alone. The globalisation of the language of development legitimises abstract normative and accepted social order representations of values and beliefs. However, the practical domain of policy, which generates confrontations, collaborations and participation among different social actors, constitutes the social and linguistic field that gives form to operational policy. This provides scope for linguistic strategies and actions by actors and groups lower down the policy chain or network.

While the abstract representations and the normative character of such language provides a degree of authority to the image of experts influencing social change, the fact remains that they are far removed from the demands and life-worlds of the recipients of development programmes. Nevertheless, these intended beneficiaries are active actors who maintain their own interests, resources and power, and who play an important role in representing their own demands and practices. This cacophony between expert and beneficiaries reflects the tendency towards a sectoral and contested linguistic encounter. This interface usually encapsulates more than one single set of representations, activities and accounts, and ultimately local actors try to keep control over their local decision-making processes, whilst attempting to get the maximum benefit from national and international development policies.

At the level of international institutions, certain policies are preferred over others, not simply in the use or misuse of rational linguistic objectification of Third World problems (see Lefwich 1994), but because some are more visible than others. The formulation and representation of what might be called 'transcendental' development activities are significant in attributing social and economic motives to people. At this stage of the argument, I want to suggest that the policy language of international institutions affects the direction, efficiency and regulation of local development processes through the attribution of certain meanings to people and their behaviour. This introduces dissonance in ongoing local political activity and undermines the position of local knowledge as a means of enunciating people's narratives of the present.

Development practice is not just a parenthesis of normative linguistic constructions – the language of development cannot stop or control actors' actions – but it does provide selected, and not necessarily correct, information, data, images, representations, idioms and interpretation of the development issues. It permits and legitimises the activity of international policy makers to misrepresent local 'realities', the agency of people and their effect on the production of identities and subjectivities in processes of development.

An encounter with the contemporary language of development: Latin American experiences

Interlude

In considering the language of development as an important representational field, priority must be given to locally situated languages. This is significant in order to define the role of representing problems and substantial issues in the field of development studies. We will present, in this section, local languages of development. These linguistic constructions are described and analysed in the context of their occurrence as situated and located representations, whose precise nature make sense to both actors and the ethnographer alike in terms of the social action these descriptions have promoted. In this sense, speech-acts of the language of development are mainly concerned with the performance of actions of various kinds. What we need to explore is how actors make intentional use of notions such as 'market-led' development, 'free enterprise', 'opening up national markets', 'competition', 'privatisation', 'liberalising resources' and 'global marketing'(see Arce 1990, Arce & Marsden 1993, Arce & Fisher 1997, 1998).

The language of development is misunderstood if it is simply treated as a static framework broadcasting and receiving cryptic messages from institutions and representatives of the world of development. The language of development should be seen as a field generating interfaces within the processes of social change in at least three ways. First, it is a field of reflexivity in which many of the contemporary perceptions about modernities feed back into the re-organisation of production, consumption and life style. Second, it is available for use as an acceptable linguistic device to legitimise the representations and technical and political constructions which make up the social dimensions of development. Finally, it mediates the field of social change by becoming its linguistic image.

We can take as an example the contemporary languages of development in Latin America, which represent the material and cultural conditions of existing notions of progress. Market-led development is organised and at the same time has been organised by actors following others' experiences and images of modernity. We must also recognise that the language of market-led development has been able to generate some local representations and metaphors to question the traditional sphere of action of the state. At best this leads to a 'language of dissonance' between and within actors and between and within national and international institutions, creating differential room for particular performances and argumentations within the language of development. The latter have a direct bearing on different dimensions and interpretations about the transferability and replicability of market representations.

The experience of modernities has somehow become separated from everyday life. Global market representations do not take into consideration the human price actors have to pay in order to become successful in the world market. Usually the language of development is presented as an abstraction that reduces and masks the paradoxical character of life to some facts, agendas for action and private experiences. 'In the past we used to have time, but we did not have information and proper organisation to establish our businesses' said the young corporate manager of a recently created foreign trade section in one of the most traditional agricultural companies in Santiago, Chile. 'Today we have to live by cellular phone and we have to be ready to react. Markets can fluctuate at any time'. This thirty-year-old executive's fetishes include fast communication and computer technology, which he describes as the 'technological development' that gives him knowledge and power to negotiate vis-à-vis other actors in the international market. This representation of the market provides us with the possibility of treating this type of actors' agency as a hologram of the corporate organisa-tion.[4]

These cultural dimensions of the official language of development are often ignored or presented only as side-effects of the seemingly more important process of capital accumulation. Usually, stress is placed on the production and distribution processes that take place on a global scale, including countries like Chile. This linguistic strategy contributes to constructing an image of constant economic progress, as an essential idiom in the successful representation of development. But let us pause for a moment: perhaps the economic 'miracle' of Chile is just a metaphor that can be de-constructed through the political contents of the thinking and positioning of a Chilean corporate manager. Indeed, when this manager speaks and enacts the language of computers, inter-continental communications and global free markets, he is referring to a pattern of organisation that is not purely natural, organic, technical or textual, but a combination of all of these and which has the potential to control people and resources on a global scale. In his language, the nature of social relations, politics, environment, and issues of social justice are seldom mentioned specifically, but instead disappear in the diffusion of a general representation. That is, the social circumstances of the emergence of local identities are treated very much as part of a cognitive cartography of globalisation. His language of life is organised privately and his agency becomes visible and interpretable only through the inscriptions read with difficulty by the ethnographer from technical devices. At this point one begins to think about how this actor visualises his subjectivity in the image of the computers, constant information and cellular phones.

Returning to reflect on the contemporary language of development

The corollary is that we have paid too much attention to the linguistic set, which refers to economics and the market, and because of this we are missing out on the greater interaction, that which occurs between the natural, the organic, the technical and the textual. In the Chilean case it is the interaction between computers and people that gives rise to the greatest forces reshaping society and life. Although I am aware that neither the Chilean corporate manager's world-view nor the use of signs can call the tune of cultural complexity alone (Hannerz 1992), information and communication are ordering Chilean society to the extent that the idiom of computers, although abstract and universal, has much to do with a representation of the market as 'virtual reality.'[5] In this new social construction of reality the manipulation of a view that, apparently, removes distortions from the 'real market' or considerations of the beneficial role of 'state intervention', is superseded. Instead new knowledge and power configurations are seen to result from the interaction between humans, nature and machines. This leads us to rethink the nature of social relationships at a point characterised by a sea change in technical and human capacities and aspirations. Our concern is to further these lines of thinking and analysis in order to add new insights into the transformative processes of multiple modernities shaping contemporary Third World scenarios.

Two brief ethnographic readings

Digital information and global traders in Chile

During a recent stay in Chile[6] I visited one of the oldest agricultural companies. Six experts in international trade were each introduced to me, first by their commodity specialisations and only later by their names. Immediately afterwards an apology was made, because they were busy concluding some business deal with Argentina and Peru and were therefore unable to give me their attention.

My host went on to say: 'Perhaps what is important for you is to see us in action rather than us telling you about our work. This, we call a commodity desk, where we are concerned with beans, raisins, and onions. To organise our trade we have these [four] computer terminals on this desk. One is connected to the commodity markets in the US. Another one gives us the transactions taking place in Chile and the names of the suppliers, and we also know with whom he is trading. That one over there [monitor] gives us the maximum and minimum price at which we can buy and sell. That other monitor provides us with information about the products we still have in our stores'. He addresses the other person opposite him. 'Are you already in contact with Argentina?' The answer was 'Yes'. Taking the phone, he said to me, 'You must listen now'. 'OK, do you need more beans there? ... .Yes, could you please double the quantity of beans you sent me? ... .Here the price is improving because the season is starting ... .OK, we will do that tomorrow'. Then he explained to me that the company has brokers in Argentina, because the Argentinian market is unreliable. 'The buyers never pay, therefore we have to control the brokers with instructions, information and prices from Santiago'. He continued: 'Five years ago we did not know the international market, so I went from country to country in Latin America with a suitcase and some ideas. I got information about the market and created a network of brokers and possible clients. To maintain these people in our network we need good and fast communications. In this office we spend a large amount of money on telephone accounts, it is the item to which we devote most of our resources'.

I drank my coffee and then said: 'I guess nowadays with all this technology it isn't important to personally know the person with whom you are trading'? He replied, 'On the contrary, although these communications are very powerful it is essential to know the other person well, otherwise you lack the element of trust'. I was surprised with this answer since so much of their business depended on computer-mediated knowledge.

Concurrently, there was a transaction going on with Peru. The person was negotiating a cargo of beans and the price was being settled over the telephone. The Peruvian trader was bargaining for a higher price, arguing that another trader was offering him a better price for the beans. The answer was clear: 'Yes, we know that "El Chino" sent beans to Peru last week but the price is not the one you are quoting'. There was silence on the other end of the line, followed by a brief negotiation over the price and the contract was closed.

The person in charge of the desk said to me: 'This deal was closed well above the minimum price, so that we will get a nice premium'. Then he adds, 'This is the power of communication, this is why we can control the market in Latin America. Ten years ago we did not have the technology, though we had a quiet life. The market has forced Chileans to modernise and we have become more efficient'.

The above observations support the view that cellular telephones, computers and commodities destined for the global market have brought about a whole new set of images, representations and subjectivities in Chile. New social relationships emerge as Chileans extract information and capitalise on the market. It is important to observe that they have been able to store information and encompass new techniques to organise through use of modern technology. This practice has constructed an instrumental language of development and power. It has led to a specific style of performance re-affirming the self-confidence and identity of Chilean entrepreneurs vis-à-vis the organisation of the market and its actors in Argentina, Peru and Japan. A new panorama unfolded in front of my eyes to reveal how ordering practices based on distant market control, fast communication and digital information have permeated actors' daily organisational practices and activities. Their agency has been configured by their interest and use of the 'perfect world' of computers. For these global traders fast translation of economic inscriptions and quick dissemination of information have become the object of knowl-edge and the only means to evaluate their performance in the 'virtual market'.

In Latin America the experience of modernity and the attainment of development has been possible in diverse ways, usually independent of the scientific control of experts and legislators. In contrast to Chile, in countries such as Colombia and Bolivia, we witness development processes that are not 'officially recognised', escape official statistics, and centre on the production of narcotics. Although defined in official discourses as 'illegal', such processes of modernisation can also be framed within the West's project of instrumental reason. A diversity of modernisations has brought different ways of experi-encing science and technologies in Latin America. They have become deeply incorporated into the life experiences of local people during the period of market-led development and generate new relations between nature, culture and technology. Moreover, the right to achieve local 'modernisation' has become the battlefield of experts, since local people are deploying practices and effecting local economic transformations of a scope not previously observed. These local practices express the emergence of diversity, choices and the performances of 'new' actors.

Today, actors are left to shape the material and immaterial conditions of social development. Representations and practices connected to neo-liberal policies provide significant clues as to how linguistic constructions can contribute to processes of ordering the world. The establishment of market representations, like other forms of representation, operates against a background of people's own strategies. In this sense, local political economies link human activity, capital and nature in specific forms.

These combinations have resulted in the generation of certain economic activities that have transgressed the 'legitimate' nature of the market. In this vein, different representations of the market and modernities are fought out locally. For example, the Colombian cartel in Medellin has established a language of development based on local drug production and a global distribution of these illegal commodities. In contrast, the USAID 'alternative' language of development for Bolivia has been based on the criminalisation of the production of coca leaves and its necessary substitution by other 'legal' crops. In this way the contemporary language of development has constructed new productive activities which have became a battleground in the attempt to manage the introduction of different modernities into local worlds, people's subjectivities and identities. All these transformations have changed the existing relations between society, technology and markets. Viewed in this way modernity is salient in present day 'Third World' scenarios, where globalisation and the language of development are part and parcel of the application of instrumental human rationalities.

The virtual reality market in Chile is an initial starting point for a 'new' language of development. This represents a technological mode of innovation and a local view of the world that has internalised, mediated and naturalised the technology of the moment. Here modernity has come to be explained in ways that reinforce the idioms of techno-science and that make existing social practices efficient, rational and legitimate. This is a commonsense language that anticipates some of science's conceptions of how to develop the world. In fact, the institutional language of development is in a semantic crisis when it is contextualised, because it does not contain enough situated knowledge or information to read the diverse working arrangements of life and techno-science.

Illegal crops in an age of global consumption

In Bolivia during the mid-1970s, a huge wave of people migrated to the Chapare region, a process which coincided with an increase in the cultivation of coca leaves (see Flores & Blandes 1984). Since this cultivation was linked to the global narco-traffic network, the region became more dependent on responding to the forces of supply and demand that emanated from the international market. It is no exaggeration to suggest that market-led development has been extremely effective in generating the production of illegal crops in Bolivia. Coca leaves have now become the economic icon that links local producers, entrepreneurs and an ever-increasing market of consumers of illegal substances in the United States and Europe.

The preconditions for the development of coca production are related to a general deterioration in the Bolivian economy during the 1980s. Policies that tried to bring the large national debt into balance consumed nearly 30 per cent of total export earnings in 1985. The programme of macroeconomic stabilisation aimed to improve economic efficiency but in practice disintegrated the Bolivian tin industry, which declined 30 per cent between 1980 and 1984. Furthermore, the general breakdown of the formal economy, coupled with a programme of austerity cutbacks in state activities and services, created favourable conditions for the development of an informal economy which engaged a great number of people seeking to secure a meagre livelihood. Coca leaf and cocaine production fitted perfectly into informal sector activities (see Laserna 1985).

Coca leaf production has become concentrated in the Chapare region of Bolivia. This region is a 'new' sourcing area for coca leaves and it is estimated that 80 per cent of the total Bolivian coca production originates from this region. Government sources acknowledge that 90 per cent of the coca cultivated in Chapare ends up as the raw material for cocaine production (Lohman 1992). Since 1985, the Chapare region has become the target for the drug eradication policy. Local Chapare farmers protest against the way the Bolivian government and the external US 'war against drugs' are intervening in their region. It is possible to identify militarisation, violation of human rights, and so-called 'alternative' development as the trilogy pitted against local coca farmers.

Local coca farmers disagree with the criminalisation of their crop practices, since for them coca production is part of their cultural heritage, and presently constitutes the only profitable crop on which producers can build their regional livelihoods and political identities (see Schoute 1994; Berger 1997). The unwillingness of local producers to give up their coca bushes is based on the fact that coca leaves remain the main income-generating crop. There are guaranteed legal and illegal markets and the yields are reliable in comparison with other crops, such as citrus, pineapples and other tropical fruits. In this region, the language of development has concentrated its effort on de-criminalising agriculture. Diversification of agriculture, credit, financial support, the organisation of an agro-industry based on tropical products, the construction of roads and the development of commerce are some of the programmes which have had only relative success in the Chapare region.

The language of development aims to transform Chapare farmers into the objects of development instead of seeing them as co-participants in the process of social change. In this, certain linguistic redefinitions of farmers' biographies and life histories have been manipulated by the government. In practice this means a displacement of the farmers' power and identity. The eradication of coca has become an abstract linguistic representation for development programmes in the Chapare region. A recent alternative for the region sees agro-industry as the magic recipe for curtailing the cultivation of illegal crops. Potential private investors are represented as embodying the solution to the problem of coca production. They are presented as agents who are able to stimulate a different economy based on the cultivation of pineapple, pepper, maracuya, bananas and palmitos. Private investment is seen as the solid backbone of a regional agro-industry. In building this representation, the Bolivian agency for alternative development and USAID (Rasnake & Painter 1989) are attempting to clean up and legalise local markets through replacing illegal crops with legal ones.

The picture of private investors is set against the background of a tropical region presented as consistently developed and expanded in terms of infrastructure. The physical space of the Chapare region is marketed to potential investors in promotional films as having drinking water, electricity, roads, airports and a strong local culture which respects private property. What this representation does not express is the fact that much of this development and these images of progress have been both the direct and indirect outcome of the production of coca leaves for narcotic global networks. In addition to this agro-export linguistic idiom, there are other competing idioms seeking to find alternatives to coca production. One of these advocates the transformation of the whole region into an area for tropical eco-tourism, directed at environmentalist and adventure tourists from the Northern industrialised societies. A second alternative is more radical than the other two and is designated in the language of development as a 'zero option'. This proposes that the Bolivian government should buy out all farmers and turn the whole region into a national park for conservation purposes.

All the above proposals try to deal with farmers' activities and commitments, and insofar as this is the case, there is a rhetorical intention to address local issues of development. In fact, these are political-cum-linguistic attempts to control the escalating issue of the influence of coca leaf production in Bolivia. Very rapidly this has become the issue that has risen to the top of the development agenda in recent years (see Leons & Sanabria 1997). Unlike the case of Chile, Bolivian authorities and development experts have focused their fight for the control of the Chapare region on the technical development of monocultures directed towards international markets. Despite the symbolic value of development with the introduction of 'new technologies', the radical substitution of coca leaf production is seen by local farmers as a threat to Bolivian sovereignty. Such grassroots opposition to development programmes has generated institutional national and international dissatisfaction with Chapare farmers. American officials usually voice serious objections to Chapare farmer associations. They argue that local farmers are merely justifying the political existence of the global narco-traffic network. Further pressure has come from the Bolivian state whose powerful militarisation of the issue has been critically viewed at international level because of its failure to make any commitments to protect human rights. So far, the Bolivian state has resisted external pressures in this direction. On the other hand, it has accepted American political and economic influences for greater co-ordinated unity against illegal crops.

Chapare farmers who reject development programmes are represented in the language of development as passive and therefore without any intention to legalise their agro-production practices (Jones 1991). These programmes do not acknowledge that farmers have recent experience of the high financial costs associated with changing crops as well as the personal costs involved in relation to macro-economic adjustment policies. In general it is possible to suggest that the language of technological development is formulated and implemented with little or no regard for local producers' participation.

Farmers complain that in meetings with development experts they are outnumbered by government and development officials and that in the end local initiatives are always ignored. This reached a point where a group of farmers began to accumulate their own collection of data and facts in order to generate what they wanted to define as their representation of 'reality'. The farmers do not trust the way they are represented in the official language of development (Schoute 1994: 94). These kinds of situations illustrate the existing gap in language between farmers and development experts in the Chapare region.

Chapare coca farmers present themselves as taking a stance against eradication policies; they do not hold that eradication can contribute to local development. In their locally situated language they do not perceive themselves as accountable or dependent on the drug barons of the cocaine industry, instead they locate themselves as innocent and the narcotic problem as a responsibility of Western culture and the existing global commodity market. In local language, Chapare production of coca is not synonymous with drug trafficking. For local people coca is a valuable and important commodity that allows them to sustain a diversified cropping system that includes manioc, corn, fruit and a few animals. Although the non-coca farming activities occupy a large amount of land and labour, it is the cash crop of coca which provides them with an income to cover the farmers' basic consumption requirements and capitalise within the household.

Social and political contradictions in the Chapare region provide us with a different local representation of the presence of the Third World in the language of development. In this, local farmers achieve a degree of economic progress and political voice through the production of an illegal crop. In so doing they reshape the local mediations of people to the Chapare tropics, global markets and the nation-state in a way that makes the established insights of development studies no longer adequate. The difference between macro-economic language in Bolivia and the local political language of the Chapare farmers, needs consideration. As some argue, the local appropriation of modern technology is resulting in the creation of 'new' ethno-scenarios of commodity production. Chapare farmers in their own language and representations are negotiating their linkage to the nation-state as citizens, as well as positioning themselves within the global network of narcotics. This is accomplished through aggressive technological modernisation of farming practices coupled with new ways of using existing political and cultural language. From a development perspective this local situation is problematic, because through their practices local farmers are decentering the legality of the Western institutional language of development. Instead they are constructing a language that combines the use of traditional 'idioms' coupled with the 'need' to exploit the opportunities that are offered by the global market. Local farmers want to be politically respected in their local translations of the signs and codes coming from the macro-economic language of structural adjustment. They care about themselves and the language that should be used in an era of post-project development consensus.

The appearance of illegal crops as global commodities calls for ethnographic studies to examine how local people embody and perform their practices in the context of social change and representations of modernity.

The study of the language of development should focus on the use of linguistic representations, researching the distribution of cultural complexity and the social contestations that are set in motion by the social life of commodities. It is an important task to ask what are the major sites of ethnographic production where significant development representations are generated as counter-tendencies to the international language of development. Ethnographers should not allow a case like Bolivia to become divorced from the links with the abstract language and practices of international development. It is cases like Bolivia that reveal so dramatically the effects and importance of globalising processes.

The fact is we are moving to a turning point where the re-positioning of the individual economic subject has dramatically shifted the boundaries of 'legal-responsibilities' to a series of 'post-privatised' regimes of experience where novel linkages between local knowledge, technology, nature, markets and violence have re-generated the economic agency of actors. We need to study whether the tendencies and counter-tendencies of development and modernity are global processes that are locally mediated, or whether they are simply specific local manifestations of more global social change. We need to theorise a vision of contingency in relation to languages of development, especially when people's performance and practices are a constant result of the interactions between distant and local worlds of knowledge, information and linguistic representations.

Conclusion

As we have demonstrated through the use of Latin American examples, actors' practices that engage with global modernities are much more complex than economic decision-making in isolation. Actors' recognition of the relevance of chemical and electronic devices, such as computers in Chile or the properties of sulphuric acid as used in cocaine production in Bolivia, prompts an increasing awareness of the role of these devices as the main actants in processes of economic development. Thanks to the labours of modernisation programmes in reviving the broad economic literature on market-led development and its distribution through the developing world, a new appreciation of the mediation of industrialised consumer demands is apparently taking place among Third World producers. Production in Third World countries has actually meant a fusion of horizons that are increasingly removed from the production of commodities in everyday life and needs. Neo-liberal commodities have acquired an esoteric quality quite different from commodities produced in 'classical' industrial times. Looking back in history, it seems that 'new' commodities possess a value not because of their objective qualities or style, but simply because they embody status and identity inscriptions. Now products become new and sought after because of what is inscribed within them, that is, because of the language of the market-in-itself.

Actors in the Chilean and Bolivian cases have created spaces within the language of development. Their experiences cannot be reduced to an abstraction within a main or hegemonic development discourse. Their diverse practices and images of modernity are differential responses to normative and abstract representations of universal free market development, and to the spread of an idea that is global in nature, but locally situated in terms of the attribution of meanings. In other words, the language of market-led development can be constructed and de-constructed in different language terms, which are difficult to assess in terms of any 'standardisation' of what constitutes modern values. This modern relativism of development discourse means that language representations generate alternative economic and political constructions where logic, private experiences and disputes describe and define the character of the battlefield and the struggle between different actors.

These processes can only properly be studied through close up ethnography of actors' practices and their use of language strategies to achieve their own private objectives and interests. Hence, any critical analysis of the language of development should concentrate on a study of the diverse discursive manifestations of 'modern reason' by 'modern actors', together with how instrumental reason is used to legitimise new linkages that connect local knowledge, technology, nature, markets, violence, authority, and power in emerging global modernities.

In the period of market-led language, the ordering processes of practical connections between bureaucrats, 'new' macro-economic contexts, computers, privatisation schemes and the cultivation of illegal crops, amongst other linkages, are related to different re-constructions of the relationship between state and society. This is a locally situated process that in itself is an outcome of global neo-liberal language, practice and ongoing development processes in a phase of economic liberalisation. Economic liberalisation has promoted new interactions between humans, nature, technologies, markets and various forms of conflict and violence, and these constitute the new parameters of global modernities. Processes of commoditisation are certainly present but in different forms and with more diverse meanings than previously. These meanings are part and parcel of socially constructed processes, whereby different local languages legitimise modernity. At the same time, they are a dimension of the agent's self-identification with a diversity of values and inscriptions, that are in turn manifestations of contested power within the language of the market itself. These actors are not global statistics or puppets that can be reduced to a technical understanding of the international division of labour, or to the global logic of the IMF and World Bank structural adjustment conditionalities. To understand the significance of the languages of development we must look at both the complicity and activities of international institutions as well as how local actors contribute to the elaboration of global modernities.

This chapter has been devoted to discussing the language of development as a representational field in which the meaning and intentionalities of development policies can be approached, observed and analysed. It is not a neutral or innocent excursion into the topic of international development institutions, their linguistic strategies and local situated outcomes. This line of analysis continues in the tradition of previous contributions in this field (Apthorpe 1984; Wood 1985; Arce & Long 1987; Ferguson 1990; Long & Long 1992; de Vries 1992; Arce 1993; Hobart 1993; and Peet & Watts 1993). In its own way each of these contributions has dealt with issues of language, practices, knowledge and to a lesser extent representations. Nevertheless, all have contributed to demythologising the meta-theoretical languages of development (modernisation, dependency and institutional theories). A major implication of this tradition in development studies has been a re-consideration of the distribution of meaning through the study of development practices while focusing on issues of power.

The era of globalisation calls for a focus on diverse language representations such as progress, rationality and development. Representations stemming from international institutions aim to regulate or stifle differential actor responses in local practices, principally in order to control the processes of development. In an attempt to explore some of these dimensions, I have stressed the need for a sociology of development and a politics of social change that address the language cartography of intervention policies and their outcomes. In short, I argue that a sociological perspective on knowledge, authority and power should not merely rediscover diversity, but rethink the whole issue of the distribution of meaning, externalisation of the idioms of modernity, and the representations and counter-representations of development intervention. It follows that any rethinking of intervention will have to engage with the question of whether or not development interventions should regulate or create diversity, and seek the active presence of Third World actors in creating global modernities.

Notes

1   A preliminary version of this paper was presented in Berkeley, California, at the Workshop Languages of Development in October 1994. Since then, this paper has evolved into its present form. During the process of the paper's mutation, I received support from my departmental colleagues. I want to thank them for their help. I want to extend a special word of thanks to Eleanor Fisher of the University of Wales, Swansea, who read and commented extensively and so critically on this paper. She helped me to clarify my thoughts and made valuable comments analytically and provided me with editorial advice. I found this extremely supportive and stimulating, she constructed a friendly environment in which I could finally finish this paper.

2   Here, I draw upon John Law's (1994) characterisation of 'modes of ordering' as strategies or modes of recursion that depend upon representation. Ordering *depends*, that is, on how it is that agents represent both themselves, and their context, *to* themselves … .[R]epresentations shape, influence and participate in

ordering practices: that ordering is not possible without representation' (Law 1994: 25). Nor, of course, without language use and translation.

3   Other forms of ordering include the use of statistics to construct, for example, human populations. These statistics may then be used as the basis for interventions (see Fisher & Arce, this volume). Mapping and cartography constitute another way of ordering reality and can facilitate the territorial occupation of space, as well as enable people to plan a safe journey (Wood 1993). A further form of ordering appears in classification and taxonomies of the natural world in order to provide us with an experimental basis for society. Criminology with its development of fingerprint data-banks and other techniques is another example of ordering. Through statistical correlation individuals are identified within a population, as the basis for practices of detection by criminologists (Stratton 1996).

4   For a full description of holographic organisation in practice, see Morgan 1986: 103–5.

5   This notion of virtual reality is taken from the computer's representation of realities. Virtual reality is a reality organised from 'other' different realities that the actor can manipulate or re-assemble according to his/her interests, information and capabilities. This is a reality without history or tradition, it is a modern and flat present, therefore to act on this or under this does not compel the actor into questions of morality or universal values. This is the privatisation of the collective consciousness, in order to allow the individual to page up or down (govern) his/her representations and desires of life.

6   This information was collected in July–August 1994.

3 Modernisation without the market?

The case of the 'Soviet East'[1]

Deniz Kandiyoti

The purpose of this chapter is to examine the nature of 'modernising' encounters between the former Soviet state and its Central Asian periphery, with a view to exploring whether an analysis of their interaction can contribute to our broader understanding of modernisation and development. Our notions of the latter in the 'less developed countries' are generally informed by a specific range of colonial encounters, namely those between the historic West and its various peripheries. A body of writing, which we may loosely define as post-colonial scholarship, has exerted considerable influence upon critical perspectives on 'modernity' as a political project. This has, in turn, inspired many critiques of development, both as theory and practice.[2] Much of this writing is based on the premise that the capitalist West is the hegemonic centre from which discourses about progress, modernisation and development emanate, while the rest is subjected to the imperial gaze and development interventions, occasionally met by local resistance and protest. The more recent emphasis on globalisation as a central analytic category would seem to point to a splintering of hegemony, with seemingly contradictory features of both greater homogeneity and interconnectedness and counter-trends of fragmentation and particularism. Yet, the backdrop to this new discourse remains an expanding capitalist world order, now much complicated by new patterns of production and consumption, flows of people and ideas, but ultimately interconnected through the medium of the market (understood in the broadest sense, as in Appadurai 1990).

I argue here that culturally contextualised analyses of attempts at modernisation-without-capitalism have a great deal to teach us. There is a degree of urgency to this analytic task, since the shift to market economies has gathered such momentum in post-communist states that the specificities of socialist experiments purporting to be transformative in the absence of market economies may soon be lost from view.

Among countries currently undergoing such transitions, those of the Muslim periphery of the former Soviet Union offer particularly striking examples since, on the face of it, they appear to have been subjected to extremes of social engineering, starting from the period of Russian colonisation in the late nineteenth century and especially after their incorporation into the Soviet regime from the 1920s. This period saw forced sedentarisation of nomadic populations, collectivisation of agriculture, the influx of non-indigenous settlers, changes in local alphabets, purges of local elites, repression of organised religion, and attempts at 'reinventing' local cultures in a Soviet mould. If modernisation implies a radical break with the past, these cases should constitute relevant illustrations.

Yet, this is also a region where two totally contradictory discourses about modernisation appear to coexist. On the one hand, we have numerous ideologically inspired celebrations of the achievements of Soviet-style modernisation, pointing, among other things, to the emancipation of women, universal literacy, and the triumph of Soviet forms of expression over 'traditional' cultures. English language reviews of Soviet sources, such as Silver (1992) and Jones and Grupp (1992), reveal themes that are thoroughly familiar to any reader well versed in the Parsonian variants of Western modernisation theory. Transcending national particularisms through assimilation into 'Soviet' culture is presented as the highest point of modernisation, and indicators of success are elaborated upon in numerous writings on so-called 'cultural convergence' (see, for instance, Dunn & Dunn 1973). On the other hand, many commentators, depending on their political proclivities, either lament or celebrate the immutability of local Muslim cultures, the relative lack of penetrative capacity of the Soviet state and the resilience of local social patterns, with an abandon that would make even the most hardened Orientalist blush.[3] How, then, may we explain such apparent contradictions? And what underlying processes do they reveal or conceal?

Before elaborating on these questions, it must be pointed out that this is in some measure a reflection of the impoverishment of social scientific analysis under the dual impact of Western Sovietology and Soviet ethnography. Caught between the political agenda of Sovietologists searching for lines of fault in the Soviet system (and looking expectantly in the direction of the Muslim periphery as an enclave of cultural resistance) and the ideological orientation of Soviet scholars intent on demonstrating the eventual triumph of progressive modernisation, the actual dynamics of change, accommodation and resistance in Central Asia were often overlooked. Now, with the dismemberment of the Soviet Union and the political independence of the Muslim-majority republics, a new geopolitics of alignment with the Muslim world and Western fears about the spread of Islamic fundamentalism (Eickelman 1993) may yet again bypass and render irrelevant any serious discussion of the Soviet legacy in favour of more pressing concerns about geopolitics and identity formation.[4] In what follows, I shall offer a review of differing evaluations of the Soviet legacy with a view to highlighting the paradoxes inherent in 'modernising' encounters in Central Asia.

Colonial onslaught or cultural stasis?

If we define loss of civilisation in the narrow sense of rupture or severance of links with religious 'great traditions', the case for treating the Soviet East as a case in point is most forcefully made by Shahrani (1993). He argues that Soviet policy in Central Asia should be evaluated as a colonial project geared to the centre's aims of economic and ideological control. On the economic front, the Muslim periphery was utilised as a source of primary commodities – petroleum in the case of Azerbaijan and cotton in Central Asia. Much has been written about the overspecialisation of the latter economies, especially Uzbekistan, in cotton production and about concomitant processes of depletion of water and soil resources with severe levels of environmental degradation and pollution (Rumer 1989; Gleason 1991; Carley 1989; Spoor 1993). Although there are special complications involved in making precise estimates of net in- or outflows between centre and periphery (Spoor 1993: 147), the fact that there were hardly any textile industries in the region, despite the dominance of cotton cultivation, clearly suggests that any value added remained outside Central Asia. On the ideological front, the modernisation of the 'backward' Central Asian populations mandated nothing short of a systematic onslaught upon existing patterns of social institutions, identities and loyalties. This onslaught took the form of territorial fragmentation and the constitution of artificial ethno-national entities, the severance of links with both the Turko-Persian heritage and the wider Muslim world through the adoption of differently modified forms of the Cyrillic alphabet, and the systematic destruction of Muslim institutions. This amounts to a 'historical trauma' which must have wrought deep and significant transformations.

Against this background, it may appear somewhat startling to learn from some Russian commentators on Central Asia that Communism barely scratched the surface and hardly penetrated under the cultural skin, so to speak. Some, like Malashenko (1993), go so far as to argue that if culture loss is what we are talking about, then the turmoil created by the Soviet regime has been far greater for the Russians, since the institutions of Russian Orthodoxy were dismantled more thoroughly than those of Islam, which, for a variety of reasons, received more support at the official level.[5] He even posits a certain cultural fit between Islam and Communism, based as they both are on strong ideas of social justice, the primacy of the community over the individual and obedience to authority. Panarin ruefully expresses a similar sentiment of loss when he talks about the ironies of a situation whereby '[a]fter severing ties with Christianity, consigning to special secret library archives half of our old Russian culture, and forfeiting many fundamental elements of popular morality, we, the Russians of the Soviet era, began to feel like genuine cultural missionaries in the East' (1993: 14). He is averse, however, to facile explanations based on the loss of Russia's pre-revolutionary cultural legacy, recognising instead tendencies for exclusiveness, revolutionary nihilism and a 'sacrilegious thrust of absolute self-alienation from the past' as important historic strands of Russian identity.

Nonetheless, one cannot help but get an occasional whiff of post-Communist nostalgia, whereby the formerly 'backward' peoples of Central Asia are being recast by Russian commentators as sturdy local cultures which have managed to retain and reproduce some immutable cultural essence. This cultural essentialism is only matched and surpassed by that of the Central Asians who are utilising the same notions of unbroken, historical ethno-cultural essence in the service of the articulation of post-Soviet nationalisms. In order to achieve a better understanding of how these positions became crystallised, it is important to search for their antecedents in Soviet policies and scholarship, particularly in Soviet ethnography.

The Soviet ethnographic 'other'

The local cultures the Russians encountered in Central Asia could readily be construed by the colonists as archetypes of 'tradition': patrilineal tribal formations among the nomads, sometimes with tribal aristocracies, sedentary populations subject to the control of the patriarchal family, local despots and the strictures of Islam, all this overlaid by the 'Asian immobility' assumed by Soviet commentators to be associated with the so-called 'Asiatic mode of production'.[6] The modernising encounter was not between two civilisations, that of the West and the 'Orient', however defined, but between a declining colonial power, uncertain about its own place of insertion into the historic West, subject to much soul-searching about its own backwardness, and diverse indigenous formations ranging from the sedentary populations of the great Islamic centres and urban settlements of the Maverannahr, literate and catechised, to the nomadic and semi-nomadic peoples of the steppes whose conversion to Islam came late and remained for a long time a thin veneer over their ancient Animistic beliefs and cosmologies. The task that fell to Soviet ethnographers of understanding, classifying and ultimately playing a role in transforming these entities, presents rather unique features that may not be assimilated to the role of anthropologists in the colonial encounters of the West, despite a similar interest in administering ethnically and religiously disparate subject populations. The quasi-missionary zeal and positivistic outlook of the Soviet ethnographer as agent of change is represented well by Snesarev (1974: 217): 'In order that the struggle to uproot survivals may receive the necessary content and be directed purposefully, a basis in scientific research must be set up for the struggle. Ethnographers can and must do this'.

Shanin offers an incisive account of the interpenetration between Soviet nationality, policy and the notions of ethnos and ethnogenesis that dominated Soviet ethnography. He draws our attention to the fact that Soviet perceptions of ethnicity and their expression in the social sciences differed significantly from their Western counterparts. The very fact that the term *natsionallnost* (which he translates as 'ethnicity' with many reservations) has no exact equivalent is quite telling in this respect.[7] Differing radically from Western approaches adopting a relativistic position, by the 1960s, Soviet ethnologists saw ethnicity as 'a culturally self-reproducing set of behavioural patterns linked to collective self-identity, which continues through different modes of production and is significantly autonomous from the forces and relations of production. A new cross-modes concept of *ethnos* was declared the *differencia specificia* of ethnology as a discipline' (Shanin 1989: 413).

Inevitably, various convolutions were necessary to make this notion of ethnos fit in with the orthodox evolutionist sequence of socioeconomic formations postulated by Stalin. Skalnik (1990) argues that the Institute of Ethnography of the USSR Academy of Sciences, under the leadership of Bromley, squared this circle by invoking the concept of 'ethno-social organism' (ESO). This subsumed both *etnikos*, namely the stable common features of language, culture, psychology and self-consciousness characterising a collectivity, and the types of broader societies (primitive, feudal, capitalist) of which they formed a part. 'It is precisely,' Bromley suggests, 'this relative conservatism and certain independence of ethnic qualities that conditions the possibility to preserve basically the same "ethnikos" over a period of several socioeconomic structures' (1974: 69). This made it possible to posit ethnos as something consistent, enduring and objectively existing, thus creating a space for traditional ethnographic research whilst at the same time paying lip service to the Marxist-Leninist sequencing of socioeconomic formations. This produced a reification of cultural diversity on the basis of arid definitional speculations rather than fieldwork and an aversion to any real discussion of the actual problems of inter-ethnic relations. Skalnik is particularly critical about the fact that this theory served as window-dressing for Soviet ethnic pluralism and as evidence of the respect of the Party for the language, culture and mentality of each ethnic group in the USSR. He suggests, furthermore, that ethnographers provided the ancient policy of Russification, inherited from the Tsarist regime, with the new wrapping of 'progressive' amalgamation into the first international (inter-ethnic) formation based on socialism. Thus, the highest point of modernisation was represented by the merging (*slianiie*) of ethnic particularisms into a new superordinate entity – the Soviet people (*sovetskii narod*) – whose *lingua franca* happened to be Russian, the language of inter-ethnic communication, universalism and civilisation.

The crafting of Soviet culture through the creation of new rituals, or the rescripting of existing ones, constitutes an intriguing chapter of Soviet modernisation (Lane 1981). Binns (1979) shows that the various phases of Soviet ritualism were complex reflections of historical contingencies (such as war), the need to legitimate political rule, the vagaries of different waves of anti-religious propaganda and popular pressures from below. Sadomskaya (1990) distinguishes between different types of anthropologists engaged in this enterprise. The so-called 'bureaucratic' anthropologists wanted, to varying degrees, to be directly involved in writing fully-scripted scenarios for new holidays and rituals, since they felt professionally best suited to sift out the 'useful' from the 'harmful' in traditional cultures. The 'traditionalist' efforts were directed at an attempt to pour the 'old wine' of ancient customs and folkloric reconstructions into the 'new wineskins' of socialist ritual. They often approached their subject with nostalgic compassion and rehabilitated some old holidays, previously banned as 'religious vestiges', decreeing them as non-church and therefore harmless. For instance, the Central Asian holiday of Navruz (the spring New Year), banned as Moslem in the 1930s, was rehabilitated as Zoroastrian (hence pre-Moslem) and as a benign holiday with folk-agrarian roots. Thus, anthropologists proceeded to harmonise the syncretism of folk holidays and rituals with the new, ideological ones justifying 'the curious marriage of convenience between paganism and the governmental cult' (Sadomskaya 1990: 250). This syncretism from above was, in this author's view, largely ineffectual in creating a new folklore and 'the people of the Soviet Union were doomed either to official parades or archaic costume shows' (*ibid*: 251).

What this author does not elaborate upon is the extent to which these representations of 'ethnic' cultures and rituals may have been internalised by those peoples of the Soviet periphery who may have had a different vocabulary to articulate their sense of identity and a less salient sense of themselves in ethnic terms. Roy (1991–2), for instance, demonstrates that what took place under the Soviet system was the reification of a play of much more open, dynamic and relational identities than either theories of ethnos or state policies could adequately reflect. For therein lies one of the most frequently cited paradoxes of Soviet nationality policy: that while officially espousing the goal of merging nationalities and transcending ethnic particularisms, it institutionalised, codified and ossified them, making 'ethnic solidarity the one dimension where political dissent and local consensus and lobbies could be organised and/or mobilised' (Shanin 1989: 420).

Numerous authors are in agreement about the Soviet Union's contribution to the process of nation-building among the non-Russian peoples (Suny 1993; Zaslavsky 1993; Bremmer and Taras 1993; Smith 1993). In Central Asia, the drawing up of new territorial boundaries in the region formerly known as Turkistan, went through several phases after 1924 leading to the creation of five union republics, which emerged as independent states in 1991 – Kazakhstan, Uzbekistan, Turkmenistan, Kyrgyzstan and Tajikistan. However artificial these demarcations might originally have been, they achieved lasting importance as the context for the development of institutions laying the groundwork for nationhood: the cultivation of local, national intelligentsia and cadres, the codification and elaboration of national languages, cultural and scientific establishments, an elaborate system of schooling in non-Russian languages, to name but a few. Anderson's (1991) suggestions concerning the colonial origins of post-colonial nation-states seem amply borne out in these examples. However, as Brubaker (1994) points out, these nation-building processes bear the hallmark of a system of institutional mismatch between ethno-cultural nation and citizenry, whereby nationhood is not related to legal citizenship of a state but is the prerogative of sub-state ethno-territorial groups. This creates, among other things, a pervasive tension between incipient national states harbouring substantial national minorities and the 'external' homeland states to which those minorities belong (by ethno-national affiliation but not by legal citizenship). It is not citizenship, moreover, but *natsionallnost*, an ascriptive legal category, that determines one's life chances; positively, if one is a member of one of the 'titular' nationalities benefiting from preferential treatment policies, and negatively, if one happens to be a member of a 'minority' nationality. Thus, as Gleason correctly points out, ethnic belonging is not merely about preferences in life styles and customs but very much related to something as crucial as expectations about the future. He suggests that '[c]alculations of an ethnic group's life chances and expectations for the future played a major role in suffusing national identity in Central Asia with a sense of urgency that by some measures exceeded that of any other region in the USSR' (Gleason 1993: 333). Roy (1994) argues persuasively that it is competition for scarce resources, not among 'traditional' ethnic groups, but among groups reconfigured within the framework of the Soviet system, that is responsible for so-called ethnic violence in Central Asia.

The persistence of tradition?

We may now return to the apparent paradox signalled in the opening section of this paper; that what appeared to some as rapid modernisation and radical change was interpreted by others as cultural stasis and immobility. I would argue that it is the nature of Soviet-style modernisation itself, some features of which were discussed above, rather than resistance from a cultural complex described by Soviet ethnographers as 'traditionalism' that has created this paradox. In order to clarify this point, it is necessary to subject the concept of 'traditionalism', which is routinely invoked in Central Asian ethnographies, to closer inspection.

The most forceful case for the continuity of the social order in rural Central Asia, despite decades of Soviet rule, is made by Sergei Poliakov (1992). His main contention is that behind the veneer of modernisation lies the reality of an untransformed traditional society, which has both resisted and subverted Soviet attempts to change property relations and the moral/cultural basis of community life. Superficially, one may discern similarities here with the 'cultural obstacles to change' literature of early modernisation theory, with its stress on endogenous factors blocking development. This impression is quite misleading, however, since Poliakov, a convinced materialist, is only willing to accord the cultural complex he describes as 'traditionalism'[8] the status of a superstructural phenomenon which could not survive outside the economic context which lends it life and substance. It is only with reference to this untransformed economic base (rather than to Islam per se) that we may understand a host of empirical phenomena: widespread petty commodity production despite collectivisation; distinct age and gender hierarchies in large rural households; the prevalence of arranged marriages and *kalym* (bride price); high fertility; the subordinate status of women; high levels of spending for life cycle rituals; the salient role of the *mahalla* (neighbourhood) and the mosque as key socialising agencies competing with formal Soviet schooling, to name but a few. Poliakov's approach is quite bold since he forsakes the language of 'remnants' and 'survivals' used by his colleagues when witnessing similar phenomena (which implies some teleological faith in an ongoing process of transition) choosing instead to present these features as endemic. He suggests that the majority of the adult rural population in Central Asia (up to 85 per cent) worked in petty commodity production and that participation in collective work was minimal and only undertaken to obtain a plot of private land which, far from being a supplemental subsistence plot, formed the basis of a thriving second economy. Furthermore, this 'illegal' economy was heavily subsidised by the state sector through the use of tools, free inputs and transport diverted from collective to private uses. This type of economy, in turn, sustained the unreconstructed domestic mores of the rural community.

In order to explain these outcomes, Poliakov felt little need to invoke the agency of social actors who might, in Scottian vein, be deploying a panoply of techniques such as diversion, pilfering, outward compliance and private resistance and concealment in order to maintain the relative autonomy of their communities in the face of politico-administrative encroachment (Scott 1985). Nor was he able to discern, as Lubin's classic study did, some solid underlying rationale behind indigenous nationalities' livelihood strategies. Indeed, Lubin (1984) suggested that there may have been more than meets the eye in ethnic occupational stratification in Uzbekistan. Although the Slav and European nationalities, overwhelmingly concentrated in urban areas, occupied jobs requiring higher levels of training in the industrial sector and received higher wages, they were not necessarily best equipped to deal with or capitalise upon shortages in the economy nor did they necessarily command the highest incomes. Preferences for work outside the socialised sector, in agriculture and the services, may have been based on solid economic reasons, since these offered much better prospects for higher incomes, earned as unofficial emoluments for scarce services and commodities, or as the result of parallel activities and unofficial markets. Poliakov, who insists on the 'irrational' nature of Central Asian social patterns, opts, instead, for a materialist/structuralist account. His starting point is that Central Asian societies constitute an instance of the Asiatic mode of production, manifesting itself in diverse forms of livelihood such as subsistence agriculture, irrigated farming and mobile stock-breeding (Poliakov 1993). This system was characterised by the absence of private property and the limited development of the forces of production. The beginnings of agrarian capitalism stimulated by incorporation into the Russian empire and the islands of private property, which it gave rise to, were swept away by collectivisation, which reached Central Asia in the 1930s in the form of 'Stalinist communal-serfdom' (*op. cit*: 126). Collectivisation restored to its former strength the local community, which had been weakened by colonial rule; and the authoritarian-patriarchal management of the collective farm system based on patron-client relations between superiors and subordinates could readily be absorbed into customary life ways. The clear conclusion emerging from this analysis is that the Soviet system in Central Asia, far from effecting a progressive transformation leading to modernity, actually reinforced and gave a longer lease of life to pre-capitalist forms of production and social organisation. This is a suggestion that must be taken seriously, despite the fact that Poliakov attributes what he interprets as cultural stasis to the arrested capitalist development of the Central Asian periphery, and the resulting strength of 'traditionalism', rather than the combination of local factors with intrinsic features of the command economy and the politico-administrative structures of the Soviet state itself.

Evidence pointing to the 'colonisation' of Soviet institutions by pre-Soviet forms of social organisation is plentiful, and cannot merely be put down to limitations in the outreach of the Soviet state. Bacon (1966) was one of the first to note a process of overlap between Soviet institutions such as *kolkhozes* and brigades and tribal formations in Central Asia. Olcott (1987) also shows that among the Kazakhs, the real structure of local power was controlled by traditional clan leaders behind a façade of Communist party organisation. Poliakov's own data on collective farms in Tajikistan points to the continuing importance of the extended family, the *avlod*, in work organisation and the constitution of work brigades. Referring to similar patrilineal groupings as *elat* among the Khorezm Uzbeks, Snesarev reluctantly acknowledges that '[t]he prevalence in our day, although in residual form, of these territorial-kinship groups introduces certain complications in the social life of the *kolkhoz*' (1974: 229). These take the concrete form of refusing to leave inhabited places for new settlements and continuing to maintain the mutual aid and ritual functions of the *elat*, even though its economic role may be marginal. Dragadze's (1988) ethnography of a Georgian village also suggests that, far from modifying and undercutting family solidarities, the Soviet system actually reinforced them as the only refuge from powerlessness and as a source of security in a shortage economy. She describes rural households as 'multiple-income management units' where the judicious deployment of household members in wage-earning and self-provisioning activities is crucial to adequate living standards, as is the cultivation of broader networks of kin who may provide favours such as loans, hospitality and residence permits. In the rather different context of Turkmenistan, Bouchet makes the observation that 'the kolkhoz does not abolish tribalism, it becomes its context' (1991–2: 66). Whereas originally tribal formations served significant socioeconomic roles and worked in pursuit of common economic objectives, under the Soviet system their role may have been reduced to the pure exchange of services, and in cases of asymmetrical exchange, to new forms of clientelism. It is in this sense that it is possible to discern a degree of capture of Soviet institutions and of possibilities of manoeuvring within them in the framework of local networks of obligation and clientelism. It would appear that if so-called 'traditionalism' did indeed exist, it was endemic rather than residual to the Soviet system.

Humphrey's (1983) ethnography of a Siberian collective farm goes furthest in identifying sources of internal contradiction within the command economy and therefore deserves detailed attention. Her observations about the nature of Buryat-Soviet encounters have broader implications and provide important illustrations of the sorts of paradoxes with which I am concerned in this chapter. On the economic front, the tight monitoring of production targets and work organisation did not prevent the creation of non-legitimate resources in materials and people. In fact some unofficial or illegitimate roles were essential to the smooth functioning of collective farms and could be deployed to perfectly legitimate ends such as procuring inputs or ensuring the sale of *kolkhoz* produce. The materials and monies thus generated, as well as the proceeds of private plots, which Humphrey calls 'manipulable resources', were not investible in a capitalist sense (given the restrictions imposed on the disposal of assets) and found their way, instead, into a system of ritualised exchange which turns individually owned goods into a means of leverage for attaining status in the public sphere. Once achieved, a more advantageous position could be used to maximise a variety of personal rights, such as greater freedom to travel, access to goods that are unavailable locally, or access to special shops. The fact that the 'Buryat gift economy' seeped into the cracks of the command economy does not, however, mean that it survived unaltered. On the contrary, the social content of reciprocity is shown to have undergone substantial modifications since collectivisation, with Buryat concepts of reciprocity being applied to totally new relationships.

Given the important changes noted by this author in most Buryat institutions, ranging from kinship to religious ritual, how is the fiction of unbroken continuity, which finds its counterpart in the Soviet concept of 'traditionalism', maintained? This is made possible, Humphrey argues, by the fact that 'the phenomena of the Soviet world appear disconnected from their theoretical origins, structured by a Buryat consciousness. Those Buryat social institutions which existed are wholly adapted to Soviet circumstances, but this is not recognised and they continue to be explained as though there had been no break with the past' (*ibid*: 441).

Is it, then, the very colonisation of Soviet institutions by local forms of organisation and consciousness which paradoxically accounts for the 'sovietisation' of the local? Bouchet would seem to concur with this evaluation when he states: 'Soviet Turkmens are not merely Turkmens living in the Soviet Union, they integrate deeply the "soviet" dimension to their identity' (*op. cit*: 66). This interpenetration of identities appears to go a long way in creating a semblance of continuity. I would like to suggest, however, that this narrative about continuity is only tenable under circumstances in which social forces acting to break down local communal networks are relatively weak or nonexistent.[9] This, indeed, appears to have been the case in a collective farm such as the one described by Humphrey where communal values support parochialism and local ties and allow the maintenance of dual and parallel communal groups, the purely Soviet and the Buryat-Soviet. A more recent ethnography of a Tajik village goes even further by suggesting that the Tajik/Soviet split may not only activate parallel networks, but actually acquires a gendered dimension since the public world of the *kolkhoz* and of politico-administrative dealings is dominated by men, while women become the custodians of religious observances and household-based rituals associated with Islam, a central component of Tajik identity (Tett 1994). Indeed, Soviet anti-religious campaigns produced a divorce between folk practices and the institutions of organised religion and public expressions of religiosity. Reduced to privatised ritual and cut off from its philosophical and institutional moorings, religion, according to Tohidi (1995), also became identified with the 'private', in Azerbaijan, particularly as a marker of 'Azeriness' centred around women's proper Muslim conduct and virtue. Reinterpreted by this author, 'traditionalism, especially in the area of gender relations, appears as a reactive or compensatory strategy for cultural self-preservation in the face of colonialist meddling, an argument quite similar to that made in connection with Muslim societies, and colonial encounters with the West more generally. 'Perhaps because Muslim Azeri men had to cede control over political power', Tohidi suggests that 'proving unable to resist Russian domination and Russification in the public arena, they have held onto the private domain the hardest as the only bastion of their power and identity' (*op. cit*: 25).

However, parallels with other colonial encounters, more specifically those between Western imperial powers and the Middle East, fail to capture the specificity of the Soviet case and disregard the extent to which various forms of parochialism and ethnic consciousness were as much creations of the system itself as responses to it. A command economy which hemmed in processes of mobility of people and goods, combined with a nationalities policy which institutionalised ethno-national difference as the basis for the distribution of social rewards and life options, could only coexist in a state of permanent contradiction with universalist ideals of modernisation, progress and equality. What, in this context, appeared as 'traditionalism' was the fictionalised and over-determined outcome of a particular path of modernisation, where to paraphrase Marx, 'everything solid' far from 'melting into air' often congealed into a strange parody of itself. This resulted, among other things, in an acute sense of 'national injury' and loss on the part of both coloniser and colonised, a sense often articulated with nostalgic reference to an antecedent civilisation, which better expressed some lost cultural essence. The socialist utopia of the future was thus replaced by a dystopia of the present and a mythical reconstruction of the past, the search for a 'golden age' that currently legitimises and lends credence to efforts at national self-assertion. As Roy perceptively points out, the discourses of coloniser and colonised became mirror-images of one another; nationalist intellectuals in

Uzbekistan, for instance, even as they reproach Moscow for suppressing their culture, use the very definitions of ethnos propounded by Stalinist ideologues in their own elaborations of national culture (1991–2: 30). It is to these deeper levels of interpenetration that one must look to discover the more disturbing effects of hegemony, those which take the insidious form of a constriction of the discursive possibilities within which choices, alternatives and aspirations for the future may be articulated in the post-Soviet space.

Notes

1   A first version of this paper was presented at the EIDOS conference on *Globalisation and Decivilisation*, 14–16 December 1995, Wageningen Agricultural University, The Netherlands. I am grateful to participants for their comments. I also owe thanks to Anthony Hyman, Ruth Mandel, Ekaterina Makarova and Faridah Garnett for helpful reactions to the first draft and to Sami Zubaida for pointing me in the direction of French language texts. The chapter is also published in *Economy and Society*, Vol. 25, no. 4, November 1996: 529–42.

2   As exemplary texts see Marglin & Marglin (1990) and Escobar (1995).

3   For instance, Carrere-d'Encausse (1979) suggested that Central Asian societies, far from producing 'homo sovieticus', remained dominated by 'homo Islamicus', which would inevitably reveal lines of fault in the Soviet system. Sergei Poliakov (1992), a leading ethnographer of Central Asia, decried the fact that 'traditionalism' had Central Asian societies in its firm grip, subverting and undermining Soviet policies. A collection of 'revisionist' interpretations by post-Soviet scholars echoes a similar sense of limitation in a far more nuanced manner (see Naumkin [1993]).

4   The question of Central Asian identities is certainly a crucial area for investigation. See, for instance, Gross (1992). However, if studies on transition to the market and economic reform adopt an exclusively technocratic tone, disregarding the social and cultural context of transformation, and if studies on Central Asian identities continue to evolve in an economic vacuum, the sterility of the Sovietology/Soviet ethnography duo may be reproduced in a different form.

5   This author points to cycles of leniency and repression based on political expediency, as in the co-optation of the Muslim clergy during World War II to establish the 'just' character of the war, followed by severe repression and atheistic propaganda from the mid-1950s.

6   I am grateful to Ron Inden for attracting my attention to a process whereby Russia gradually came to be defined with reference to 'feudalism' while the concept of the Asiatic mode of production migrated to Central Asia.

7   It is also significant that Ernest Gellner's Preface to *Soviet and Western Anthropology* (1980) is, in large part, devoted to terminological differences and the non-comparability of superficially similar terms. For a further elucidation of the term 'ethnos' in the Soviet context, see also Tamara Dragadze in the same collection.

8   He defines 'traditionalism' as follows: 'the complete rejection of anything new introduced from the outside into the familiar, "traditional" way of life … . The only thing that is important is that society must not depart from its "ideal form"' (Poliakov *op. cit*: 4).

9   This stands in stark contrast to rural communities in the global South, which have experienced rapid processes of transformation and dislocation under the impact of commodification of agriculture and massive migration to urban centres and across national boundaries.

4 Islamisms and the decivilising processes of globalisation

Azza M. Karam

Introduction

On 15 November 1995, 42-year-old Egyptian diplomat Ahmad Nazmi was returning home from work. As he got out of his car, parked in the underground garage of his home, he was shot six times.

The organisation which later claimed responsibility – an unknown 'International Group for Justice' – is reportedly linked with the *Jihad* Islamist organisation in Egypt. Mr Nazmi's murder was carried out in the early evening in Geneva, Switzerland, the hiding place of *Jihad's* exiled leader, Ayman Al-Zawahri. The organisation claimed to be taking revenge for arrested Islamist colleagues being tried in military courts in Egypt. More ominously, however, it vowed to kill many more Egyptian diplomats. Less than a week later, the Egyptian embassy in Karachi, Pakistan, was devastated by a bomb which killed seventeen people. In this case, three different Islamist groups hastened to claim the 'honour'. It would come as no great surprise were it to be revealed that the killers were Egyptians, trained in Afghanistan, who had acquired Russian, Czech, or American weapons from a European country.

One of the arguments put forward for this increased activity of Egyptian Islamists outside Egypt is the rather optimistic and naive claim that it is because their activism has been curtailed by government security forces in Egypt itself. As if to underline the contrary, on the day of the embassy attack in Karachi, a train crossing Egypt from Cairo to Aswan was blown up by Islamist militants. There is, however, another explanation for this transnational Islamist activism which I put forward and which shapes the argument of this paper. Islamism is in itself a transnational/global phenomenon, tied to the migration of people, information, and commodities, i.e. the increasing compression of time–space that is a feature of post-modernity (Harvey 1989: 159–72). In other words, Harvey's notion of the compression of social relationships so that spatial distance becomes unimportant, is applicable in this understanding of globalisation. It is not only social relationships – in this case between one religio-political group and its exiled members – but also the compression of access to means, resources and information which can be used without any control. It is not inconceivable that a command given in Cairo can be implemented only minutes later in New York, with tools/weapons acquired in Zagreb.

To take this logic one step further, the argument thus materialises into forces which are globally active in a manner that is as unpredictable as it is potentially murderous. It is interesting to note that the Egyptian government gave no official comment or reaction to the killing of the diplomat. One might ask if this silence was the privilege of those who formulate the discourse of knowledge/ignorance – perhaps hoping it was a one-off incident which would somehow disappear from memory. On the other hand, the Egyptian government could not but react to the bombing of its embassy, since that event hit global news headlines almost immediately. And that reaction was even more interesting, since it revolved around a global call for help in the search to find those responsible. Hence, these incidents alone are evidence of the global scale of politics.

When Prime Minister Yitzhak Rabin was assassinated in November 1995 by a 'Jewish extremist', the responses to this event were as mixed as they were telling. There were those who were relieved that the killer was not a Palestinian, Arab, Muslim and/or Islamist, and there were those (Jews, Israelis, Arabs and Muslims) who wished for the honour of this redoubtable 'achievement'. On the other hand, a general sense of shock resounded among those who are far more comfortable with the belief that Islamism is the only form of religious extremism around, or at least the only form that is capable of both local and global atrocities.

The realisation that religious 'extremisms', whether Jewish, Christian, Muslim, or Hindu, are part and parcel of contemporary life, is slowly dawning on 'citizens of the world'. Not only that, religious identities have become an important aspect of globalisation, though often misrepresented. They are variously ignored or magnified, generalised or regionally located, or seen as an impending threat to 'civilisation' because they are linked to poverty, underdevelopment, and irrationality, or they are seen as simply transitory phenomena. In short, in the light of an increasingly worldwide revival of religion, the importance of religious identities is insufficiently analysed and little understood. But, whether in the large number of Islamic banks in Egypt, or the varied Church responses to AIDS in Brazil, or the militancy of Jewish settlers in Israel, religious identity, whatever its manifestation, is definitely on the scene.

Unfortunately, religious identity tends to get confused with politically religious movements and organisations. The latter indeed propagate some forms of religious identity, but they do so in connection with the specific aspirations of, or links to, state power. The emphasis of these ideologies, therefore, tends to centre around 'community' solidarity activities, as opposed to individual development. The reasons for this confusion between political and personal religious identities are many. On the one hand, it may be because it has been convenient for interested parties to generalise and oversimplify matters, and on the other, due to the tendency to think and view in terms of binary oppositions – a legacy of modernist thought – a tendency which remains embedded in much of the discursive practices of global politics.

In this chapter the links between Islamism – specifically those operative in the Arab world[1] – and globalisation will be analysed by reference to Islamist viewpoints concerning notions of 'civilisation'. Civilisation, as understood and propagated by Islamists, is often presented as an alternative formulation for modernity. Hence, the relationship between Islamism and post-modernity is explored. In the second part of the chapter, the viewpoints of Islamist ideologues will be analysed in the light of ideas on (de)civilisation. And in the third and final part, an evaluation of the relationship between Arab Islamism, decivilisation and development will sum up the arguments presented.

Post-modernism and Islamisms

Post-modernism cannot be encapsulated in a few sentences or claim a uniform definition. Rather, it is a mixture of fluid and often intentionally ambiguous ideas. In his book *The Postmodern Condition*, Jean-Francois Lyotard (1986) summarises the post-modern condition as one in which grand narratives lose their legitimacy and credibility. What post-modernists do, he argues, is to question the assumptions of the modern age, particularly those that maintain that rational thought and technological innovation can guarantee progress and enlightenment to humanity. Later, on the theme of civilisation, Lyotard (in During 1993: 172) states that 'after two centuries, we are more sensitive to signs that signify the contrary. Neither economic nor political liberalism, nor the various Marxisms, emerge from the sanguinary last two centuries free from suspicion of crimes against mankind'.

There is not one post-modern condition, as Lyotard implies, but many, which are different and contain different characteristics. The diminishing importance of meta-narratives has not only taken place in the Western world, but globally. Moreover, the phenomena of religious fundamentalism involve the proliferation of not one grand narrative of religion but many subnarratives. In that respect, Western civilisational discourses are globally in crisis. Islamisms must therefore be seen as an aspect of religious fundamentalism world-wide, closely tied to the collapse of the validity of any one Western global civilisational discourse.

In effect, meta-narratives are no longer seen as 'truth', but rather as authorised discourses that deny and silence competing voices. The struggle for universalised knowledge has been abandoned in favour of the search for previously marginalised and unheard voices, for the specificity and power of language and meaning, and their relationship to knowledge, context and locality.

In that regard, Michel Foucault, one of the leading post-modernists/ post-structuralists, has emphasised the shortcomings of grand narratives, and the need to examine the specificities of power in relation to discourse (knowledge and language). He dismisses 'reason' as fiction and views 'truth' as historically constructed. Discourse – a historically, institutionally, and socially specific structure of statements, terms, categories and beliefs – is the site where meaning is both constructed and contested, and power relations defined. Power relations and their exercise in a society can be understood, Foucault contends, through studying the ability to control knowledge and meaning through writing, as well as disciplinary and professional institutions and social relations. According to Foucault, and using a Gramscian understanding, the false power of hegemonic knowledge can be challenged by counter-hegemonic discourses which offer alternative understandings of 'reality' (Foucault 1972, 1979, 1980).

Reality, however, is shaped by language, or by discourse which gives meaning and 'explains' the concrete experiences of daily life for the individual. This has, in turn, led to the call for deconstructing discourse in order to discover the ways in which meanings are constructed and used. A proponent of this, Jacques Derrida (1976), emphasises the important role played by binary oppositions, such as rational/irrational, truth/falsehood, man/woman in Western thought. Meaning is given in such a way that primacy, legitimacy and superiority is allotted to the first term of each of these oppositions. These binary categories shape understanding in complex and often unrecognised ways. In order to better understand this process, Derrida and others have argued for the critical deconstructing of texts (both written and oral) and for greater attention to the way differences are constructed and maintained (see Marchand & Parpart 1995).

As far as Islamism is concerned, a definition is equally untenable. Islamisms are political phenomena par excellence. They cannot easily be summarised into one pattern since they vary according to ideology and ends (i.e. Islamise society and only gradually the state; Islamise the state first; which Islam, which Islamic law or *shari'a* etc.) and means and methods. The Islamisms operant in Saudi Arabia (see Asad 1993: 209–227), cannot be said to be the same as those in Indonesia or yet again in Egypt. But bearing in mind these diversities, what these groups do have in common is some form of political quest for (state) power.

Post-modernity in this context is understood in the same fashion that Sayyid (in Laclau 1994) formulates it. Sayyid sees post-modernity as a 'decentering of the West' (Sayyid 1994: 276). This is also the same sense in which Young (1990: 19- 21) talks about post-structuralism and an awareness of the specificity of European culture. In this respect, post-modernity partly coincides with the project of the post-colonial, since both take up the deconstruction of the centralised, master narratives of European culture, and aim to break down the centre/periphery opposition of imperial discourse. Sayyid develops the concept of post-modernity in such a way as to make it applicable to Islamism, or the politics of the periphery. Basically, he argues that 'it is the change in the relationship between periphery and centre which is constitutive of post-modernity' (Sayyid 1994: 277). This change, he terms 'decentering', since modernity itself is another means of privileging and prioritising the West. That is, 'modernity is a way of saying: "only in the West"'. Post-modernity is a shift from the centrality of the discourse of modernisation/Westernisation. Another means of describing this decentering is by looking at it in terms of decolonisation. The latter is by no means a homogeneous process, but is one of the 'main impetuses behind post-modernity and the revelation of the West's particularity behind its universalist façade' (*ibid*: 278). Sayyid argues that the decentering of the West should be seen in Gramscian terms wherein 'the hegemonic order that naturalised and sedimented a certain narrative structure has broken down, even though tremendously unequal power structures are still in place' (*ibid*: 281). In other words, the West is being decentred to the extent that its claim that there can be no other narrative of development, emancipation or progress other than its own, becomes irrelevant and inaccurate. In fact, seen in this light, 'Islamism does not become the 'other' of post-modernity, but one of the possibilities of decentering of the West. Islamist movements are a *continuation and radicalisation of the process of decolonisation*' [original emphasis].

Indeed, Islamist discourses can be seen as part and parcel of post-modernity, insofar as their proliferation and legitimation derive from the 'failure' of Westernisation, and all its incumbent narrative baggage of modernisation. It is the recognition of the non-universality of Western discourse, of the ability to think difference in a different way, which promotes the validity of Islamist discourse. Ironically, it is the globalisation of Western discourse which has also globalised its failure as an overarching story of the development of humankind.

Islamism and decivilisation

However, to assume that Islamism is possible only because post-modernism is *decentering from the West* – or decolonising – is to ignore a large body of epistemological work that has gone into indigenising knowledge in the non-West. It is to de-legitimise the large body of material that may well have started from the East to the West. In the search for some form of epistemological soundness, one must make room to question the assumption that 'in the beginning was the West'. One of the main tenets of Islamist thought is that 'Islamic civilisation' is in fact the precursor to Western civilisation.

This belief is adhered to quite strongly by most Islamist ideologues. The kind of narrative woven by them can be summarised as follows. There was once a time of ignorance/unbelief (*Jahiliyya*) before the coming of Islam. Then came a golden era following the establishment and spread of the Islamic civilisation, which, in turn, became the source of inspiration and enlightenment for what are today's 'Western' civilisations. Then the moral, social and economic decline of this Islamic civilisation set in, that is, the process of decivilisation, which has been explained in a variety of ways.[2] This is then understood to have led to the undoing of the Islamic civilisation by decivilising influences – i.e. of hegemonic Western civilisation. In fact, some elements within the Islamist movement go so far as to see this characteristic of modern times as a return to another form of *Jahiliyya* (cf. Qutb 1981). Sayyid Qutb, one of the earliest Islamist ideologues of the Egyptian Muslim Brotherhood, whose writings continue to influence and be debated by many today, was executed by the Nasser regime. In his most cited political manifesto *Ma'alim fil Tariq* (Signposts), Qutb argues:

> The struggle between the Believers and their enemies is in essence a struggle of belief, and not in any way of anything else. This was not a political or an economic or a racial struggle; had it been any of these, its settlement would have been easy, the solution of its difficulties would have been simple. But essentially it was a struggle between beliefs – either unbelief or faith, either *Jahiliyyah* or Islam.
>
> (Qutb 1981: 301)

Westernisation, seen by many Islamists as synonymous with modernisation, colonialism and globalisation, is a new imperialism. Western is also equated with Christian. As Qutb describes:

> We see an example of this [i.e. efforts to crush Believers] today in the attempts of Christendom to try to deceive us by distorting history and saying that the crusades were a form of imperialism. *The truth of the matter is that the latter-day imperialism is but a mask for the crusading spirit*, since it is not possible for it to appear in its true form, as it was possible in the Middle Ages.
>
> (*ibid*: 303, emphasis added)

Qutb's essentialist views on *Jahiliyya* and the likening to the Middle Age crusades, however, is not espoused by all Islamists. In fact, other prominent Islamist ideologues such as Howaidi (1994) and Al-Qaradawi (1994), specifically reject Qutb's description of latter-day Islamic societies as *Jahili*. These thinkers point out that today's Muslims are merely ignorant and in need of guidance, as opposed to being unbelievers. Their ignorance is a result of both internal as well as external problematics. As Tunisian Rashid Al-Ghanoushi (1992) claims, inner moral corruption of Muslims is due to all manner of despotisms (political, religious, cultural and ideological). Al-Ghanoushi also elaborates that the outer barriers causing ignorance stem from the Zionist movement which is a danger 'to all humanity and civilisation' (*ibid*: 28). Al-Ghanoushi describes the current reality of Muslims as one in which they are in a state of 'being behind/following, being influenced' which is, in turn, related to being 'slaves of the West', as opposed to a 'situation of civilisation, a situation of action and impact' (*ibid*: 25–6).

Al-Ghanoushi's point is elaborated further by Egyptian Salah Abdel Metaal. Abdel Metaal argues that Islamism is facing enormous civilisational challenges. In his opinion the most important challenge is that the Islamic *umma* (nation) 'cannot achieve a civilisational revival [...] as long as it is colonised by Western countries tainted by modern crusaders and hegemonic Zionism' (Abdel Metaal 1992: 38). But, he continues, 'these challenges are related not only to external global factors, but also to the choices made by ruling regimes and internal economic forces. These choices are made precisely to fill in a civilisational vacuum created by the world order, and thus to organise the lives of Arab and Muslim peoples politically, socially, economically, and technologically' (*ibid*: 38–9).

Sudanese Hassan Al-Turabi, arguing along similar, if not identical lines, calls for a unified Islamic move to reify the role of Islam. Al-Turabi stresses that 'we are in a world of connections in which there is no room to be cut off', and 'the Islamic movement is a global phenomenon transgressing borders and regions'. Hence, the imperative of unification – among the different Islamist movements – in order to lead the (alternative) civilisation process not just of the Islamic, but the whole world (Al-Turabi 1992: 22).

For these Islamists, globalisation in post-modern times has meant the spread of Western values, norms, economics and politics, all of which effectively led to the downgrading of Islamic civilisation. In other words, for some Islamists, globalisation has entailed a form of decivilisation. The project facing Muslims then, according to them, is one of reviving Islamic civilisation, or in other words, one of *recivilising* the Islamic world. As an alternative to present forms of globalised Western modernities, these Islamists are arguing for a unified form of Islamist modernity.

Nevertheless, almost all Islamists would agree that this process of recivilisation should not involve total rejection of all things 'Western'. Qutb is perhaps one of the notable exceptions to this, when he argues that since Islam is a way of life,

> Other societies do not give it any opportunity to organise its followers according to its own method, and hence it is the duty of Islam to annihilate all such systems, as they are obstacles in the way of universal freedom. Only in this manner can the way of life be wholly dedicated to God, so that neither any human authority nor the question of servitude remains, as is the case in all other systems which are based on man's servitude to man.
>
> (Qutb 1981: 137–8)

On the other hand, Fahmi Howaidi, another Egyptian Islamist scholar, takes up the call for a selective mimesis of Western cultures,[3] made earlier by the Indian Mohammed Iqbal, and by Al-Afghani. Howaidi acknowledges that some precautions against all-out imitation are necessary, but argues that: 'What is important is what we take and what we leave. What is important is that if we change our clothes, we do not change our skins or our minds. What is important is to take theirs which is most valuable, and not to lose the dearest of what we possess (Howaidi 1991: 67).

In a similar vein, Egyptian Islamist Yussuf Al-Qaradawi argues that the West is not all evil or aberration. In fact, he praises its possession of 'good works, good behaviour, great achievements, and great possibilities which can be used to better the lot of humans, all humans' (Al-Qaradawi 1994: 90). What he also calls for is a selectivity in the process of cultural acquisition. A selectivity which, in his words,

> may necessitate a process of reformulation and contextualisation – by sometimes adding and detracting – from that which we adapt until it appears beneficial for us, in accord with the principles of our shari'a, the system of our lives, the conditions of our environment, and [this adaptation] with reform and contextualisation, could become a part of our moral existence, our cultural essence, and lose its original affiliation
>
> (*ibid*: 91)

Al-Qaradawi then gives specific examples of what it is possible to select from the West, namely, democracy (which agrees with the Islamic principle of *shura* (consultation) and holds rulers accountable to the ruled), legal systems (which accord with and can carry out Islamic justice), and cultural tools such as cinema, theatre and television and radio 'as long as their content agrees with our aims and ideals' (*ibid*: 92).

Others, such as Abdel Metaal, argue for a recivilisation that ignores any reference to the West. The only exception to this intentional ignorance is made in the context of being able to critique whatever comes from the West 'that is inimical to Islamic civilisation such as atheistic Marxism and materialistic secularism which argue for separation of religion from state, religion from life, and faith from knowledge' (Abdel Metaal 1992: 40).

Yet other Islamists, such as Al-Ghanoushi and Al-Turabi, speak of reifying Islamic civilisation only in the context of a greater hegemonic Western framework. This overarching Western context has to be countered on all levels – moral, religious, social, economic and political. Both advocate that the best means of doing so is through a gradual, concerted and unified effort to reach and preach to the masses on the relevance of Islam.

Islamism, decivilisation and development

Post-modernity, as a decentering of the West and the loss of the legitimacy of the grand narrative, provides interesting insights into the possibility of Islamism, which is, in turn, a collection of 'smaller' narratives. Globalisation, in terms of the compression of time–space, has meant that good news and bad news travel equally fast. This has meant that post-modernity's message, regarding the collapse of Western meta-narratives, reached Islamists at around the same time that Islamists were working on what they regarded as the decivilising effects of precisely these same narratives.

Decivilisations, then, is a provoking concept with which to highlight the particularities in the visions of Islamists vis-à-vis Westernisation. Yet, it is equally plausible to argue that decivilisation, coupled with post-modern critiques of binary oppositions, provides a further insight, namely, how Islamist recivilisation strategies can themselves be critiqued. For Islamist proposals seem to revolve around the creation of a variety of counter-discourses, each of which can be argued to be a reaction to a hegemonic West. In other words, binary oppositions continue to persist in Islamist thought and advocated means – good/evil, Islamic/Western, authentic/foreign, ours/theirs and knowledge/ignorance. Thus, I would argue that, insofar as Islamists continue to promote a rebuilding of an Islamic civilisation from a supremacist standpoint of us/them – where the 'us', Muslims (or Arabs), are better than the 'them', Westerners – they are effectively replicating the same aspects of decivilising modernist strategies, but simply reversing them. I maintain that such an Islamism is, in effect, itself decivilising.

It is nevertheless important to query the Islamists' own discourses on development. Hobart (1993) argues that discourses of development are in some ways tied to the problematic of knowledge, embedded within which is the implication of a parallel growth of ignorance. Development as rational, systematic and embodied/embodying knowledge alludes to the important relationship between knowledge and power (Hobart 1993: 1–30). Based on that, I argue that Islamist discourses on development, themselves yet to be fully developed, would not differ radically from Western ones insofar as they are both premised on the binary opposition knowledge/ignorance. Islamists operate under the assumption that much of Western development discourses are an extension of earlier imperialist decivilisation mechanisms, whereby the non-West wallows in ignorance and the West has the task of informing, that is, disseminating knowledge and civilisation. The Islamist counter-discourses of development, therefore, would run along similar lines to their earlier problematisation. In other words, we (the Muslims) know (or know better) and they (the Westerners) do not. Or to put it differently, Islamist thinking assumes the superior rationality – presumably that of God – which must triumph over Western rationality. Apart from its qualities of essentialism and generalisation, such a counter-discourse is also not new. Limited to inverting binarisms, it is in effect a perpetuation of an Islamist modernist discourse, in the name of either recreating or reviving 'an Islamic civilisation'.

Discourses of development themselves need some reformulating and contextualising in order to fit the many different realities and problematics that the nature of development entails. Decivilisation highlights the faults of both 'Western' trajectories, as well as Islamist counter-discourses. Post-modernity serves to point out the continuities and similarities of these drawbacks. What remains unattempted is the development of several historically, culturally and perhaps religiously specific (counter)-discourses of development. Such discourses cannot afford to use any hegemonic notions of rationality or knowledge. Indeed, a presumption of rationality, whether human or divine, need not feature in such alternative development discourses. Situated knowledge (Hobart 1993) would be a reasonable *beginning* – though by no means the end. Such a form of knowledge would need to be placed within a framework that takes diversity as its starting point. And simultaneous and consistent reflexive communication – as opposed to a communication which denies the legitimacy of the 'other' – is a *sine qua non* of any further developments of development discourses.

Notes

1   Islamism is a heterogeneous phenomenon, which is to be differentiated from 'Islamic fundamentalism'. The latter is misleading as a term, since not all those who wish to better their lives by following the basic precepts of their religion, are necessarily either approving of or involved with political movements.
2   These range from faulty adherence of Muslims to religious tenets, to a conspiracy against Islam by Westernism, Zionism and the like.
3   Or any other culture, since this call was in the gist of trying to counter the sense of hostility and fear propagated by some extremist Islamists against anything they regarded as 'foreign'.

5   The spectacle of modernity

Blood, microscopes and mirrors in colonial Tanganyika[1]

Eleanor Fisher and Alberto Arce[2]

Introduction

The colonial project in Africa was surrounded by technology, ideology, and representations of modernity based on the application of instrumental rationality. In this chapter we focus on how this project evolved in what was the British Protectorate of Tanganyika through attempts to change and improve the material circumstances of the subjects of the colonial regime. An important perspective on colonialism as a cultural and administrative enterprise is that of Comaroff & Comaroff (1992). They argue that colonialism was paralleled by the development and use of the biomedical episteme,[3] in that a European cosmology of 'health as social and bodily order' was extended to Africa through the medium of relieving people from suffering (*ibid*: 216). This notion of healthy living was used to demarcate Western values from 'native contaminated' values, which were not capable of controlling pain, the spread of diseases, or the unhealthy 'dirty' conditions (see Vaughan 1991).

In Tanganyika these processes can be illustrated by the way the colonial administration responded to the incidence of sleeping sickness prevalent in particular regions. This led to both administrative and medical intervention, the former characterised by the implementation of a programme of resettlement of selected populations, and the latter by the widespread use of medical instruments such as the microscope[4] and various, often experimental, diagnostic and curative measures. These interventions brought about considerable dislocations in local societies in respect to community and spatial organisation, people's understandings of the relationships between nature, the spirit worlds and witchcraft practices, as well as concerning their perceptions of the 'powers 'of their colonial 'masters'.

In this chapter we tell the story of the microscope and how its use generated a complex set of relationships between people and the forest, supernatural beings and diseases, and blood, vectors and human hosts. This allows us to understand the role of colonial administrative and medical practices in response to sleeping sickness, and to define the nature and the scale of the 'epidemic', which not only formed part of a wide process of reshaping the landscape and settlement patterns, but also attempted to modernise and 'purify' the African colonial subject. Western medical knowledge and practices aimed at controlling sleeping sickness provided a powerful means of negating local forms of knowledge and livelihoods, which were perceived to facilitate the continuous spread of the disease (cf. Haraway 1988). In response to these colonial actions local people devised a number of pragmatic and evasive strategies to avoid detection and medical treatment, and escape from the surveillance and control of district officers, medical personnel and game scouts, and from being moved under the resettlement programme. These organised counter-tendencies, sometimes authorised by chiefs and local headmen, were accompanied by the emergence of a number of anti-witchcraft movements that, as we document later, offered some explanations for the predicaments of the human condition consequent upon the colonial experience.

Human Trypanosomiasis in Tanganyika

The following discussion explores issues concerned with the spread of human Trypanosomiasis and colonial control measures in Western Tanganyika between 1919 and around 1940 (see for comparative studies: Lyons 1992; Worboys 1994; White 1995; Hoppe 1997; MacKenzie 1990; Headrick 1994).

Following the First World War, German East Africa became the UN Mandated Tanganyika Territory under British control. Between 1920–5 three major sleeping sickness epidemics erupted, one in Mwanza (around 1921–3), another in Liwale (around 1924), and the third in Ufipa-Tabora (around 1921, identified in 1924) (Fairbairn 1948; Maclean 1926, 1927, 1928, 1929; Swynnerton 1924–5). They were followed by numerous outbreaks in other areas of the territory. Our examples will focus on the Ufipa-Tabora sleeping sickness epidemic. The sleeping sickness epidemics arose at a time when the colonial bureaucratic apparatus was becoming established and later consolidated, features that are critical to our analysis.[5]

Forms of Trypanosomiasis (sleeping sickness) affect both humans and cattle with fatal consequences. Here, we focus on human sleeping sickness, although the animal form of the disease, *nagana*, was also extensive during the period in question. In Tanganyika, interventions regarding human and cattle Trypanosomiasis were divided between two different administrative sectors, the Tsetse Control & Wildlife Department, and the Medical & Sanitary Services, which concerns us.[6]

Trypanosomiasis is caused by a parasite of the blood or trypanosome of which there are many different species (Ford 1971; Giblin 1990). In the 1920s, during the period on which this paper focuses, it was understood that only two species of trypanosome – T. gambiense and T. rhodesiense – led to the spread of sleeping sickness in Tanganyika. The trypanosome for sleeping sickness has a complex life cycle. It is transmitted from one vertebrate host (natural host), usually the larger species of wild animal, to another by means of an invertebrate host (the vector), namely different species of tsetse fly. Sometimes an infected fly will bite man or cattle (adventitious hosts), leading them to harbour the trypanosome and become sick. By implication, complex relationships exist between the parasite, the host, the vector and the adventitious hosts. These relationships are enacted within the habitats of the forest, home of the natural hosts and the vector, and the settlement, home of the adventitious hosts, man and domestic animals.

The different living contexts and physical habitats which compose the life cycle of the sleeping sickness trypanosome became the focus for colonial control measures. These measures sought to break up the life cycle of the parasite and in so doing prevent the infection of people or cattle. In the case of sleeping sickness, controls were biased towards the man/fly relationship, seeking to prevent people from having contact with the tsetse fly. In this focus 'the fly' became isolated by colonial officers as the administrative 'problem', which was described as 'our most formidable opponent' [2]. The Provincial Commissioner wrote in 1932: '[I]t is certain that tsetse and sleeping sickness are the main problems and the governing factors in every problem of native administration in the Western Province' [25]. Tsetse continued to be held as the 'greatest single obstacle to the economic development of the region in the 1950s' [3].

It was not fully understood why sleeping sickness erupted so extensively in Tanganyika after the First World War, nor was it known whether it was endemic or had been brought into the region. Certainly, migratory theses were popular and struck a chord in colonial ideas of the period (Kjekshus 1977: 164–8). Underpinning the concerns of many administrators was a belief that the spread of tsetse flies – hence human and cattle trypanosomiasis – were ultimately the consequence of bad land use practices and internecine tribal warfare [4, 20]. Population upheavals generated by the East Africa Campaign during the First World War were also held to have contributed to the expansion.[7]

Sleeping sickness measures implemented by the Medical & Sanitary Services attempted to integrate prevention with treatment. Prevention was based on a policy of moving whole human populations into 'sleeping sickness concentrations' or 'settlements' and instituting quarantine restrictions on people in the settlements and over recently evacuated areas.[8] Between 1922 and 1945 approximately 140,000 people were resettled into sleeping sickness concentrations in Tanganyika (see Fairbairn 1948: 8). This was apparently in order to break the 'man–fly' relationship, although restrictions were in keeping with the wider policy context of colonial population control measures (see Iliffe 1979; Mbilinyi 1988). Dr Maclean and Dr Fairbairn were the government Sleeping Sickness Officers in charge of concentration measures in the Western Province of Tanganyika between 1924 and the 1940s. Both men were instrumental in developing treatment in 'the field' that involved microscopal diagnosis, and testing and perfecting the use of drugs developed in Europe, such as 'Bayer 205' and 'Tryparsamide'. These drugs were brutal to the bodies of patients, being in the 'experimental stages' of development. They could cure but not with certainty.

Medical controls were linked to interventions generated by the Tsetse Control Department. In 1914 the Desart Committee, set up by the British in 1911 to advise on such interventions, had concluded that in order to eliminate tsetse-borne diseases it was necessary to wipe out the tsetse fly. From this arose a policy of tsetse eradication in Tanganyika whose wisdom was not fundamentally challenged until the 1950s. During the period in question, tsetse eradication policies were under the jurisdiction of C.F.M. Swynnerton, the Director of Game Preservation and Tsetse Control. In practical terms, Swynnerton conceived 'tsetse reclamation' as a 'broad ecological investigation' combined with an 'experimental attack on the fly' [28]. This involved bush clearing, controlled late burning, localised measures against game, barriers (cleared strips), pickets of 'fly-boys' to capture tsetses, game eradication experiments, and chemical measures [5]. Many of these techniques were incorporated into the establishment and maintenance of sleeping sickness concentrations.

The idea of sleeping sickness settlements was underpinned by the notion that contacts between people and tsetse flies needed to be irrevocably broken. By implication this meant critical interventions in the way people lived, as well as into economic activities which brought individuals into sustained contact with tsetse flies. Maclean, Sleeping Sickness Officer for Western Province, held that during the nineteenth century tribal warfare compelled people to live in large settlements centered within cleared areas of land used for agriculture and pastoral activities. In effect, he argued, tsetse flies were kept well away from all but occasional contact with inhabitants because the bush – where the tsetse fly and wild animal hosts lived – was 'pushed back' (Maclean 1929).

According to Maclean, suppression of tribal warfare by the Germans, together with depopulation through famine, epidemics, and labour migration led to a change in settlement patterns: people started to live in 'forest villages' – family settlements dispersed through the woodland. Scattered communities in close and prolonged contact with tsetse flies provided the ideal environment for sleeping sickness to spread in epidemic form: '[T]he protection afforded by cleared and cultivated or grazed land is lost and at certain times of the year tsetse is found almost everywhere, occasionally even inside the houses' (Maclean 1929: 43). Human settlement patterns and the productive activities that transformed woodland to open country were considered key to pre-colonial tsetse control, and therefore something which sleeping sickness control policies should emulate (Fairbairn 1948; Maclean 1929, 1930, 1933). Implicit in this argument rests the idea that by creating settlement concentrations the colonial regime could reproduce African 'tradition' and therefore such interventions would be acceptable to the people concerned.

The model sleeping sickness concentration was considered to need a human population of one thousand or more to make it viable. This figure was based on the calculation that the most suitable conditions for sleeping sickness epidemics arose when human population densities were between 16.5 people and 82.5 people per square mile (Fairbairn 1944: 1; Maclean 1933). If the population density was lower, the infection would be self-limiting, whereas a higher density was likely to imply that extensive areas of bush were reduced, diminishing the presence of tsetse flies. According to the model, a settlement site would be chosen in the tribal homelands, which had a water supply and good arable land or would be placed on the edge of a previously open area, though in the end neither was implemented [20] (Maclean 1929, 1930, 1933). The establishment of schools (state and missionary), clinics capable of treating sleeping sickness, churches, and agricultural and veterinary extension work were incorporated into settlement plans. Through modernity the problems associated with 'decadent and disease stricken primitives' could be overcome [23].

In Tabora and Ufipa in the 1920s, Maclean, acting on behalf of the Medical & Sanitary Services, chose a policy of making new clearings in forest areas because people apparently objected to being removed from their tribal homelands. Bush clearing and game eradication took place near the settlements in an effort to wipe out the natural host of the trypanosome and in so doing to break its life cycle.

Epidemics, maps and people in Tabora and Ufipa

In this section we are going to document the spread of sleeping sickness from a few undiagnosed cases of illness to the construction of an epidemic. The storyline begins with the account of Dr Maclean, Medical Officer for the Western Province and the District Administrative Officer for Ufipa, G.W. Hatchell, both civil servants under the British Colonial Office.

The chronological beginning of the epidemic's narrative is November 1924 following Maclean's appointment to the position of Medical Officer. Maclean states in a published account that in 1915 possible 'sporadic cases could occur unrecognised' (Maclean 1926: 330), however it was not until 1920–1 that 'a fatal disease established itself', the 'high incidence' of the disease being regarded as something different (*ibid*: 330). Apparently, people in the area were almost unanimous in their characterisation of the disease as something new, although 'it is a common experience to find natives confusing sleeping sickness with other diseases' (*ibid*: 330). By interpreting 'native accounts', Maclean and Hatchell traced in minute detail the 'starting point' of the disease from the village of Tumbu in Ufipa, to its spread by the 'constant intercommunication between different settlements' to the point where it 'radiated' northwards through the 'stampede of panic-stricken refugees'. It was reported that 'emaciation, swelling of the legs, and fatal termination' were the different stages that characterised the disease. Men seemed to be more affected than women and children, thought to be because of their bush activities, though it may have been that women were 'invisible' (Fairbairn 1948). Outbreaks were occurring in other parts of the same forest, but a common connection could not be established and therefore Maclean explicitly excluded mention of these outbreaks from his account (*ibid*: 334). The fact that these outbreaks might have called into question the migratory thesis that formed the premise for his characterisation of the epidemic was not considered.

After the medical officer became aware of the presence of the disease, a survey was instituted with all cases being diagnosed microscopically. According to the Annual Report [21: 15–16], 'the most serious matter affecting the public health of the district is sleeping sickness in the south ... its presence was definitely established early in January 1925. By that time a number of natives had already died.' It appears that the use of the microscope was of primary importance in providing a diagnosis and in quantifying the number of cases. This optic positioned the previous invisibility of the illness to a specific disease form, and became central to verifying the existence of an epidemic. In so doing, the microscope provided the Medical Officer with expertise and legitimacy.

The statistical data used to enumerate the number of cases of the epidemic in Tabora-Ufipa between November 1924 and December 1925 are surprising. In some settlements its presence was high (35 per cent), but in others it was low (+/-1 per cent) or non-existent (two areas) and of 563 people tested (described as 'the population'), 62 people (11 per cent), were infected. In spite of this being the area most 'thoroughly surveyed, and, possibly, also the most heavily infected', the low number of positive cases and their differential distribution did not lead to alternative explanations.[9] Instead the data were aggregated to present the disease as an epidemic. This critical event contributed to establishing the character of the health experts as moral entrepreneurs central to the sleeping sickness drama.

As suggested above, medical cures for sleeping sickness were in the experimental stages. Diagnosis and treatment of the disease involved the sterilisation and re-sterilisation of blood through the use of 'Bayer 205' or Tryparsamide. In the process, blood had to be regularly checked with the microscope. In this mission, different cases of sleeping sickness, with different degrees and symptoms of the disease, were treated in an experimental way in order to achieve a process of purification through sterilisation of the blood. In some cases a cure was provided, in others the sheer efficacy of the toxic substances regularly resulted in death.

Although the microscope was a central instrument in drawing the lines against the disease, nowhere in published or unpublished accounts can a critical assessment of its use in Tanganyika be found. In Europe at that time its optical capacity and use was coming under critical examination. During this period many examples of microscopy techniques were developed, including new types of microscope (Clay 1924); examination of the formation of images, optical capacity, and the resolving power of the microscope (Heimstädt 1927; Mallock 1923; Porter 1929); new techniques in mounting slides and manipulating organisms (Klugh 1922; Pratt 1921); and experimentation involving the use of polarised light for resolving power of compound microscopes, and background illumination (Smiles 1924; Stump 1921).

In our view, a lack of critical assessment of the capacity of the microscope in Western Tanganyika tended to functionalise the use of a particular instrument in the practices associated with the job of the colonial health officers. It appears that colonial administrators focused their attention on the organisation of the health service and the formulation of policies that could arise from the instrumental use of the microscope and from their interpretation of the biomedical episteme (Latour 1988, 1984; Comaroff & Comaroff 1992), and did not attempt to gain a critical understanding of the instrument itself. One can imagine that colonial health officers were surrounded by the logistical difficulties of making proper use of the instrument (e.g. access to blood, trained dressers, location of the clinic, validity of the sample, etc.). In a context where there existed a high probability of failure in the use of the instrument, the role of the microscope becomes more significant as a symbol of legitimacy within a 'hierarchy of credibilities'.[10] This political legitimacy was more important than questioning the performance of the instrument per se.

The knowledge of the microscope can also be viewed from the perspectives of people caught up in the event of forced resettlement. It should be emphasised that we draw on people's accounts, not in order to search for one encompassing truth, nor to become historical relativists, but to highlight the complexity and multifaceted nature of the topic at hand. In this case, the stories arose from the oral historical accounts of informants, who were evacuated from the region surrounding the Ugalla River by the British medical authorities (in southern Tabora district north of the initial focus of the epidemic reported by Maclean above)[11]. People from the area were resettled to seven sleeping sickness concentrations in the dry seasons, June to October of 1925, 1926, and 1927. The evacuation took place systematically according to minor territorial units, '*gunguli*', each under a headman and chief.[12] These accounts give an insight into the way that biomedical knowledge, when combined with political power and administrative legitimacy, could be used to deny the knowledge, experiences, desires and life styles of people who were exposed to the disease. People's lives were moulded into a particular 'problem' that warranted a particular solution, namely human population resettlement.

According to local historical accounts, a new disease, with which people were unfamiliar, came to the area.[13] It was reasoned that their misfortunes were a punishment inflicted by local spirits and would continue until they were placated. Chiefs and ritual experts slaughtered cows to the spirits of the land and to the ancestors (Hatchell 1949: 62; Wagner 1996: 194, citing Gwassa, 'Tunza papers' 1967: 47).

When Dr Maclean and Hatchell arrived in Ugalla many people had died of an unknown sickness that had been present for some time. Apparently the officials demanded to know whether anyone was ill. Although people had been experiencing illness, the first reaction of the locals was to deny the sickness and hide it from the Europeans. Sick people were kept out of sight or made to walk back and forth in front of their houses, pretending to be well. Their fears may have related to previous experiences and imaginary associations with coercive European labour recruitment, to German and Belgian armies stationed in the area, and to tax collection measures in the late nineteenth and early twentieth centuries (*vide* Iliffe 1979). Europeans were thus not safe to deal with. It perhaps revived fears relating to stories that 'certain Europeans wandered about the country seeking human blood for the purpose of making medicine ... ' As mentioned below, this interpretation might later have been reinforced by the practice of taking blood in sleeping sickness diagnosis. (TNA. Morogoro District, vol.1, part A, sheets 25–6, August 1931, film no. MF15; cited in White 1993: 46).

Dr Maclean stayed in Ugalla and tried to convince people that their illness was inflicted by tsetse flies. He told them they should not repair their houses as was usual in the dry season, but instead make bark sacks in which to carry their possessions when they were evacuated. People did not believe this, as Mzee George Ntiyama has stated: 'there were tsetse flies before the illness came, and people thought that the sickness was inflicted by the spirits' (Kakola Village, May 10 1993). When he told them they had to move, inevitably 'people did not want to move because they were being asked to move away from all that their lives were built from'. In this encounter, although the illness resonated as a chord between the local people and the experts, the cause of the illness created a cacophony of difficulties: the local people could not understand the significance of the vector in transmitting the disease; and the experts could not understand the significance of the ancestral and natural spirits, or the concept of disease as punishment. The encounter reinforced many of the original perceptions of the different parties, perceptions whose discontinuities continue today. For example, informants who keep bees near the Ugalla River reason that there are still tsetse fly but no disease. One of the authors' informants reasoned that although they had been resettled because many people were sick, 'after we were moved there were still very strong tsetse fly here and we have come every year [to keep bees and to fish], therefore how could Bwana Makeleni [Maclean] have been correct' (Juma Lugovi & Katanga Mboga, Senga 2 camp, field notes 10 July 1994).

In Tabora and Ufipa in the mid-1920s, colonial officers tried to survey and map the extent, density, and movement of the disease. In order to do this the microscope was central for identification and subsequent interventions. The analysis of blood samples became vital to assessing the cartography of the disease. One of the problems that the experts experienced was gaining access to people's blood. In this vein, a large repertoire of stories about blood emerged as dimensions of the Africans' bestiary of science, technology and occupations in colonial Tanganyika. These stories can be seen to represent the different beliefs of colonisers and colonised, 'blood is the most ambiguous of bodily fluids, according to context it can signify life and death' (White 1993a: 3), a medium with fluid boundaries through which people could express their fears and resistance (see also Law & Mol 1994 on anaemia in Africa).

In the case of sleeping sickness, the desire of medical administrators to extract blood, and people's incomprehension of microscopal analysis, exposed a foreign kind of relationship between the illness, the tsetse fly and blood. According to certain local informants, the breakthrough came for the medical authorities when some people learned that if they gave blood they could obtain a source of income, because payments were given for blood samples. For example, one local informant, a Moravian preacher, who was born in Ugalla before the First World War, described the sampling of blood:

> The medical doctors they took blood and went to test and then they brought back the reply to people. One day I can remember my father, may he rest in peace, he was brutally assaulted … they came and they took blood and they went to test it. Afterwards they came to speak with him himself and they said 'aah do you see this blood it is a source of gain (profit, employment)'. They came here, they took blood and then they gave 50 shillings to him. He said to the person 'and you, would you give 100 shillings for my body?' this I would not like! But people they took money for blood.
>
> They came and they said 'we want sick people', and you would reply 'what sick people?'. Many people were being hidden and towards the end many were dying. And when they came those medical doctors they walked inside houses and around the back and inside another house and around the back and inside another house in order to see whether there were sick people, or what? But really the officials they tried their level best until the whole of our country had been stirred up.
>
> Myself, many times I think that it really was the assistance of God to give [?me] religion. You see that it was really a hard life in our country to get the word of God. It was really difficult because you could leave here, for example, and go as far as Ndono and there you would encounter missionaries, and then you would leave Ndono and it was not until you reached Igange that you would find another missionary. There were so few in our country, they would walk all around to spread the word of God, but in our country I remember that there were so few Christians … God assisted to bring things here … 'I am retired but I still love God' [By implication he was arguing that it was an act of God to take them to the sleeping sickness settlements where missions became established and large numbers of people became Moravians and Catholics, especially children in the process of formal education in the mission schools.]

When we were moved we were moved by government vehicles. In 1925, 1926, and 1927. It was cars that could move people with such strength. Others came on foot, they completely refused to climb on the lorry [because] you understand that custom is very strong. Other people died on the road. My father for his own stubbornness he walked and he died on the road and was eaten by hyenas. Four old people remained who did not want to move, three of them died and when people passed later on in the dry season, I don't know whether it was hyenas or what, but the people found that the old people were already dead ... they just encountered clothes and bones!

He came to stay, the *mzungu* (white person). He stayed for almost two months to hasten people to make them move. He arrived many times and he would go to see the chief and tell him or her that they had to tell the people not to build houses and to tell people to make bark sacks. People said 'that one is a madman'. [Fisher]: "Do you remember his name? The *mzungu*"? Makeleni, Doctari Makeleni aah I remember him very well because I saw him with my own eyes.'

(Field-work recorded interview with Teophilo Sizya Mapolo: 24.9.93. From Fisher field diary 1994)

It is important to note that nowhere in the colonial administrative archives is it mentioned that payments were made for blood, the emphasis being placed on the notion of 'voluntary' testing [20]. Once blood samples started to be 'volunteered', native dressers were stationed with a microscope, samples were taken by these dressers (colonial government employees and private mission personnel) and the blood was diagnosed by European doctors (most of whom were attached to the missions – Catholic and Moravian). This procedure was used in the tabulation of information in order to map out the positive and negative number of cases by year, where the disease was likely to have been contracted, and whether it was increasing or decreasing in given areas. Finally, this generated a style of report (narrative) based on the microscope and analysis of blood.

Cases for the region around the Ugalla River are given as 99 in 1925, and 87 in 1926 (the number of people living in the area at the time is not known, although see below), after which people were evacuated. Interestingly, the highest number of cases from a single location in each year, 76 and 59 respectively, were from Ugunda where a medical doctor attached to the Moravian church hospital specialised in treating sleeping sickness. Although the data are limited, this might imply that the number of samples were less a reflection of exceptionally high incidences of the disease, than of the relative closeness of centres of diagnosis and treatment to where people lived [20]. On the basis of these figures, the Senior Commissioner for Tabora District commented to the government Chief Secretary in Dar Es Salaam: '[I]t is with the greatest satisfaction I am able to report that the disease is still confined to the southern and thinly populated areas. It was decided to evacuate the whole of the affected area and so far some 3,000 to 4,000 people have been removed which is probably half the total number it is necessary to evacuate' [19]. In fact this was an underestimate: between 1925 and 1927 a population of approximately 19,000 people were forcibly resettled from the region around the Ugalla River into seven different sleeping sickness settlements ranging in size from 1,000 to 5,000 people [21].

The resettlement move was incomprehensible to local people because they did not make the same associations between death, disease and the need to abandon the area where they lived. For the colonial administrators, the numerical increase in deaths warranted public health measures in the form of forced resettlement, whereas for local people death, 'the fly', constituted a part of everyday life. This does not mean that it was an insignificant event in the lives of the people concerned, but rather it was not seen as a failure of social organisation that warranted a vehement physical intervention, which in their terms could evoke further retribution from the spirits. Certainly in informants' accounts today it is the event of evacuation that is emphasised, not the disease. Stories abound of the burning of huts, fear of the lorries that came to take them away, old people who refused to leave and were eaten by hyenas, and the difficulties of life after the move:

> My uncle he left [was resettled from Ugalla] and he came to Uyumbu. He was a sick man you realise this [he had sleeping sickness], but you couldn't live with all those injections, injections and injections and injections. After we had been evacuated and arrived here all the people who were sick got better, but he remained sick, having injection after injection until he was tired and then took up a gun and shot himself.
>
> Mzee Katanga (Fisher, field diary, July 1994)

After the move, people experienced extensive material hardship. Resettlement also generated political conflicts. For instance, the settlement of Kakola (also known as 'Ugalla') was in the powerful Unyanyembe chiefdom.[14] The move effectively subordinated the people of Ugalla to Unyanyembe, a situation which generated intensive disputes over a period of twenty years. In 1942 the Ugalla chiefs gained administrative permission to return to Ugalla, but the site was not the original location. The older Kakola people continue to refer to the new site, even though it keeps the original name 'Ugalla', as 'a place without a soul' (Teophilo Sizya Mapolo & George Ntiyama, both Christians, Kakola village, 10.5.93) [19]. Trying to reorganise the soul of the people had in any case been only partially successful. According to contemporary oral accounts, people had always returned seasonally to hold their *ngoma* (drumming and dancing), to drink beer, hunt, fish and gather honey, whilst the chiefs returned annually to worship their ancestors.

The hopes of many administrators are echoed in the sentiments expressed by the Provincial Commissioner for Western Province: '[I]n their ignorance bush natives must realise that the advantages of safe community life properly administered, must eventually out-weigh the joys of being left alone.'[25]. Dimensions of modernity expressed through Christian missions, education (state and mission), health care (state and mission), agricultural and veterinary extension work (state) all gravitated towards the spaces delimited by the resettlement schemes.[15] For colonial administrators, these settlements were to become centres where people's identity could be repositioned in relation to new trajectories of time, modernity, markets or forms of organisation such as co-operatives, different farming methods and the production of cash crops.

The aspirations of administrators for the people under their control should not imply that some did not resist these new centralised trajectories. One such tendency was an outright rejection of the resettlement schemes. Some simply ran away from intervention measures and made themselves invisible in the forest. Awareness of their actions appears in the colonial archives: for example, see sections on attempts to improve agricultural methods by rotation of crops, 'it was tried in a few settlements, and not only failed but produced discontent and unrest, with a tendency for the settlers to run into the bush…" (Fairbairn 1914: 4). Many comments of this nature are repeated in the Provincial Commissioner's diary and official reports from the region [26].

By the 1930s a community of British administrators, experts employed by the Colonial Office and missionaries (predominantly British, German, French and Dutch) experienced in tsetse reclamation work and sleeping sickness issues had become well established in the region. In Tabora District alone Drs Maclean and Fairbairn were employed as Sleeping Sickness Officers. There was the Moravian hospital in Ipole, and another in Usoke where two 'European lady medical assistants' were based; at Sikonge there was another Moravian hospital where a certain Dr Keevil specialised in sleeping sickness cases. All mission hospitals were deemed to be on the boundaries of sleeping sickness areas and 'rendered much valued assistance in relation to the disease'. At Tabora there was the government 'native hospital' and twelve government-trained and -employed Sanitation Inspectors. Each settlement had a native dresser (a government employee), microscope and health centre (both state and mission). This formed the foundation for a technoscientific practice concerned with public health.

The microscope seems to have legitimised the need to try to control and purify the infected areas and people. In this sense the microscope was not only capable of creating a network between different things, elements and people, but also generated a new field of action, drawing on organising processes that had implications well beyond the biomedical language and practices. The form of some of these interventions, such as settlement concentrations, were established by the Desart Committee in 1914 and were taken into British government policy in Tanganyika after the First World War.

One of the issues then becomes, how to understand the political importance of microscopal diagnosis for the practices of the civil servants? The figures given in the above text convey the impression that the overall sample, certainly in the Tabora-Ufipa region, was too small to warrant the panic that there was an uncontrollable epidemic raging through the area. This is not to doubt that there was a disease present of which people were dying, or that the microscope played a central role in scientifically establishing the existence of contaminated blood and providing the evidence to link this to the vector, the tsetse fly – which it should be remembered was the 'enemy' of progress and represented the threat of uncontrolled land use practices.

The microscope was used to locate the boundaries of the disease. It was not, however, the docile technology that it may appear to have been at first sight. The instrumentality of the microscope was constituted through a tortuous set of procedures, whose critical points were: an adequate supply of blood, the geographical location of patients and microscopes, whether dressers had a disciplined eye to identify trypanosome-infected blood and, finally, diagnosis of infection levels in order to administer drug treatments. The commoditisation of blood allowed for its extraction. Its subsequent use enabled medical officers to disembody the epidemic from people. In effect, this transformed the locally situated social life of the disease into its expression as clinical cases that became the basis for medical and public health procedures.

The statistical data generated by those engaged in the sphere of sleeping sickness control in the Western Province of Tanganyika are highly revealing, not only in terms of the information they purport to convey, but also because they are based on the aggregation of people into units of 'population'. For a disease to exist in the form of an 'epidemic' ('affecting at once a large number … a disease attacking many persons at the same time', Concise English Dictionary 1992), a population must exist which can be enumerated and subsumed within statistical data by officials (whose role encompasses a legitimacy to carry this out). Once this has occurred it is a short step to institute radical changes in the way people live, in the name of disease prevention, 'hygiene' ('the art of health … the science of the prevention of disease … sanitary science', *ibid*.), in the form of 'public health measures'.

Moore (1996: 10–12) argues that through the development of specific techniques, knowledge and expertise, science and public health have been particularly powerful means of managing populations. She draws on Foucault (1991: 99–100) to make connections between public health measures and the purpose of government. As in the case of human sleeping sickness, forms and techniques of knowledge, generated in relation to 'the welfare of the population', become a means to establish the layers of a bureaucracy and to tie people into processes beyond their control but in which they are forced to participate directly or indirectly (*ibid*: 10).

Resettlement schemes can be seen as purifying attempts to establish modernity in the area. On the one hand, they were legitimised as places where local people's bodies could receive protection from the sleeping sickness and contact with the fly; on the other, their minds could become receptive to proper training in order to remove the contamination of primitiveness and instil the pursuit of progress. There were, however, parallel manifestations of locally situated modernities and purification acts that can be seen as counter-tendencies to the above processes. One such manifestation was the popularity of the witch-finding movement known as 'Muchape', which entered the sleeping sickness realm in Western Tanganyika in the 1930s.

Practices of purification, sleeping sickness and modernities

Witchcraft is typically associated with 'affairs of the earth': issues of power, personal conflict, misfortune and the need to distribute blame and seek redress. Mary Douglas argues that considerations pertaining to witchcraft can give insight into disease; it can be suggested that these considerations also provide an entry point into local situations, where objects and properties of modernity, brought by Europeans, were drawn on and combined in new ways by Africans (Douglas 1992, 1994: 85).

In the 1930s, a witch-finding movement known as 'Muchape' was brought from Malawi and Northern Rhodesia into southern Tanganyika and became very popular in the area that was resettled under the direction of Dr Maclean and Mr Hatchell in the mid-1920s.[16] It can be argued that this witch-finding movement was an expression of modernity at the local level, and in this context, a local fight against sleeping sickness and sleeping sickness interventions. The tsetse fly itself had become a sorcerer's familiar that could be sent to cause fatal injury from a distance (Willis 1968: 4). The Muchape witch-finding movement was notably different from other local ways of dealing with witchcraft, namely through private, individual accusations between known parties. Muchape, in contrast, was public, collective and mobilised large numbers of people.

An account of a Muchape witch-finding ceremony in Sumbawanga on 22 August 1933 is described by a certain Edward Shaba, an African clerk originating from Sumbawanga and employed by the colonial service [26]. In Shaba's account some 2,000 people assisted in the public ceremony near Sumbawanga, males and females sat outside in a large circle:

> inside the circle is a collection of horns, gourds and other items used by people to keep their medicines in. This circle is called a 'guard', if a man has been searched or examined and found to be a bad person he sits inside the circle which is a sign to others that he is a human flesh eater. The men are in a long row on one side and women the other. The Mganga Mkubwa (big doctor) is feared by people and honoured by chiefs. He carries a zebra tail decorated with beads, and a large *Ilizi* round his neck and a whistle in hand. The whistle is blown for silence. The

Mganga Mkubwa stands in the centre of the horns containing *dawa* (medicine) collected from accused people.

The big doctor does not speak directly to the people. A spokesperson for the Mganga Mkubwa preaches and explains the work and says: 'We are here to purge the country and to save people. Missionaries have not succeeded. We follow the commandment of God who says thou shalt not kill.' In this narrative, white missionaries are presented as powerless to stop people from dying. The big doctor portrays himself as part of the Christian tradition, while the ceremony is directed towards persuading people to show their medicines publicly to the big doctor, whose authority finally resides in the act of gazing at the medicines. Medicine is clearly an idiom of power and the act of medicine surveillance is central in the Muchape ceremony to resist poisoning. The spokesman for the Mganga Mkubwa clearly states that if people refuse to produce medicines for examination they will die. The narrative emphasises that the witch-finding movement has come to the country to save people from dying or being poisoned by friends. If a man drinks this medicine '*mchapi*' he will never die, even when given poisonous food to eat.

This description clearly highlights a conflict over who has the power to carry out purification practices and protect people. Missionaries are portrayed as unable to identify polluted 'human flesh eaters', and therefore less powerful than the Mganga Mkubwa who is honoured by local authorities. The big doctor is able to construct a discourse with past and present images, making visible the way in which semantic manoeuvres challenged the authority of white missionaries and by implication the colonial administration.

'Mchapi' refers to the 'resisting poison' that is central to the ceremony, of which there were two kinds, a brown medicine and pure clear water. According to Shaba, a notice was issued by the chiefs of the district saying that a big doctor (Mganga Mkubwa) would come to search both young and old people for witchcraft medicines. Failure to participate, whether they were Christian or not, would brand someone as a witch (*mchawi*). The witch doctors who came into the locality from elsewhere said they had been sent by the government to find wizards.

The Muchape movement in Ufipa in the 1930s was a locally situated purification process. We can clearly observe the use of devices and ideas that can be recognised as appropriated from European colonialism (for an interesting treatment of similitude, reflection and mirrors see Foucault 1970/74: 17–45). The use of modern elements has resonances of a history of previous encounters with missionaries and bureaucrats as well as evoking the people's own past. For example, the witch-finders drew on claims to legitimacy based on the government, and potency based on the failures of the missionaries in their purification attempts, constructing a powerful counter-narrative. Similarly, objects of apparent European power such as mirrors and glass bottles featured prominently during the ceremony (Comaroff &

Comaroff 1993: 227). Furthermore, these practices also drew on potent local traditions, such as making medicinal incisions in the skin for protective medicine. In this sense the Muchape movement can be interpreted as a ceremony embedding and locally situating modernity, a process of blending together and relocating people's beliefs and practices. The Muchape allowed people to engage in a counter-work to both colonial and localised discourses and values. This is clearly delineated in the following account of Edward Shaba:

> The Mganga stands and says that clean people will not be caught but wizards will. The Mganga alone will choose between good and bad. He says that the Christians argue against the Muchape, but some of the native ministers have been found in possession of a skull of a European lady. So don't trust Christians, he said, they are great wizards.
>
> Then the whistle is blown again for total silence. The Mganga Mkubwa calls a follower who brings a bottle of brown liquid and a glass. He sprinkles medicine on a glass [mirror] and wipes it off with a handkerchief. The Mganga calls people by numbers, not mentioning a single name. He turns his back to the men and gazes at the glass, and says 'Number One, get away from the row.' You are clean or not a *mchawi* and the person leaves with vigelegele [?] from his relatives. The Waganga know by looking in the mirror that someone is a wizard. Then someone will have the 'guard' said instead of being clean and his followers will drag him into the circle of medicine horns. In this case the person resists saying he is not a *mchawi*, but he is beaten until he yields. As he enters the circle people taunt him as a flesh eater. To others he would say this man has some human flesh in his stomach and the audience mock. The Mganga blows his whistle before searching the women's side. The same things happened. When finished he blows his whistle and says: 'I now tell you that these people are wizards that eat human flesh and have reduced tax and have caused loss to people by killing your friends and eating them.' Now, says the Mganga Mkubwa, 'I will give them *mchapi* to drink and make each one eat the poison they have used to kill people. They will not die because they will first drink the *mchapi*.' He gives each his own medicine and then these people are kicked and made to dance witch songs while eating and chewing medicine. He beats each with a tail and then sprinkles brown *mchapi* to show that they are clean and will not bewitch people. The Mganga's followers then cook *ugali* (maize meal) cutting it into small round pieces and placing it on the ground in rows, with a mixture of hair from the man's forehead who is going to take that dose, they also scrape the toenail of the man who will swallow the *ugali*. People then go home happy and sure that they have overcome their difficulties and that no one will attempt to poison them or bewitch them.
>
> After drinking *mchapi* no one will attempt to bewitch others or they themselves may die. A wizard would die that day if he drank the medicine

and then tried to practice his art. He will never be angry at any offence, or disappointed, always happy with anybody, even with his enemies. No one will attempt to have sex with a woman in the bush or they will both die at the same time. A wizard who has drunk Mchapi will be declared clean and no one afraid, congratulated for casting his medicine away.

After a person has drunk brown *mchapi* he must then drink another *mchapi* to protect him from poisonous food, etc. This costs 1d – 4d [old pence]. Brown *mchapi* costs 4d, and the clear water 1d any size. Also *mchapi* followers prepare Ilizi (protective charm) for 1/- to 6/-. After drinking the bottle of water it must not be filled with common water but you must wait for the rains in the bush and not drink from the river where people draw water. This will renew your medicine and will be a safeguard against all dangerous poison taken.

These people mostly accuse poor, old, and feeble men and women, and those with an ugly face, and dirty. If they see a young man clean and well clothed they simply pass by. We were there, but they never took notice of us as we were sitting near the chiefs noting down what we saw and heard. Some chiefs were not accused at the ceremony but privately in their huts at night-time. Provided of course they pay the Mganga good money then it will prevent him from exposing people, even though some of them were badly suspected by their own people to be great wizards. The witch-finders are only after money that is all, nothing else but money.

The writer questioned the Mganga to prove [that] the woman who had been exposed had human flesh in or near her house and the man had flesh in his stomach. To this the Mganga failed and said 'I know you Christians, you come to interfere'. The Mganga said that the *mchawi* would not now be caught because of this interference. These men were arrested by the government [D.C. J. O'Brien] and sentenced to three years with a fine of £15 to be distributed as compensation to those exposed as *mchawi*. The chief was deposed by the government.

(Thus concluded the account of the clerk, Edward Shaba).

A good illustration of the Muchape, as an expression of people's capacity to reposition modernity within the familiar is the case of Chief Katonda (Mwami Katonda) of Uruwira. Uruwira was a sleeping sickness settlement for people evacuated from near the Ugalla River. Mwami Katonda apparently became a professional exponent of Muchape, and an expert at dealing with sleeping sickness, having obtained some bottles and mirrors from Father Osther at Uruwira Mission. He apparently published far and wide that he practised Muchape with the approval of Father Osther.

Mirrors as a device of European potency were repositioned within the cosmology of the Muchape ceremony. The mirror contributed to producing a different representation of sleeping sickness phenomena than the one put forward by the colonial administration based on the use of the microscope. It seems that the ceremonial use of the mirror was significant in breaking the chain of connection between infected blood, the vector and the construction of the epidemic. Although the Muchape movement was not against modernity per se, it no longer reproduced the dominant belief in the need to resettle people, and in so doing the Muchape movement eroded trust in the colonial experts and their purifying measures. The Muchape movement was making partial connections between discursive and material elements and the critical events taking place at the local level, signalling with the ceremony and the presence of the 'big doctor' the distance between people's experiences and the experts' use of sophisticated instruments like the microscope. In this fashion local people were re-drawing boundaries from the other end of the knowledge spectrum to make sense of sleeping sickness.

By the use of mirrors, the Muchape ceremony eroded the social distance that the Europeans had created through the boundaries of administrative control and public health measures. Through the use of reflections on everyday life, the Muchape movement questioned the enlightenment of the microscope to generate explanations for contaminated spaces. It postulated that sleeping sickness was a result of the power of witchcraft. The Muchape movement presented a reality that was experienced not as a disintegration of their 'old world' but rather as a living ensemble of imagined and felt experiences that encountered and reassembled aspects of science and witchcraft. In this situation, enlightenment and witchcraft were part of two worlds that somehow emulated each other in a natural duplication of realities and images; and one would find it impossible to say which of these had the dominant say in constructing the boundaries[17] that located modernity. From the West one might say that the microscope has a stronger influence than the receptive mirror of the Muchape ceremony; nevertheless we should not forget that the microscope itself is constituted by mirrors and the use of light. However, the symmetrical rivalry between colonial administrators and local witch-finders about how to use mirrors, were not equal tournaments of value or dignity. This asymmetry is expressed in the manner in which colonial administrators reported the Muchape movement and tried to contain it through arresting the practitioners of the cult. But one thing is clear, the clear reflection of the mirror reproduced different locally situated forms of purification.

This interface provided locals with a particular way of appropriating and circulating elements and devices of modernity. It positioned local people in wider fields of action than those arising from the immediate contact with missionaries, colonial bureaucrats of the region, and other Europeans. These wider fields of action were the construction of arenas of conflict where the local people were able to fight against witches opposed to modernity, and create forums where they could have a dialogue with missionaries and gain an ability to negotiate with colonial administrators. Local emporiums were present in which the Muchapi medicine was transacted. In engaging with these elements, Africans were enrolled at one and the same time in the witch-finding cult and in monetary exchanges. This confronts us with a history of engagements and counterworks that take place with the spread of modernity.

Sleeping sickness was used as a property in different ways by local people and bureaucrats. For those engaged in the ceremony, Muchape created a materialistic base from which to consider the disease as an accusation against modernity at the local level. For the local administrators the disease was the outcome of ignorance and bad practices by local people and warranted public health measures. In this sense the Muchape movement against witches was trying to neutralise, through processes of purification, threats to the establishment of modernity. The sleeping sickness resettlement concentrations provided particularly fertile ground for the movement because of the number of people located together, the ways their lives were reorganised, and the forms of education, religion and extension work that people were submitted to [5]. This generated processes of tension, fear and anxiety.

In contrast to purification practices such as Muchape, public health and tsetse eradication measures epitomised scientific purification methods used by some colonial administrators in the construction of the project of modernisation. A wider range of practices was put to purification ends, for example: the resettlement of the human population and imposition of quarantine measures on people and land; bush destruction through clearing, burning and poisoning; game destruction through traps, poison and shooting; the sterilisation of people's blood through drugs such as Bayer 205 and Tryparsamide, and for cattle through Tartar emetic, and experiments with arsenic compounds to render cattle poisonous to the tsetse fly. An interesting and central feature of the tsetse eradication experiments is how science, in the form of 'the experiment', was used in order to legitimise expert practices. This comes across clearly in another example, the case of the famous 'Shinyanga experiment', where, apparently, bush was totally cleared over an area of 24 square miles and the game shot. The shooting of game was not indiscriminate, but involved the killing of specific species at pre-determined times, with success measured in death counts, analysis of blood and tsetse counts [6].

The images of the experiments in purification to eradicate the fly warrant inclusion:

> [i]ntestines [livestock] filled with blood and water have been dropped on the backs of men and each has been probed by flies (morsitans) coming to the latter as (probably) would have fed anyhow. Pieces of newly-flayed ox-skin carried on the shoulders of men have been probed fairly freely both from the hairy side and the flesh side even when a day old (but still moist) [6].

The use of pickets of 'fly-boys' draped with wet skins smeared with glue or blood in order to attract and trap tsetse flies was the subject of extensive experiments.

Colonial administrative purification practices tried to simplify unknown local complexities, separating elements from elements and people from people. Through a range of techno-scientific devices, colonial bureaucrats were able to build for themselves a sense of moral integrity and an exclusive inter-subjectivity. This generated the basis on which to design a vantage point that could be used to reorganise and develop people's lives and locally situated spaces and resources. The new associations were directed towards the creation of a pure and predictable landscape, together with more familiar social relationships and processes of governance. Purification through science in Africa was possibly one of the last historical stands of the West's nightmares against imaginary entities – monsters, epidemics and vectors – which had previously populated the dark ages of Europe. For the critical mind of modernity, security and prediction rested in burning the arenas of uncontrollable demons that could challenge the pilgrimage toward modernity. The light of the purifying flames of science brought onto a world-scenario the reflections of nostalgic shadows performing the final embodiment of experimental purification, but when boundaries were crossed, the Muchape experience contested the authority of science, as a prelude to a new era of local power claims.

Conclusion

The constitution of a community of administrators and soul managers

In our argument we have suggested that the establishment of the colonial administration was in part the result of a set of practices generated in an unknown and 'hostile' local context after the British took over control of Tanganyika Territory from the Germans. The encounter between the administrators and the local situation implied first the need to explore the boundaries of the territorial unit and its 'problems'. This was done through administrative practices (i.e. tour of duty). These practices generated a rich repertoire of information, facts, description, native ethnographies, surveys of natural resources and the demarcation of judicial administration. The information that was obtained allowed administrators to imagine differences and organise other relationships between nature, society, and the boundaries of the colonial project. The use of the information and associations constituted the local administration and administrative practices. This generated a language of report writing, in particular the District Books and Annual Reports, that bound together a hierarchy of credibility of different authorities in the colonial civil service. Health administrative practices forced the officials to create pockets of techno-scientific knowledge in order to legitimise their policy implementation. In so doing, the role of the microscope, we have argued, was central.

The microscope's use facilitated the British policy of sleeping sickness resettlement concentrations. The resettlement schemes not only transformed the physical landscape but generated possibilities for local people to experience and internalise the diffusion of modernity. Some unintended consequences of these processes, such as the Muchape witch-finding movement, lead us to question the capacity of the colonial administrators to translate directly the use of Western instrumentality to explain local realities: one has only to note the difficulties that arose in trying to verify, quantify and map sleeping sickness. It is possible to argue that these 'difficulties' generated semi-autonomous fields of action from the point of view of local health officers (cf. Moore 1973). On the one hand administrators had to face and deal with situations with which they had no previous experience or administrative guidelines. This lack of a blueprint provided them with wide powers of decision making and discretion. On the other hand, administrators were part of a hierarchy of authority to which they were answerable. This hierarchy was rapidly generating standardised practices and creating fixed administrative offices, such as those of the 'Native Authorities', through which 'indirect rule' was implemented. As offices were established, and foreign civil servants and local power holders moved through the ranks, 'the office' itself came to embody an agency internalised by the office holder, who re-embodied modernity in standardised patterns of local action, and attended to the cultural construction of the intent and interpretation of modernity.[18]

The fight against diseases set up organising processes that in fifteen or so years consolidated boundaries and filled them from within, through critical interventions which had the role of purifying the contaminated character of the area and people within the administration, and created a cartography of tsetse control based on the reconstruction of people and landscapes. Intervention attempted to diminish diversity and ordered the reconstruction of elements so as to make people and events predictable. In these actions, techno-scientific instruments such as the microscope were used to establish the bureaucratic service, rather than to add new knowledge to existing bodies of knowledge as an end in itself. This generated reinforcements of colonial authority in the practice of governing the soul of the natives, although it did not necessarily create a total monopoly of power and knowledge. During this period, government emphasis shifted away from an administration trying to keep 'the forests at bay', to the actual management of modern people.

Colonialism was a process in which different elements – such as maps, microscopes and blood – were assembled together in new ways which put together both European and African 'tradition', and in so doing, established particular local situations of modernity. In this process of transformation, blood, the fly and resettlement schemes generated a different local complexity. The colonial administrator was in a difficult and sometimes personally uncomfortable position, but one that was never in tune with the local people and their environments. The final transition of a biomedical episteme to a development economic one coincided with the entrenchment of a colonial administration that sought to politically control space and people. Our concern in looking for partial connections lies in the intention to understand the counter-tendencies generated by the fight against sleeping sickness and the creation of modernity in Tanganyika.

Archival sources

Tanzania National Archives (Secretariat Files unless otherwise stated)

1   2551. Report of the District Political Officer, Tabora to the Secretary of the Administration, Dar es Salaam, 1919.
2   42398/2. Annual Veterinary Report for Tanganyika Territory, 1920.
3   42398/2. Unyamwezi Development Report, by Rodger, J.T.R.C., 1954.
4   31351. Compulsory Resettlement of Africans: General, n.d.
5   11825. vol.1. Swynnerton, C.F.M. n.d.
6   7538, vol.2. The Game Experiment, Shinyanga, Jackson, 11.5.46.
7   21261. Tanganyika Territory Legislative Council, the Sleeping Sickness Problem in the Western and Lake Provinces, and in Relation to Uganda, 1933.
8   11307. Sleeping Sickness: General Principles of Treatment, Quarantine.
9   31731. Resettlement as a Preventative Measure Against Sleeping Sickness.
10   21709. Sleeping Sickness Concentration Commitee: Minutes of Meetings.
11   31598. Principles of Tsetse Reclamation.
12   10599. Volumes 1 & 2. General Correspondence on Sleeping Sickness, n.d.
13   11307. Sleeping Sickness: General Principles of Treatment, Quarantines, 1927–1933.
14   11515. Sleeping Sickness Outbreak Western Province, Volumes 1, 2, 3, 1927–1932.
15   21710. Sleeping Sickness Concentrations: Medical Arrangements Concerning, n.d.
16   21711. Sleeping Sickness Concentrations: Educational Arrangements Concerning, n.d.
17   21712. Sleeping Sickness Concentrations: Economic and Development Concerning, n.d.
18   40876. Tsetse Operations in Western Province, n.d.
19   1733/4 (52). Annual Report for Tabora District, 1925.
20   1733/9 (69). Annual Report for Tabora District, 1926.
21   1733/20 (105). Tabora sub-District Annual Report, 1926.
22   1733/-(5). Tabora District Annual Report 1921.
23   21475. Annual Report for Western Province, 1932.
24   Morogoro District, Vol. 1, Part A, Sheets 25–6, August 1931, film no. MF15. E.E. Hutchins.

Rhodes House Archives, Oxford

25 Mss.Afr.s. 279–306. Bagshawe Papers. Bagshawe, F.J.E., Provincial Commissioner for the Western Province: Annual Provincial Report for the Western Province, 1932. Private Diary, volumes xv, xix, xvi, xvii, xviii, xix, xx (1932–1937).

26 Mss.Afr.s. 3059. Bagshawe Papers. Photographs, Urambo Concentration 1936 and Uyowa and Bugoma Concentrations 1937.

27 Mss.Afr.s. 622. Maclean, G., Abstracts from Tanganyika Diary (1926–61).

28 Mss.Afr.s. 1259. Potts, W.H., Tsetse Research in Tanganyika Territory, 1925–1952.

29 Mss.Afr.Tanganyika Provincial & District Books, Microfilm Reels No.19 and 20.

30 Mss.Afr.s. 1897. Tsetse Research in Tanganyika 1919–1938 and the role of C.F.M. Swynnerton.

Notes

1   To facilitate reading, the chapter does not give named references in the text for all archival and other secondary source material. However, a complete list of these sources appears above, with corresponding numbers in square brackets in the text.

2   We would like to thank Norman Long for a valuable conversation on mirrors, witchcraft and religion whose convivial circumstances stimulated us to continue. We extend our gratitude to Jan den Ouden for a thoughtful reading of the text and to Julia Guivant for her comments on an earlier draft. Our thanks also to Gerard Verschoor whose Latourian perspective has provided a springboard for thought.

3   The biomedical episteme represented a sense of order, which was in itself carrying the spirit and agent of modernity. This was represented by the link between the reaction against diseases, dirt and the sense of control and purification of the colonial administrators, expressed at this time through the identification, control and re-organisation of people's lives and places, that contributed to the establishment of the foreign civil service and the construction of sleeping sickness settlements, the posts of modernity. In this sense the language of medicine is a representation of modernity and the need to reconstruct through biology and medicine the control and organisation of Africa's nature. See also Foucault 1974: 71.

4   The use of magnifying lenses has been traced to Roman and Greek times and arguably earlier. However, an instrument that can be held to be an early prototype of the microscope first began to be used to examine minute objects in the late sixteenth century when it was introduced to the public view by Zacharias Jansens and his son. It was not until the latter part of the seventeenth century that magnifying instruments started to be technically developed and used for scientific purposes when descriptions began to emerge of objects examined through the microscope and classified, such as 'The Parts of a Bee' by Stelluti, in 1685 (Hogg 1858).

In the eighteenth century advances in microscope construction started to make visible the invisibility of nature by providing the expert with a means to access 'those specks of life' (Baker 1753. Vol. 2: 229). It also contributed to the establishment of epistemic communities ... by affording a new source of rational amusement... (Hogg 1858: 9).

5 An unknown disease, later thought to be human Trypanosomiasis, was reported in Uganda in 1901. By 1906 this is held to have claimed 200,000 lives. The disease was also present in Mozambique, the Congo, and the Zambezi valley, as well as other areas of Central and West Africa. Sleeping sickness was 'discovered' in Tanganyika around Lake Victoria in 1904. There were subsequent outbreaks along the shores of Lake Tanganyika and the Rovuma River in the south (Fairbairn 1948; Kjekshus 1977: 165–6). Before the First World War the German government in German East Africa (Tanganyika) erected treatment centres where sick people could be isolated, 'reclaimed' areas of bush from tsetse and shot wild animals in the field. They did not resettle people as a sleeping sickness measure (Maclean 1930). Extensive cases of sleeping sickness only appear to have occurred after the First World War.

6 Tsetse control was initially under the Department of Tsetse Control and Game Preservation. This was later split into two separate departments, one for tsetse research and control, the other for wildlife conservation and game control (1929).

7 There are maps from as early as 1913 which trace the 'advance of the fly' within 'tsetse belts' (Kjekshus 1977: 164) through German and British colonial times. The idea that the fly could be identified in a particular location, within bounded units known as 'tsetse belts', implied that the fly was the vanguard of the return of nature against civilisation. The idea was that if the fly could not be contained then the forest would take over, as the Provincial Commissioner for the Western Province pessimistically anticipated in 1932: 'in a few years time the bulk of the province entrusted to his care will be uninhabited wilderness' (TNA, 21575, 1932, administrative comment at back of file). In this respect, maps performed the role of making visible the invisible threat, and in doing so, visibility became the first step towards keeping a record on policy implementation. This is a clear case where cartography became integrated with administrative procedures in the colonial civil service.

8 For example, no person could leave a sleeping sickness concentration without a road pass issued free by the local dresser or dispenser after a medical examination (1933). Or, labour recruits from Tabora District were quarantined for two weeks after a visit to a medical officer before they could be registered (1937) (Tabora District Book, Microfiche, Rhodes House).

9 Low numbers of diagnosed sleeping sickness cases relative to the size of the human population and vast numbers of people who were concentrated into sleeping sickness settlements continue in later statistics. For example, in Tabora District: 1925, 99 cases: 1926, 223 cases: 1927, 102 cases: 1928, 411 cases: 1929, 85 cases: 1930, 469 cases: 1931, 357 cases 1932, 424 cases (Tabora District Book, microfiche, Rhodes House, Oxford). In 1925/7 and 1936/7 a total of 28,500 people were resettled in this area (Fairbairn 1948) on the basis of these cases.

10 For example, Bagshawe, the Provincial Commissioner for Western Province, commented in his diary that there were practically no new cases of sleeping sickness reported at Nyonga in 1935 due to blindness on the part of a certain Dr Richards, who later retired (RH. Mss.Afr.s. 279–306, Private Diary, vol. xvii, 16 November 1934).

11 This information is based on research carried out on people who go to the Ugalla River to fish and keep bees in the dry season, and was collected by Fisher between 1992 and 1994. A large number of discussions referred to the sleeping sickness evacuation, deemed as an important collective event and historical reference point. Detailed interviews with five male informants are of note in this context. They are Chief Nsokoro Mvulla, Mzee George Ntiyama, Mzee Teophilo Sizya Mapolo, Mzee Martin Mpenta Chalamila, and Mzee Lucas Songo, each of whom was born before the First World War and can remember the move.

12 Colonial administrators worked through the structure of the 'Native Authorities', African chiefs, drawn into the colonial bureaucratic structure (see Abrahams 1967). This led to tensions in the allegiances of the respective chiefs as they tried to balance relationships with colonial administrators with their relationships to people who did not want to be moved. Mtemi Nsokoro Mvulla, who became a Galla chief following his father's death shortly after being resettled, said that the chiefs were consulted about the move and where they wished to move to, but at the same time their houses were burnt and they had no choice as to whether they actually wanted to move or not (Interview notes, July 1994).

13 The lack of knowledge of sleeping sickness might indicate that it was a new disease to the area as informants gave extensive details about other diseases and how they were treated. For example, if a person contracted small-pox they were sent to live or die in the forest and food would be left for them at a distance from their camp. If a person had hook-worm, the last piece of millet meal from the meal would be thrown at the place where the person had sat and the hook-worm told to stay away. Venereal disease became bad in the area after people went to work on the railway (early twentieth century). If a stranger visited they would be offered food, but afterwards the stool they sat on would be turned upside down until it was known whether they were in good health.

14 Kakola settlement was an area on the border of open country which was cleared for sleeping sickness resettlement. Three thousand local inhabitants were used as labour for nearly a month to clear the land. They were supervised by Mr Stiebel, the District Administrative Officer. Mr Swynnerton, the Director of Game Preservation, visited the settlement to evaluate progress. In 1925, 1,350 people were resettled in an area of eight square miles, which was extended to nine square miles in 1926, when a further 50–100 people were moved into the area, totalling approximately 1,400 inhabitants.

15 The importance of the sleeping sickness settlement as a focus for modernising concerns is conveyed in the case of sleeping sickness settlements in Buha to the west of the area with which we are concerned. In the 1930s an intensive wrangle occurred between the Neukurchen Mission, the Christian Missionary Society and the Society of Missionaries for Africa (White Fathers) over which mission should gain the rights to establish their schools within each settlement. The White Fathers started to build schools very rapidly in an active attempt to exclude the other missions (TNA.21711, n.d. see correspondence).

16 Muchape has been known by various terms in East Africa (Muchappe, Ranger 1969; Kamcape, Willis 1968). Forms of Muchape reappeared in the region in 1943–4, 1954, and 1963–4 (Willis 1968). According to a minute from the Secretary for Native Affairs (Bagshawe, RH.Mss. 3059, report held with private diary, vols. xv and xvi) Muchape was held to have started in Nyasaland in 1930 when a chief obtained and sold a drug manufactured from millet and bark extracts. This drug was used in public witch-finding ceremonies that relied on the use of mirrors to find out who possessed witchcraft substances and provide the medicine as an antidote. Significantly, the drug entered into commoditised relations of exchange, to the extent that '[t]he chief's business and profits were so great that he was unable to dispose of his wares himself so he confined his energies to manufacturing the stuff and employed his agents to hawk [it] ... '.

17 A key means of dealing with misfortune and witchcraft accusations was for people to move house. People were unable to move from the sleeping sickness concentrations but many informants whose families were evacuated from Ugalla suggest today that they moved from the concentrations at a later date due to problems of witchcraft. Similar situations are reported in the case of villagisation (government-led post Independence population resettlements) around the 1970s.

18 A good example of the entrenchment of bureaucratic procedures and practices appears in the autobiography of F.G. 'Beeswax' Smith (*Three Cells of Honey Comb* 1994) describing his experiences in Tabora Region, Tanganyika from 1949 to 1961. 'The correct way of doing things was laid down in GENERAL ORDERS and FINANCIAL ORDERS, from the addressing of letters right through to the various allowances which officers of various ranks could claim for travelling, hire of porters for foot safaris, hotel allowances and so forth'. He describes how each officer was responsible for the expenditure of government funds allocated to him for his work, and the way that details were carefully recorded in what was called 'The Vote Book'. Stores were also carefully controlled. 'Every officer had to write a monthly report and submit it to his immediate superior. I received simple but very informative reports from the African beekeeping instructors, written in Swahili, some in Arabic script. In turn I wrote my monthly report to my Head of Department. I found this an excellent exercise for organising one's thoughts. The monthly reports made the building blocks for the all important Annual Report, and helped to make sure nothing of importance was overlooked. I have made some mention of these routine matters because from what I have seen of some other civil services, the flaws of which rose to headline dimensions in the 1980s, governments could learn much from the Colonial Service, later known as Her Majesty's Overseas Civil Service. My final, really big achievement of that first tour was to get my research station built in 1952. Built to my design, it contained two offices, one for me and one for my clerk, a microscope laboratory with storage for an herbarium, a chemical laboratory and a photographic darkroom' (Smith 1994: 46–8). In an interview with one of Smith's clerks, later to become the first Tanzanian Director of the Beekeeping Department, he chuckled: 'Yes, I remember the laboratory, I used to brew honey beer there and compare notes with Father Chuck (a White Father) at the beekeepers' co-operative' (Mr Ntenga, 9 September 1993, Fisher, field diary).

6 Development discourse and its subversion

Decivilisation, depoliticisation and dispossession in West Africa[1]

James Fairhead

Introduction

In this chapter, I merely want to add to a now extensive literature which exemplifies again and again how the elaboration of problems and solutions in development policy interlocks with, and stabilises, the production of natural and social scientific 'knowledge' which is demonstrably wrong, or at least highly partial.

Focusing on the environment and development nexus in West Africa, and 'anthropogenic impact', I want to sketch how such precarious knowledge is held (in the sense of stabilised and reproduced) within both the institutional structures of science and policy, and their reasoning. But I want also to consider whether other parameters are not implicated which enable the false not to be falsified. In particular, I want to explore three processes often linked with development, but themselves linked by a sense of on-going diminishment – decivilisation, depoliticisation and dispossession.

The concept of decivilisation focuses on the detachment of 'development discourse' from the philosophy of the subject, and when doing so it becomes 'disengaged and disarticulated from processes of thinking, arguing and acting which we call civilisation' (Hobart 1995: 3; cf. Baudrillard *et al.* 1988: 214). Put bluntly, the concept reminds us that in becoming knowledge's subjects, one becomes subjected. Depoliticisation is best exemplified in development by Ferguson (1990; see also Escobar 1984), who argued that the disjuncture between development realities, and realities as expressed 'within the field' is an expression of development as 'anti-politics machine'. In his words:

> Interventions are organised on the basis of this structure of [development] knowledge, which, while failing on their own terms, nonetheless have regular effects, which include the expansion and entrenchment of bureaucratic state power, side by side with the projection of a representation of economic and social life which denies 'politics' and, to the extent that it is successful, suspends its effects ... The 'development apparatus' is an 'anti-politics machine' depoliticising everything it touches, everywhere

whisking political realities out of sight, all the while performing, almost unnoticed, its own pre-eminently political operation of expanding bureaucratic state power.

(Ferguson 1990: xv)

Depoliticisation as a concept reminds us how ideas of 'objectivity' support the hand of bureaucratic management, and of bureaucratic managers.

The third concept, dispossession, is blunt enough to need little elaboration. Nevertheless, it reminds us not to forget the material effects when recalling what might otherwise be rather lofty concepts of decivilisation and depoliticisation. As Roe has argued, narratives of environmental crisis as portrayed by development organisations and fuelled with their associated sciences – are 'the primary means whereby development experts and the institutions for which they work claim rights to stewardship over land and resources which they do not own' (Roe 1995: 1066). The appropriateness of the term 'stewardship' here affirms the links between dispossession, the anti-politics machine, and decivilisation. In 'development', bureaucratic stewardship, which claims objective 'rationality' in resource management, gains rights to usurp personal control, and to suspend it until people in social action themselves become 'rational' – in other words, indefinitely.

Thus formulated, these three processes might reasonably be considered as linked. It can be argued further that at the heart of processes of decivilisation, depoliticisation or dispossession in the field of environment and development lurks a conceptual object of Cartesian beauty: 'nature', an idea which in its conservationist incarnation encourages people to think themselves out of the world when considering it. On reflection, this particular nature is in essence anti-civilisation, anti-politics and anti-possession.

If science is predicated on this nature being 'rational', predictable, hence 'knowable', then conservation or environment-and-development is predicated on it being 'rational', predictable and bureaucratically 'manageable'. So in a very real sense, 'globalisation' in environment-and-development circles happened long ago; at the time when the nature it dealt with became constituted as independent of time, space and subjective perspective. The 'natural' sciences (and nature itself) became defined around ideas of replicability, and modes of simulation, modelling and coherence.[2] Such replicability is today a major concern in development research, where it inheres in the idea of 'pilot projects' and of 'scaling up' of locally-specific development actions. Simulation, modelling and coherence are the tools of planning and the stuff of analytical 'overviews' designed to tease out generalities.[3] Indeed development studies frequently aspire to 'natural science' status.

In the particular cases which I want to examine briefly, the way 'anthropogenic impact' has been constituted within the natural science canon of environment-and-development has obscured (a) how different locations and ecologies may respond to use in very different ways, and (b) how the landscape responds to use today may depend upon how it responded to use before; in short, how the impact of land use may be both locationally and historically contingent, and how local consideration and use of landscape may respond to this. This is the stuff of post-modern natural science; of non-equilibrium ecology, but it is far from the science driving development policy.

Today, and perhaps as never before, nature is exemplified in tropical rainforests. As I wander home from Brighton railway station, I am greeted by the daubed slogan 'Dig Up The Roads – Global Forest Now'. Forests have become the lungs of the world, turning car fumes into biomass and oxygen. They are the kidneys of the world, returning polluted ground-water, purified to the atmosphere to fall once again as fresh rain. They are the world's immune system, set to provide an infinity of cures to an infinity of as yet unknown diseases. And if homogenisation is the late twentieth century's anxiety, forests have come to represent its antithesis, the guardians of diversity, not merely 'bio-diversity', but also social diversity. For it is here that one finds 'forest people' – living archives of inspiration for music, fashion, ritual and drug use. Here, conservation agencies not only conserve places, but conserve 'protected people in protected places', to crib the title of a recent IUCN publication. Captured by conservation, a 'forest people's' authenticity – its fundamental identity – comes to depend on a continuing forest location.

Ecologists have become the other *bona fide* forest inhabitants, in their quest to understand 'natural' dynamics in the raw, beyond human influence. In a world without people, nature can achieve states of 'optimality', 'climax', 'balance', and 'equilibrium'. With people come sub-optima, sub-climax, and degradation and disequilibrium. 'Good management' (whether proper 'common property resource management' or proper state regulation) seeks to limit this, as such lesser realities constitute a problem for 'sustainability'.

Nature in West Africa

To see how nature has operated in West Africa in the company of decivilisa- tion, depoliticisation and dispossession, we really need look no further than the analysis of rainfall in Sierra Leone made by Alfred Moloney C.M.G. in 1887. In his *Sketch of the Forestry of West Africa*, he introduces nature in the same crisis as that infusing modern policy documents: he tabulates the steady decline in rainfall over the four years 1878–82:[4]

> It is desirable that the attention of the community be drawn to the facts ... showing a remarkable and steady decrease in the amount of rainfall in this district during the last four years ... The only cause that can be assigned for this decrease is the wholesale destruction of the woods and forests, which are at once the collectors and reservoirs of its water supply. This has occurred in other tropical regions, and when the cause was learned, by fatal experience through famine, the result of drought, then

the forests were taken under Government protection and replanted, with the best results, but at great expense. I have added the [higher] rainfall statistics for 1883, 1884 and 1885 which point to an improvement in the direction of greater conservancy or more extended planting: perhaps of both.

(Moloney 1887: 240–1)

Never has there been such a clear expression of bureaucracy's role in nature's stabilisation. To achieve it – forests are to be 'taken under Government protection'. This shaping of nature in the interaction of forest and climate had been driving forest policy in India, to which Moloney alludes. Both Moloney himself, and later the father of forestry in Nigeria and Ghana, H. N. 'Timber' Thompson, had experience in the Indian Forestry Service where the rational bureaucratic response to natural crisis and the 'climate-forest-famine' nexus had been to impose forestry regulations and fines, and to establish strategic reserves. Such fines defrayed the expenses of the forestry service, and land alienation gave it lands to expand upon.

The long history of ideas about forest–climate relationships has been traced by Grove (1995) to an emergent coterie of professional scientists from the seventeenth century, drawn especially from the Dutch, French and English maritime empires. Ideas concerning the climatic impact of deforestation were firmly established in European scientific circles long before West African colonisation. In French-colonised West Africa, it was the colonial botanist Auguste Chevalier who introduced into policy the idea of climatic crisis linked to deforestation. In his report on forests in Cote d'Ivoire (1909), for example, he quotes directly the eighteenth-century writer Poivre:

Nature made every effort for the Isle de France [i.e. Mauritius]; man destroyed everything there. The magnificent forests which covered the soil, in their movement once shook the passing clouds and made them dissolve into a fecund rain. The lands which are still uncultivated have not ceased to experience the same favours of nature; but the plains which were the first to be cleared, and which were so by fire, and without any woodland being saved ... are today of a surprising aridity, and consequently less fertile; even the rivers, considerably diminished, are insufficient throughout the year to irrigate their thirsty sides; the sky, in refusing them rain, abundant elsewhere, seems to be avenging the outrages made to nature and to reason.

(Poivre, P. 1768. *Voyages d'un philosophe*: 123, cited in Chevalier 1909; my translation)

These two citations sum up much of subsequent analysis to date of the deleterious effects of forest loss, and what to do about it. Indeed, this simple narrative story linking deforestation, climatic desiccation and soil sterilisation to impoverishment by humans has shaped and justified West African forest reservation and conservation policy ever since.

It is, however, worth detailing a little more the form that 'nature' has taken in West African policy circles. First, natural sciences have held that the present state of vegetation can be examined in relation to the 'climax' vegetation that could grow given the climatic and soil conditions. Thus West Africa divides up into broad climatic zones with correspondingly different vegetation climaxes. Today's vegetation can be seen as unilineal, sub-optimal divergence from this original climax, and which – in the absence of further disturbance and the goodness of time – would re-establish. Such vegetation zonation and the nature of climax communities was formally elaborated across West Africa first by Chevalier (e.g. 1912) and has subsequently been elaborated upon endlessly.

Second, it is also in the 'nature' of West Africa that deforestation causes local and regional climatic desiccation, hence there is a southern movement of vegetation zones: desertification, as the Sahara moves south into Guinea savanna, and savannisation, as savannas move south into forest. Desertification was already on administrators' lips in the first decade of this century: in 1909 an administrator in Niger writes, for example: 'The Sahara walks south at a giant's pace, and the phenomenon which disturbed atmospheric air conditions soon after the arrival of its first inhabitants, manifests itself to the present, with the same intensity and the same causes' (cited in Aubreville 1938). This analysis has been much fleshed out since then. In anglophone literature it was the focus of Bovill's (1921) 'The Encroachment of the Sahara on the Sudan', and in the francophone literature of Hubert's 'Progressive Desiccation in West Africa' in 1920. This was reasserted by Stebbing (1935) in the 1930s, by Aubreville (1949) in the 1940s, by Chevalier again in the 1950s, and by countless subsequent publications and closing speeches of inter-governmental organisations.

Savannisation of forest was also a problem from the outset. I particularly like the words of a young French colonial administrator who worked in the forest-savanna transition zone of what is today the Republic of Guinea, and who wrote after only six months' residence that:

> Never, I believe, has a year so dry occurred in Kissidougou. I am left to say that from year to year, rain becomes scarcer and scarcer. And this I do not find extraordinary – even the contrary would astonish me – given the considerable and even total deforestation in certain parts of this region. ... all has been cut ... the effects of this de-wooding are disastrous; one will soon see nothing more than entirely naked blocks of granite. A region so fertile become a complete desert.[5]

Third, it is also in the nature of West Africa, as claimed in scientific and policy texts, that its soils, once stripped of their vegetation, farmed and burnt, erode.

They thus begin an irrevocable transition from fertility to sterility, a process which itself renders the southern shift of vegetation zones irrevocable.

Together these three images form a compelling narrative of crisis which has driven agricultural, forestry and environment-and-development programmes throughout West Africa. Blame for these processes is invariably placed on shifting cultivators and pastoralists, presumed either to be ignorant of, to ignore, or to be unable to counter the deleterious, unsustainable effects of their practices.

These ideas had been preformulated, and then applied, without dialogue with, hence denying, land users' own perspectives about their impact on land and vegetation. This exemplifies the process of decivilisation as considered here. And these truths about people's impact on West African nature were known and came to operate rapidly within the colonial bureaucracy, with dispossessing effects, long before any detailed investigation of West African ecology.

In Ghana, Guinea and Nigeria, for example, attempts were made at forest reservation within the first decade of colonial administrative establishment. At this time, the colonial powers – and more particularly forestry services within them – were not administratively powerful enough to overcome 'immediate and strident' resistance to reservation (Hall 1987). But by the 1930s, the scales had turned. In Guinea, Côte d'Ivoire, and Ghana – at least – percentage land-cover targets concerning the amount of forest to be reserved were made, and legislation was altered to enable reservation without consultation where it was deemed 'in the public interest'. Targets were enforced, despite the hostility of land holders and earlier inhabitants of reserved areas. Such was the perceived 'threat of fire induced savannisation', that the French and British administrations united to institute a 'curtain' of forest reserves along the forest-savanna transition from Guinea across Cote d'Ivoire and Ghana. Notably in these cases, the reserves were made 'for nature' and 'in the public interest', whether to safeguard the water supply of the district, or to assist the well being of agricultural crops on the land or in the vicinity. They were not made overtly – as one might have imagined – to secure timber for sale to concessionaries, although that has been one of their principal effects.

As Hall remarks for Ghana, 'The men responsible for demarcating the reserves were, almost exclusively, tough, resolute Scotsmen, inured to hardship, and unmoved by the frequent manifestations of hostility from local people ... The belief of foresters in the ability of forest to ameliorate the climate almost amounted to religious dogma' (Hall 1987: 37) He goes on:[6] 'The chiefs and people remained suspicious, and found the utmost difficulty in following the argument that the felling of trees would alter the climate, lower the water table and threaten the cocoa industry. The educated element could follow the evidence, but found the practical issue too hot to handle' (*ibid*: 37).

Already by 1934, plans had been made to 'rehabilitate' the vegetation in the huge watershed of the Niger river; to 'reinstate regular flow'. Poivre's eighteenth-century analysis of river flow in Mauritius had been fully transferred to the vast Niger catchment. The scheme was finally financed in 1991.

Colonial regimes have not been noted for their civilised approach to those they dominated; nor for their engagement with locally voiced interest and dissent, let alone with comprehending how subjects conceptualised their own world and problematics. And colonial regimes have not been noted for their hands-off approach to the resources of the colonised. When colonial environment-and-development policy was implemented, it was done 'in the public interest', and in the interest of future generations. Present 'environment-and-development' policy is legitimated in a similar way, and relies upon exactly the same analysis of 'nature' and modelling of 'anthropogenic impact'.

Environment and development in West Africa: two cases

But are these narratives about vegetation, climate and soils not all true? Isn't it merely that the truth was known long ago? Isn't it the right and duty of the state and international community to act in the broader public good, even at the expense of locally voiced interest?

Here I want to illustrate in two brief cases[7] how nature and people's impact on it is represented in development organisations – and by the natural science which informs them – and then contrast this with ideas about the same sort of phenomena represented by development's subjects. From these it will be possible to evaluate orders of effects – decivilisation, depoliticisation, and dispossession. I doubt if this 'detachment' of development discourse from the thinking, arguing and acting of its subjects in West Africa can be shown more clearly than in administrative and developmentalist concerns with deforestation in the forest region of Guinea, from where the two cases are taken.

The first case relates to the prefecture of Kissidougou, where, ever since colonial occupation more than a hundred years ago, agricultural and forestry policy has held uniformly, and without debate, that the original dense, humid, natural, climax tropical forest cover is disappearing, and rapidly at that. The forest patches which surround the 800 or so villages, dotting otherwise extensive savannas, are taken to be all that remains of this once extensive forest. Such deforestation, it is argued, is not only itself a direct economic loss, but entails other economic losses due to (i) the loss of a humid micro-climate for tree crops, (ii) the erosion and impoverishment of the region's soils, and (iii) the desiccation of local and regional climate, water courses and wells. The deforestation is caused, planners hold, both by existing farming practices and fire-setting, and more indirectly by population increase, and 'social break-down' associated with the political, religious and economic changes linked to 'modernity'. Sustainable development, it is argued, will be achieved only if farming is made more 'rational', intensive and sedentarised, and population increase 'brought under control'. By 1956, so bad was deforestation and soil impoverishment that Kissidougou's master plan for rural development stated up-front that 'all must be subordinated to the conservation of soils and forests'.[8] Today, the most heavily funded organisation in the area is an environmental rehabilitation programme.

Yet inhabitants of the two villages in Kissidougou where I have recently lived and worked for about eighteen months, and in about thirty other villages which my colleagues[9] or I visited, suggest a very different reading of their landscape and of what would keep it productive. Local debate concerning landscape history turns on why forest cover in people's village territories has been *increasing* over the years, and how the patches of forest surrounding their villages have been established or enlarged. Many elders recount how at the time when the village was settled, it was in savanna. Debates turn on whether it is cattle or farming practices which are responsible for an increase in woody cover there. That it is prudent, even lucrative to fell a few large trees in forest islands from time to time, and that forest bush provides a better fallow for subsequent rice fields, is not much disputed, but this is no cause for concern as people are confident of regeneration, and were it problematic, take steps to ensure it. It is almost axiomatic in local thought that empty savannas, once peopled and farmed, become more woody. Crucially, old aerial photographs and photographs from the 1950s and before, and documentation of the landscape from the late nineteenth century support villagers in their experience of landscape change, and clearly falsify the assertions being made in development circles.

The second example, also in Guinea, but slightly further south, concerns what is today (since the 1930s) a national forest reserve, the 'Forêt Classée de Ziama', which acquired international renown as a UNESCO Biosphere Reserve in 1981. The opinion held within scientific and policy documents is that this is one of the last remaining vestiges of primary, or at least hardly disturbed forest of the once intact Upper Guinean forest block, and the guardian of local and regional hydrology and soil conditions (the reason for its reservation) and of biodiversity (the principal reason for today's global interest). Policy documents consider that it is endangered due to land demand by greater populations (of local inhabitants, of immigrants from the northern savannas, and of refugees from Liberia), and that local inhabitants have themselves changed in their economic activities from a forest-benign, extractive livelihood, to a forest-degrading farming one. At present, conservation is ensured through a well-funded World Bank project.

Once again this 'reality' is not shared by the inhabitants of enclave villages, or those neighbouring the reserve. To these people, the forest overlies what prior to the late nineteenth century was a populous and savanna area which was depopulated during pre-colonial and colonial wars, and on which the present forest soon became established. This forest is no cathedral to nature, but a memorial to depopulation and lost social power. And it belongs to the descendants of these once-powerful inhabitants who now seek to renew their land claims. Today's conservationists are incredulous that the land was savanna, and heavily populated. Yet the accounts of three separate Liberian missionaries who passed through the very enclave villages in this reserve, in 1858, 1868 and 1874 show conclusively that this was the case (Seymour 1860; Anderson 1870, 1912; cf. Fairhead & Leach 1994).

In the two examples presented here I have used the analysis of 'disarticulation' strongly when considering how the elaboration of 'problems' within development discourse differed from that on the ground. This may be overly simplistic. Elsewhere, I have discussed at length the scientific, social and institutional circumstances which have led to erroneous analyses of ecological change to be maintained within development circles in Kissidougou, and have argued how the conditions for its maintenance now derive not only from the science and institutions of the development community, but *also from the particular ways that this has articulated with society, polity and education in Kissidougou over a century* (Fairhead & Leach 1996). Nowadays, the degradation hypothesis finds adherents within Kissidougou. It would be odd were it to be otherwise, as it has been taught in primary and secondary schools and in the universities for as long as these have existed. In a recent 'environment day' in Kissidougou, elders and youth delegates from a hundred villages were invited to discuss environmental change in their region with administrators, forestry service agents, school teachers and leaders of the nascent local branch of 'Friends of Nature'. A presentation made by delegates of the latter contextualised Kissidougou as part of 'the African continent' and globe, and analysed local environmental change as a subset of processes understood at a more global level. They cited FAO deforestation data – heavy with the authority of a global organisation – and set ecological processes in Kissidougou firmly within processes of desertification. Arguing the local from the global (both geographically and scientifically) in this way is surely linked to a sense of identity with the globalised scientific community, and the seal of social authority which it confers.[10] So whilst it may have been possible to distinguish landscape readings among those claiming 'development' agency, and those over whom they claim it early in the colonial period, to argue in this way is increasingly misleading.

Depoliticisation, dispossession and decivilisation

These examples from Guinea may be extreme, but they cannot be considered unique. Indeed, it would appear that the assumptions concerning the southwards movement of the savanna zone associated with desiccation and soil impoverishment are fundamentally incorrect in this part of West Africa at least (Fairhead & Leach, forthcoming). In today's forest savanna transition, there is indeed ample, if scattered evidence (a) that forest vegetation has a tendency to encroach on savanna (Vigne 1937; Foggie 1958; Aubreville 1962; Spichiger & Blanc-Pamard 1973; Adjanohoun 1964; Spichiger & Lassailly 1981; Menaut & Cesar 1979); (b) that farming may assist (not hinder) this process either in the effect of converting savanna to forest vegetation

(Spichiger & Blanc Pamard 1973; Markham & Babbedge 1979) or in increasing savanna woody vegetation (Mitja & Puig 1991). In short, there is by now ample ecological evidence to support the view that the area occupied by forest or forest fallow relative to savanna has a tendency to increase, not diminish, and that this may be associated with the presence (not absence) of people as land managers. Furthermore, and in accordance with what we have found in Guinea, oral accounts suggest the past existence of savannas far into what is today the 'forest zone' in Sierra Leone, Côte d'Ivoire and Ghana (Ekanza 1981; Willans 1909). To date, such assertions have been either ignored or rejected by historians and ecologists alike as 'impossible' – effectively binned as 'mythic'. However, it would seem that evidence for their veracity is building, and more importantly, that the narrative driving forest policy concerning deforestation due to land use, climatic desiccation, hydrological and soil impoverishment and savannisation seriously miscon- strues local realities. Yet – and now despite this ecological and historical evidence – it is still this perspective which provides the raison d'être of environment-and-development policy in the region.

In considering the implications of the cases from Guinea, let us recall in more detail Hobart's characterisation of the decivilisation effect which inheres in development in operation. Derived from Baudrillard, he considers development:

> as an emergent set of practices, [which] has become increasingly detached from (and even at times incompatible with) what has been called 'the philosophy of the subject': will, representation, choice, liberty, delibera- tion, knowledge, and desire (Baudrillard 1988: 214). In other words, it is disengaged and disarticulated from processes of thinking, arguing, and acting which we call 'civilization'.
>
> (Hobart 1995: 2–3)

The extent of such decivilisation can be assessed in these examples. If 'total disjuncture' could be conceived of, it is exemplified here. And in both cases, truths circulating in policy circles are easily falsified. But processes of decivilisation should perhaps not be isolated from those of depoliticisation and dispossession. Inhabitants who used to manage their own fallows, fire- setting, pasture management and hunting – disputes and resolutions over which constituted part of their own 'civilisation' – have lost virtually all control over this to forestry officials. Inhabitants who used to collect a large variety of produce from forest tracts now find that these same rights are in the offer of the forestry department. Land in the Ziama forest reserve has been alienated from its ancestral holders without compensation. Inhabitants have not only lost these resources, but are also fined for contravening new regulations. One elder from Kissidougou sadly reflected how he used to be fined when fire swept through his fields when they were savanna, and is now fined for clearing the forest fallow which has come to dominate these same fields. That inhabitants have become criminals in their own land uses is exemplified in a law instituted in 1974, in which fire setting came to carry the death penalty. Dispossession does not end with land, resources and life, but extends to knowledge. Since the 1910s, inhabitants have been the subject of intensive programmes to educate them out of destructive land uses, and on the end of assorted 'stick and carrot' policies to rationalise their farming.

In both of these cases, environment-and-development activities have been met by various forms of resistance (ranging from non-compliance, to burning tree nurseries etc.) but such political realities engendered have been 'whisked out of sight' (cf. Ferguson 1990). Within development circles, resistance has been accommodated and dismissed whether in anti-civilisatory (sinful) categories of ignorance or greed, or in the relocation of agency for action away from those who are actually dissenting, and onto the processes by which they came to be there (such as demographic change, migration, forced migration) or came to be like that (such as impoverishment, the unfortunate legacy of *past* regimes, the penetration of capitalism, modernity etc., etc.). This is the sort of bureaucratic reasoning which at once comprehends resistance, and 'invalidates' its real presence and obviates any need to respond to it. Rather it is to be met with other indirect policy approaches − not direct negotiation which would require listening to − and responding to − local terms of debate. Civilised engagement, in other words.

The need for civilised dialogue over forest resources has sometimes been expressed by inhabitants to project staff, but such expressions tend to have been marginalised completely. In one socio-economic report concerning the Ziama reserve, the following statement made by the customary chief of the region smuggles itself into an appendix, and is never referred to in the main text which considers problems in terms of demographic change, carrying capacity and the rationalisation of farming. The chiefly politician states that:

> This forest problem is complicated. If you see that we no longer have control over the forest, it is because of the forest agents who come with their papers and delimit the forest. If we are given responsibility for the forest, we are ready to act in the interests of conservation … . Whatever the issue, it suffices that N'zebela [the village holding customary authority in the region] gives the order for it to be done…. [The villages within the forest reserve of] Boo and Baimani were created before the first delimitation of the forest boundary by a stranger called Mr. Adam. After delineating the forest, Adam also delimited the zone [enclaves] of Boo and Baimani. The part of the land occupied by Boo and Baimaini cannot be influenced by N'Zebela. We have a customary influence over Boo and Baimani, but not an administrative one. If we had full responsibility for the management of the forest, we could give you the assurance of protecting it. But as long as control is left in the hands of the state, we can do nothing'.[11]

A recent policy document concerning the Ziama reserve, which was elaborated with full access to our work and evidence highlighting local realities concerning the forest past, was still able to ignore it all, and once again construct in its report a mythic past. To the extent that the political consequences of environment-and-development initiatives remain unresolved, and are rendered a technical problem to be met by further bureaucratic intervention, anger and resentment clearly build. One might argue that the myopia of development has denied the political field which it itself engenders, and within which it operates, so much that – like the unsuccessful parasite – it may eventually kill its host.

Notes

1 The research on which this article is based was funded by generous grants made by the British Overseas Development Administration (ESCOR), and the Economic and Social Research Council of Great Britain (Global Environmental Change Research Fellowship L32027313393). I should like to thank all those who commented on an earlier version of this paper during the EIDOS Conference, Wageningen, December 1995. I should also like to acknowledge Melissa Leach with whom much of this research was conducted. I am deeply grateful to her for her comments on an earlier draft. As ever, sole responsibility for any fact or interpretation remains with the author.
2 Earlier, 'nature', even when conceptually separated was frequently personified; a capricious, unpredictable, irrational (chaotic?) element.
3 One could, additionally, critique the idea of 'sustainable development' from this perspective, since – although fraught with definitional problems – it generally presumes socio-cultural coherence across generations and thus denies historical contingency and unpredictability.
4 In much of this he is quoting 'Dr Hart of the *West African Reporter*'.
5 Nicolas, Etat de cultures indigènes, August 1914, National Archives of the Republic of Guinea, Conakry, 1R12.
6 Here he relies on other sources, but it is unclear which, as the references seem to have been finalised posthumously.
7 These are developed at length in Fairhead & Leach (1996), and Fairhead & Leach (1994).
8 Plan de Cercle pour Kissidougou 1956, National Archives of the Republic of Guinea, Conakry 2D431(7).
9 Research was undertaken with Melissa Leach, as co-researcher, and by Dominique Millimouno and Marie Kamano, our Guinean research counterparts.
10 It has been argued by Grove (1995) and others that colonial ecologists gained much of their ecological knowledge from inhabitants of the countries in which they worked. While this indeed appears also to be the case for much of the botanical, and micro-ecological information known by foresters in Guinea, I have not found evidence to suggest that local sources had any early influence on the narrative driving forest policy, concerning deforestation due to land use, climatic desiccation, hydrological and soil impoverishment and savannisation. Were such evidence to be found, the argument presented here would need to be nuanced further.
11 Declaration of village of N'Zebela, after the notes taken by M. A. Barry, in Baum & Weimer 1992: annex 4, p. 3.

7 On the anticipation of violence

Modernity and identity in Southern Sri Lanka[1]

Pradeep Jeganathan

In this chapter, I will attempt to interrupt master narratives of progress and development, by locating a particular form of identity in relation to those narratives. Such narratives are allied with narratives of the possibility of modernity, so my challenge extends to those narratives as well. I claim in the pages that follow, that the end product of progress and development, that is to say the texture of modernity available to everyday life, may not be what it seems to be: terror might lurk in the interstices of the modern. My argument is not that modernity's texture is violent; this claim, while true, does not interrupt the logic of modernity. The claim of the modern is to control violence legally and rationally. In this framing, the perpetration of violence is authored by the state, or is replied to 'justly' by the state. My argument seeks to alter the term that constitutes these claims. I claim that the anticipation of violence – rather than its perpetration – occupies an incomprehensible place in the logic of the modern. It is a place that cannot easily be marked, quantified and responded to. It is the place from which I write.[2]

This chapter, then, does not seek to analyse violence itself; its semiotics or practice. Rather, I am concerned with those who lived through violence to live on: the Tamils of Southern Sri Lanka. Given my concern with 'Tamilness', my anthropological objects in this chapter will be a set of signifying practices that are constituted by and constitutive of the Tamil self. There is, as there must necessarily be, a large terrain of practices that are imbricated in the production of a particular identity, and Tamilness is not an exception. My analysis, then, will only attend to one moment in this larger terrain of practices, and so will necessarily be incomplete. That said, let me specify the character and kind of signifying practices that concern me in this discussion.

I will focus on a set of signifying practices of Tamilness that are only visible in relation to the presence of violence in the ethnographic landscape of Sri Lanka. An examination of these practices, I suggest, will allow for a fore-grounding of a particular aspect of Tamil identity that has emerged in recent years, which is crucial to understanding that identity, and moreover Sri Lankan modernity in general. Tamilness in Southern Sri Lanka, I will argue in the body of this chapter, is produced in the shadow of violence. Or, in other words, in anticipation of violence. So I examine a repertoire of practices that are produced by Tamils given an anticipation of violence. I will call these practices 'tactics of anticipation' and they will be the primary anthropological object of the discussion.

Reversing the common location of violence as a category that must be explained, given its emergence, I will situate it as unavailable for explanation.[3] I shall do so because I think there is the possibility of losing the density, the opacity, the very presence of the object – violence – by attempting to explain its emergence. The shadow of violence then, will hover over this text – its very density casting a long, dark, fuzzy pall over it. There will be no 'getting beyond' violence; no explaining it away. Rather than be explained – and thereby be worked upon – the category of violence in this chapter, since it is unavailable for explanation, may help in the analytical work of the chapter itself. The presence of violence in this text will be used to foreground a set of particular signifying practices of Tamilness.

The kind of violence at stake is urban collective violence – what might be called riots – that have taken place with some regularity in Southern Sri Lanka.[4] At the end of July 1983, Tamils living in Southern Sri Lanka experienced a week-long period of direct, overwhelming violence.[5] That week remains an extraordinary punctuation point in our modern history, the profound significance of which, I believe, we are yet to fully understand.[6] Tamil Sri Lankans, who were living in the south of the country during the violence, found their lives changed for ever, as they found their 'Tamilness' re-made, first in relation to this violence, and then repeatedly, in its wake, in the months and years after. Valli Kanapathipillai (1990) in her pioneering efforts, has examined, sensitively and closely, the (female) survivor of this violence, tracing the effect an event of violence had on particular life histories, and telling of particular reconfigurations in the wake of that event. This kind of work is rare in the Sri Lankan ethnographic field, as it positions violence as unavailable for explanation, just as I would like to, instead of positioning its emergence as a problematic in itself. But my explicit concern with the analytical place of violence, is not Kanapathipillai's; the place of violence is not thought through anew in her work, emerging rather through the received anthropological category of the survivor. This analytic category of the survivor is produced through (oral) biographies of the survival of direct violence. As such, then, the place of violence in this work is that of a 'cause.' It is through this causal relationship that the 'survivor' is produced: the 'survivor' exists because she has experienced violence. Such efforts are now familiar in the anthropology of violence,[7] for they operate in relation to an object that is always already visible to the ethnographic eye sensitive to the effects of violence, an object whose existence is indisputable to the ethnographer because it is marked out prior to her arrival in the field, an object, in other words, that is always already available to an anthropology of violence.

I want to draw a distinction between Kanapathipillai's work, and my own here. My concern is with the anticipation of violence, not with the experience of survival and the survivor of violence. There is, therefore, an analytic distinction to be drawn between our objects, and subtle though it may seem, I would plead its importance. By refusing to position violence in a direct causal relationship with the categories of my investigation – Tamilness in Southern Sri Lanka – I am able to both think the texture of the relationship between the categories of violence and Tamilness in a way that may not have been possible before. But even in so doing, the riskier, uncharted nature of my undertaking may become apparent. The signifying practices of the anticipation of violence, are not, it seems to me, as coherently available to the ethnographic eye, or to the anthropological project, as might be practices of survival. The practices I want to think through here are both ever present and ephemeral; they may seem visible, but then may fade away; they may shift position, but seem always to be centered; they may disappear quickly, and reappear even more strongly and suddenly. The practice of anticipating violence, I want to suggest, flitters across the landscape of Sri Lanka like the shadow cast on a cloudy day by the setting sun. The production of such a category does not come easily to anthropology; it will emerge only through and within my analysis, spreading through it darkly and pervasively.

Three chronological and interlocking clusters of practices provide a grid on which my analysis rests. First, I explore narrations of the anticipation of violence that are located within the space of the July riots; second, I mark the explicit production of 'tactics of anticipation,' in expectation of more civilian-directed violence in the south, in the years after 1983; and third, I comment on the self-conscious production of these tactics of anticipation by southern Tamils, for circulation through the metropolitan West. Throughout my analysis I will draw upon extensive, recent ethnographic research carried out in Colombo.

An introductory digression that sketches out networks of social power in Patupara,[8] a neighbourhood in which I lived and learned about for two years, will be necessary before the position of Tamils, and the location of Tamilness in that community, can be delineated. Patupara is a small lane that leads up from a vast, and uninhabited marshy plain – to a major road that falls on to Galle Road.[9] Up until the 1950s Patupara was a footpath cutting across the farms of the Pereras, a Sinhala Christian family, that had bought land in the area in the early part of this century.[10] While the Pereras had capitalised their grass fields with coconut trees, a coconut processing mill and sheds of cattle that stood on the high land surrounding Patupara, the lower reaches of the fields, especially where the path trailed off into the great marsh, became, in the rainy season, a small lake of water. It was here that the now middle-aged Perera brothers had come down from their exclusive public school, 'to do a spot of fishing', during the holidays. But old Mr Perera passed on, Colombo expanded south, and country, slowly but surely became city. The farm ceased to function, and the value of the land was transformed into urban real estate. Property, which had existed in an abstract, jural sense since the seventeenth century, began to take on the yet newer inflection of the urban: a 'novel social space' simultaneously defined by 'unprecedented proximity', and 'privatisation'. (Sayer 1991: 45). Land is now measured in perches, not acres. The new plots of land became the grounds of new family homes: the bungalow, self-contained with a defined boundary marked by a wall or fence, had come into being. Here, 'spatial distance reflected social distance' (King 1989: 35). Some of the Perera children built family homes on their shares of land, and others sold parcels to other bourgeois families. Importantly, this was simultaneous with Patupara's transformation into a 'real' road from its early beginnings as a footpath. The chief quality of a 'real' road, in my use here, is its representability on the maps of the Municipal Council, where Patupara (the road) emerges uncertainly in the late 1960s. The road was then tarred, its drains measured, municipal taxes levied, and crucially, bourgeois families that lived down the road got 'real' addresses: numbers and street names, marking the privatisation of space. A road is a vector of capital.[11] The road challenged, but did not completely displace, the claim of the 'Walauwe' – the manor house of the Pereras, to be the symbolic centre of the community. The road is where the grocery stores and the public taps are: one cannot, therefore, avoid the road if one lives in the community. It defines my basic unit of analysis.

Yet, the transformation of the value of land was inevitably uneven. In the days of the farm, the workers had lived where they worked. These old, retired workers – their children now factory workers, in the main – were gifted small pieces of low-lying land in inconvenient spots: on the banks of storm water drains, or near garbage dumps. Their shacks – always small – and which in contemporary Sri Lankan urban planning discourses are called shanties, are now crowded together, sandwiched in-between the bungalows. Since many of the gifts had been informal in the naturalised relationship between the 'lord' and his 'servants', the time-consuming and expensive survey plans and 'deeds of gift' were not drawn up for the workers.[12] The land parcels of the workers, a product of modernity, lacked the complete realisation of commodification: exchangeability. In fact, a worker lived on a small plot at the over-arching sufferance of his/her lords with whom lay the ultimate possibility of denying the gift, and declaring the workers 'squatters'.

If we turn now to two particular plots of land, the specificities of the intersections of authority and ethnicity will be apparent. The first of these plots – about 0.75 acres in extent – had been marsh, overgrown with shrubs. Michael Perera, who owned it, wanting to raise cash, sold the entire plot to a real estate development company – a subsidiary of an enormous conglomerate of intersecting, publicly-quoted holding companies. Earth-filled trucks, bulldozers and power rollers transformed that piece of marsh into 'buildable land' in a matter of weeks. The company proceeded to build a high, white wall around the entire plot – so that the shanties around its edges could not be seen – blocked it out with coloured markers into eight perch plots and settled down to sell it off at ten, yes, ten times what they paid for it. The snag, however, was Carolis' family. They occupied 7.5 perches at the eastern end of the plot, steadfastly maintaining that John Hamu had given them the land before he died. John Hamu, one of the Perera brothers who had been both an alcoholic and a leftist, might have indeed given them the land except it was not ever his to give: it was his brother's. Neither Perera persuasion, nor company offers of money (well below selling price) worked, and Carolis' family did not move. So, now, the white wall zig zags at the east end of the land.

This issue of Carolis' land had soured relationships with the Pereras considerably. All the Perera children now thought of Carolis' family as those who were 'squatting on Michael's land,' and Carolis, in turn, had stopped visiting the Pereras at Sinhala Avurudhu (New Year Week). And there was yet an added dimension to this relationship that further complicated it: Carolis' daughter Leela had married a Tamil, Muttiah. Now Muttiah and his family lived on the same plot of land that Carolis was 'squatting' on; they had just built a new shack, abutting the old one upon marriage. It was not the marriage, as much as their growing family, that made it imperative that the land not be handed over to the Pereras or their nominees; and Muttiah, a newcomer to the intricate relations between this particular master and his servants, was caught in an uncomfortable middle. His Tamilness had never figured explicitly in the dispute, but he had felt, as he told me later, that it might.

The question of property was crucial in the case of another Tamil family that had lived in the neighbourhood for a decade. The Josephs were a middle class family that had rented a house from one of the Perera brothers. A few years before the riots they had been asked to leave by the landlord, but they had stayed on, citing the high rentals in new houses and apartments. The house the Josephs occupied was rent controlled, and Sri Lanka's strong tenant protection laws made it nearly impossible for the Pereras to force the issue legally. Here, too, the question of the Josephs' Tamilness had not been directly addressed by the Pereras, who in any event liked to think of themselves as cosmopolitan people whose best friends, as the old cliché goes, were Tamils.

Then came the riots. That massive anti-Tamil violence that shook urban Sri Lanka for one week in July 1983. This chapter is not about the political economy of that event or its ideological place in a Lankan national space. I would like to set those questions aside to consider another which will take us to the heart of this matter – the texture of 'Tamilness' in the midst of that violence, and its re-making in the years after. Muttiah, who talked to me about those times during the two years I lived in Patupara, narrates that time vividly.

Many of these conversations took place under particular circumstances that are constitutive of methodological sites, that are crucial to my ethnographic representations here. These were particular moments during the long calm of the early 1990s, when Tamils like Muttiah expected another riot to be around the corner. One such important moment was in mid-1992, when a militant bomb, in the north of the country, blew up nearly the entire commanding staff of the Sri Lankan armed forces. A big military funeral was planned the next day at the national cemetery in Colombo. In 1983, the long week of violence had begun after a similar military funeral. We seemed to teeter, briefly but palpably, at the edge of a space for violence within which a riot could take place. It was at times like this that Muttiah would speak to me of 1983 – and seeing as he did its sharply etched shadow across his life – he produced then in his narratives a rich texture of detail that was not available at other times. These narratives are not then, merely about the past; and they do not in my representation here serve as 'evidence' produced in an effort to investigate the 'event.' On the contrary, these narratives – like all history – are about the past as well as the present; about recollections as well as anticipation. They are made, like Tamilness itself, in the shadow of violence.

'I didn't know what would happen,' Muttiah remembered, 'maybe they would come for me, just me, or they would burn the house, also. If it was just me, it would be all right, but without the house we would have nowhere to live. I thought if I wasn't in the house when they came, things would be all right. So I left.' Suddenly, Muttiah, who usually saw himself as the protector and master of his family, becomes in his own eyes, its liability. It was his own Tamilness that made him want to banish himself from their midst, acting as if his presence were a taint on their being. Even as he left home, warning his wife and two daughters to be careful, he stopped by the Josephs, to warn them of the impending danger. This was unusual; in the ordinary course of events, Muttiah – who drove a garbage truck for the Municipal Council – had little to say, except in submissive greeting to Joseph, who had a white collar job in the city. What is more, Muttiah would trace his ancestry to India, within a depth of a few generations, while Joseph would do the same to Jaffna, marking himself and his family as 'Sri Lanka Tamil' on a census form. But here and now, in the face of violence, class and origin did not matter as much as they might have on another day: Muttiah opened the gate to the Josephs' house, and knocked on the door.

Only Joseph was home: his family had been sent away that very hour, with a few documents they had thought were invaluable, to a Sinhala friend's house in another neighbourhood. Joseph had stayed behind, as he told Muttiah, 'as the man of the house to keep the house safe'. There is an obvious reversal of movement here, when Joseph is contrasted with Muttiah's own departure from home; here Joseph is not a liability, rather despite his 'Tamilness', he remains a true patriarch, a protector of hearth and home. But what I find significant here is the nexus of masculinity and ethnicity which emerges in each case, and which emerges in others I know of as well. To wait for a riot is to wait in a space for violence, at its shifting, porous boundaries. A space for violence is a space of danger, one in which particular masculinities can emerge.[13] And in Muttiah's subordinated, sacrificial leaving home in an attempt to save the house, to Joseph's desire to face down any intruders single-handedly, we have similar but different plays of masculinity and ethnicity at the boundary of a space of violence.

But Muttiah talked Joseph out of it. Exercising the rare authority of street-wiseness that his working class status gave him, Muttiah told Joseph that it was unwise to stay; so unwise that he could risk death. Joseph capitulated slowly, but then in the inevitable unravelling of the logic of bourgeois order in the face of violence, asked for time to put a few belongings into a bag. And as Muttiah waited, Joseph scuttered about the house first picking up one, and then another possession, commodity, heirloom, keepsake or knick-knack, only to put it down again in confusion. Such uncertainty is familiar, I would argue, to Tamilness in Sri Lanka; to be a Tamil is to both remember and anticipate the destruction of property so treasured by bourgeois society. The many Tamils who have safe deposit boxes, deep in the vaults of banks in York Street, live in the vice of this anxiety, of not knowing what in their lives must fit into a box two feet by three. It is not – as Joseph's dilemma demonstrates – easy to know what from one's home, that terrain of lived detail made over years, must be fitted into a box or shoulder bag.

They went off together, Muttiah and Joseph, to hide, deep in the marsh, until the danger had passed. They walked far, until their bodies had sunk in up to their waists, shrouding their heads with banana leaves. Joseph who had rarely been near the marsh before, and certainly not this far, had been appalled by the grime and the stench, but Muttiah knew it was their safest bet. What Muttiah remembers about that day is the smoke. First, it looked like a rain cloud darkening the sky, but then it grew larger, blackening not just the sky but the earth as well. It filled the air with the smell of charring, and tiny particles of ash. By tracing the movement of smoke, they could tell the neighbourhoods that were on fire, and those that were yet untouched. They waited in the marsh for the fires to come to them.

A common Tamilness emerges here in this example, between Muttiah and Joseph – despite differences of class – as it did among thousands of southern Tamils in that week. Two men, who even though they lived a few hundred yards from each other had never done anything together, who had, in every sense of the phrase, 'kept their distance' from each other, now crouched close and together. It was, of course, a momentary proximity, yet it is worth noting that it is ethnicity, with its ability to promise equality in the face of its impossibility, that does that work.[14]

On that day, in a complex set of events that I have described and analysed elsewhere, the Josephs' house was attacked and looted by a group of neighbourhood toughs.[15] I suggest here that the violence perpetrated in this neighbourhood depended on a particular, unstable class alliance between the men who carried out the violence, and the Pereras, the overlords of the neighbourhood. The Josephs had been marked as enemies in local, working class memory, before the riots, in a way that Muttiah or his family had not been. So the Tamilness of the Josephs was made to matter, by both the toughs and the Pereras, while with Muttiah, local working class solidarities were too strong for rupture. As the leader of that particular gang of thugs, Gunadasa, told me when I asked him about Muttiah, one night, nearly ten years later: 'he had nothing to be afraid of, we would never touch one of our own'. But Muttiah was not to know that, with any certainty. All of us, if we are Tamil, live in anticipation of violence to come.

My larger point is this. There is, in the shadow of violence, a repertoire of signifying practices that is positioned in relation to that shadow, that are very centrally about Tamilness as such. In this chapter I will call these practices 'tactics of anticipation'. These tactics are not merely produced in relation to one event of violence – July 1983 – they are produced in relation to a chronological series of events of violence, the last being the July violence.

For Tamils in Southern Sri Lanka the violence of 1983 was sudden and extraordinary, but not unexpected. The Muttiahs and the Josephs, like so many other Tamils in the South, did not know when and how violence would be upon them, or even perhaps what shape it would take. But they would have known it was coming; all they could do was wait. The possibility of violence would have been real before 1983, given that Tamil civilians had experienced collective violence, years ago in 1958, and more recently, in 1977 and 1981.[16] But it is the overwhelming nature of the last riot that makes this very history of violence visible. And that visibility, now – after 1983 – acquires a new depth, not of ten years but of forty.

I will try to both distil and reinforce my point here with recourse to a well crafted literary text that concerns itself with Tamilness in Southern Sri Lanka: *Rasanayagam's Last Riot* (Macintyre 1993). In this play – which is set on 25 July 1983 – Rasanayagam's 'Tamilness' is constructed in relationship to what I have called the 'tactics of anticipation' that are available to him. He visits (the Sinhala) Philip Fernando, an old university room-mate, on occasions when a riot is imminent. Their friendship is then made manifest during these regular interludes of violence; as Rasanayagam is, on each occasion, sheltered from the 'mob' in the streets outside. On these occasions of sheltered intimacy with the Fernandos, Rasanayagam – apart from his case of belongings – also brings bottles of liquor with him; the number of bottles corresponding to the possible duration of the violence.

Sita [Fernando]: I must say Rasa and you do some marathon boozing, whenever these riots take place!

Philip [Fernando]: What do you expect, confined here days on end with all the murder going on around us!

Sita: But still, it is bad to drink so much!

Philip: Don't exaggerate Sita, how frequent is that, '56 '58 '61 '74 '77 '81 …

Sita: Don't play the fool, Philip, you are trying to make a comedy of the whole thing

(Macintyre 1993: 4)

The string of dates ''56 '58 '61 ... ' that emerge here, are repeated in this and other forms, throughout the play; as such they are succinct markers of the intense visibility of prior events of violence, that the current riot – now available to be added to the end of the list – makes available as chronology. 'Tactics of anticipation', then, can be produced in relation to this visible chronology of violence. In the play I am reading here, many parts of Rasanaygam's self are produced through these tactics: so the bottles of alcohol that fill his bag, in each successive visit, and the 'boozing' they produce, are gentle parodies of that repertoire of practices.

The most succinct example of a 'tactic of anticipation' emerges in this text both as farce and tragedy. It is what might be called a 'master' tactic of anticipation, the kind of tactic that is learnt by us Tamils, so that we may be mobilised when confronted, during a riot, by a Sinhala mob. Rasanayagam has learnt, over the years, to pronounce the Sinhala word Baldiya (Bucket) the Sinhala way, as opposed to what might be thought of as a distinctively Tamil way of pronunciation – Valdiya. The point for Rasanayagam is this: when he is confronted with a Sinhala 'mob' who present him with a bucket and ask him to 'name' it, he is able to perform his Tamilness as Sinhalaness, given the tactics of anticipation he has learnt. He continues to perform these tactics throughout the text, negotiating the line between the serious and the parodic, until finally, as it were, he refuses in one profound moment to do it any more – refuses to perform his Tamilness as Sinhalaness – and is then killed by a 'mob' that has surrounded him. I have dwelt on this text to bring into relief the remaking of Tamilness, in the wake of 1983. The story of Rasanayagam's life and death focuses on the central importance of a repertoire of practices, tactics of anticipation, for those Tamils who have lived on. The simple point is this: to be a Tamil in Southern Sri Lanka, after 1983, is to produce one's identity, one's Tamilness in relation to the anticipation of violence. To live as a Tamil then, is to learn such a repertoire of tactics.

Muttiah and his family, who stayed on in Sri Lanka, are then, such Tamils. Like many working class Tamils in Colombo they could not muster the capital, symbolic and otherwise, to plan migration.[17] When I got to know Muttiah and his family in the early 1990s, the consequences of this position had slowly but subtly manifested themselves. His children were becoming Sinhala and Buddhist. Such an assimilatory movement in working class, urban Sri Lanka has a history as old as migration itself, with the intensive movements of Indian Malayali labour in the early twentieth century and subsequent inter-marriages being a good example.[18] In fact, Muttiah's own marriage to a Sinhala woman had not provoked a social crisis on either affinal side, and the relationship, as noted before, did not provoke comment in ordinary community life. Yet the emerging configuration of Sinhalaness and Tamilness in the lives of Muttiah and Leela's children seemed to have undergone remarkable shifts in the space of a decade. There are five children in question here: two girls born five and three years before the riots, and three others born in rapid succession after a long hiatus, in the four years following 1983. The elder two, young women when I knew them, had been given two names each, one with a Sinhala ring to it, and another with a Tamil ring. Such names, of course, are official appellations only invoked at sites of government power such as the school, hospital or the courts. But urban working class people take such institutions seriously, and the question of a name, and the practice of naming have similar importance. With the first two children, 'he [Muttiah] named them his way, and I named them my way,' said Leela, when I asked her. Then the couple had just put in the two names in the certificate of birth, that crucial piece of government paper. But the other three children, including the much awaited boy child that was the reason for the couple's remarkable fertility had only Sinhala names. 'He still names them his way,' said Leela, 'but we don't write the names on the certificate.' Muttiah, she said, thought it would be a way to avoid trouble in the future.

The presence of violence, in relation to tactics of its anticipation, emerges, also in relation to the practice of 'religion' in Southern Lanka. The ethnographic terrain at stake here is one which Jonathan Walters (1995: 29) has recently called a 'multireligious field,' that is to say a field where the practices of 'multireligion' can be thought through. The specific field in question here is that of the 'Vel festival' – where Hindus and Buddhists perform public acts of faith as a 'sacred spear' moves between two temples in the city in a complex ritual procession. The Vel festival itself can be seen both historically, and anthropologically in relation to the multireligious field of Kataragama, which has of course drawn significant scholarly attention.[19] What I want to point to is the place of this multireligious field in relation to the anticipation of violence. Observing the festival in the summer of 1993, for example, what was dramatically apparent was the shrunken nature of the celebrations. An event that had flowed and overflowed along the main thoroughfares of Colombo producing an orgy of petty consumption for the middle and working classes, that rivalled the spectacular displays of faith that accompanied the fulfilment of vows by the believers, had retreated almost entirely into non-public spaces, the grounds of the temples themselves. After 1983, the hoopla of Vel – not the movement of the spear itself, but its associated practices, could not be public, out there on the city streets any more, it had to be contained inside a demarcated and defined boundary. Given that the festival had not even been held for several years after the riots, it would be possible to argue that there is here a clear cause and effect relationship: Vel was not held because of the riot. But to my mind – as I have suggested before – this causal relationship does not sufficiently illuminate the ethnographic field in this case. I want to think of the multireligious field as produced in anticipation of violence. In this reading, the revived, but now non-public and withdrawn nature of the event is a sign of its self-effacement, a way of positioning it as something other than a public celebration of Tamilness and Hinduness, which would be unwise given the constant anticipation of the possibility of violence.

In the period before the riots, the Muttiahs regularly attended the Vel festival in the city. But they do not do so any more and that annual event is only a distant memory for the elder children; and the family hasn't been to 'see Vel' since the riots. They have felt, and this was expressed with some subtlety to me, that to go and 'see Vel' might not be 'safe'. They were right in their anticipation. In July 1993, when I visited the temples concerned with Vel and spent time there, anthropologising that ethnographic field with a senior and distinguished colleague, a bomb exploded in that very space just minutes after we had left. Tamils I talked to believed that the bomb had been planted there by the army, as a disapproving warning against even limited celebrations of Tamilness.

Leaving events like Vel behind, the Muttiah family have moved cautiously into the sphere of Buddhism. Most inhabitants of Patupara are nominally Buddhists, but as in many urban neighbourhoods only the very old and the very young display any interest in regular temple visits. What matters for everyone else is the observation of festivals like Vesak and Poson, with great energy and display. The older Muttiah children have begun to participate in these events, and the younger children now go to Daham Pasal, the Buddhist 'Sunday School' at the local temple, with other neighbourhood children. It is not my suggestion here that all working class Tamils have moved to assimilate Sinhala Buddhist socio-cultural practices after the experience of collective violence. On the contrary, there are other communities where spaces of 'multireligion', and 'multiethnicity' operate with success.[20] Yet the options Muttiah's family have exercised are not idiosyncratic, rather, in my experience, they are becoming increasingly common.

I turn now to another aspect of the re-production of Tamilness in the face of collective violence, by way of another Tamil family that moved to Patupara after 1983, the Pathmanathans. They made no bones about it, they were Jaffna Tamils, their interests in Colombo were commercial. They were not wealthy, but hoped, I think, to get there some day. The family, who had recently moved to Colombo from the north, had found it very hard to find adequate housing, especially since their son Ravi was seventeen. Young Tamil boys were under suspicion in the city, and cordon and search operations were frequent, while all Tamils were stopped routinely at check points everywhere. No landlord wanted to be accused of harbouring a Tiger, and the few who would agree wanted inflated rents. The Pathmanathans' accommodation in Patupara was such an arrangement, but Pathmanathan thought it was a good deal, since the neighbourhood was 'quiet', and 'safe'. They were outsiders in the neighbourhood, with no social links to other families in Patupara, such as the Pereras, who were central to the lives of many. They had little idea that anything at all had 'happened' in Patupara in 1983, accepting on face value the bland, oft repeated assertion that everything had been 'fine'. But still Pathmanathan liked the location of the house they rented because it was hidden from the road, and therefore shrouded his wife's Hindu ritual practices – which were carried out indoors – from Sinhala eyes. The possibility of violence, the position of the Pathmanathans in relation to it, remained an unsaid, but not an unthought denominator in all this.

After the Pathmanathans had lived for about a year at the place, the land-lords, no relations of the Pereras, decided to raise the rent on the house. Now this was understandable since price inflation in Colombo had to be coun-tered; yet the rise was steeper than might have been expected. For the Pathmanathans who had rented the place on the understanding that the rent would be constant for two years, the demand seemed unjust. They refused to pay, until one day, not altogether by accident, they heard about the Josephs: the long standing dispute the Josephs had had over the rented house with the Pereras, and their sorry plight after the violence. This story was merely hinted at, not told in stark cause and effect tones or terms; but it struck right at the heart of life. Nearly ten years after the riot, the possibility of renewed civilian-directed violence was as real as it was terrifying. The rules of the game, between landlord and tenant, were suddenly suspended: the Pathmanathans paid up silently.[21]

Things changed for the Pathmanathans after that; they grew cautious and wary; said little and walked quickly. For the old man and his wife, this was just another burden to bear, just another facet to their being, in a Sinhala land. Their son, Ravi, however, responded differently. I realised this one night in mid-1992, when a militant bomb, in the north of the country, blew up nearly the entire commanding staff of the Sri Lankan armed forces; a moment I have marked before. I note once again, the peculiarities of this methodological site: a moment framed by an event of violence, which then positions Tamilness firmly in the shadow of violence. The anticipation of violence, then, is both intense and representable in these particular moments, which are always experienced in relation to a chronology of events of civilian-directed violence that might be represented as a string of dates – '58, '77, '81, '83; on that night I wondered if '92 would be added to that list. Old Pathmanathan and his wife were, of course, worried, and I tried to reassure them that things would be all right.

But Ravi disagreed. There was going to be a riot, he said, and it is going to make 1983 look puny. As we argued late into the evening it became increasingly clear that there was a great deal at stake for Ravi in this discussion. He, unlike his parents, was not in mortal fear of a riot. He had his papers in a bank vault, and a few clothes in a case. He lived in anticipation of a riot, not with helpless anger, but with clear foresight: it would help him to leave Lanka and migrate to the West. Ravi's cousin Bala was in Canada; he was doing well with his own grocery store, and would take Ravi in. Except he had little chance of obtaining political asylum, given the relatively peaceful conditions in Southern Sri Lanka. Ravi wanted a riot. It was then, and only then, that his Tamilness would be worth something in the West. Ravi is not alone; there are many like him. The possibility of violence has loomed large for southern Tamils for too long for such a response to be unthinkable. But the possibility of violence is not enough for a visa: for embassy doors to open, people must die.[22]

A consideration of Ravi, and similarly positioned Tamils is crucial to understanding the practices I have been calling 'tactics of anticipation' in this chapter, both politically and analytically. The proximity of Tamilness to the possibility of violence, is not for me, and should not in general, be a sign of its political righteousness, or its positioning on a moral high ground. If this were so, then the narratives I have produced, and the ethnographic field I have constructed here, would merely be part of the growing story of Tamil 'suffering', that is now told repeatedly in different contexts. Ravi's intervention demonstrates the complexity of such narratives of 'suffering'. It is my contention, that 'tactics of anticipation' can also be politically positioned, produced as they are in a field of power. Practices of the anticipation of violence, and humanist narratives of suffering that are associated with them, I want to stress, can be both self-conscious and interested, and produced performatively in different contexts. Hence, my effort to encompass a series of very differently situated practices of anticipation as tactics, which allow, finally, for the Tamilness of Ravi to emerge in relation to the Tamilness of Joseph, Muttiah, Pathmanathan and that extraordinary fictional figure, Rasanayagam. My conclusion is this: a life that is always already to be lived under the shadow of violence – in other words, the very proximity to violence of Tamilness – can itself be objectified, and made available to the repertoire of practices I have called 'tactics of anticipation'.

These tactics, I want to stress finally, are made visible not in relation to the presence of violence in Southern Sri Lanka, but its possibility. There has not been, for the last thirteen years, widespread collective anti-Tamil violence in Southern Sri Lanka that is comparable to the events of 1983. In relation to that kind of violence, the institutions of modernity have stood firm; the 'rule of law' has prevailed. The claim of modernity to control violence has indeed been met in Southern Sri Lanka. Yet, the possibility of violence is real; for some, 'tactics of anticipation' are part of their everyday lives. It is not part or place that is quantifiable, or easily defined: its scope cannot be evaluated by a UN covenant on human rights, nor can it be examined by Amnesty International. The anticipation of violence produces a way of being that lies in the interstices of the modern, almost beneath its cognisance. All I have tried to do in this chapter is to think over that condition again and again, and touch its texture in different ways.

Notes

1 Significant support for this work has been provided by a Centenary Fellowship awarded by the University of Chicago, a Research Fellowship funded by the John D. and Catherine T. MacArthur Foundation, an International Dissertation Fellowship awarded by the Joint Committee on South Asia of the American Council of Learned Societies and the Social Science Research Council funded by the Ford and Andrew Mellon Foundations, a Visiting Fellowship provided by the

International Centre for Ethnic Studies, and a Dissertation Fellowship awarded by the Guggenheim Foundation. This paper was presented at the EIDOS conference on 'Globalisation and Decivilisation' held in Wageningen, the Netherlands, in December 1995. I am grateful to James Fairhead, Mark Hobart, Ronald Inden, Norman Long and Quarles van Ufford for their comments during that occasion, and Malathi de Alwis, Qadri Ismail, Nick de Genova, David Scott and Jonathan Walters for commenting with such care on a different version of this essay.

2 This chapter is conceptually indebted to two important interventions: Gyan Pandey's work (1992 & 1994) on the impossible place of violence in the historiography of modern India, and Michael Tausig's (1992) anthropological representations of the trace terror, in the metropole.

3 As an aside, let me be clear here that I am not arguing for the impossibility of producing an analytic of violence, or for that matter, for understanding its 'causes'. Such work is both important and possible, but is not my task here.

4 By separating out this kind of violence, from other, important and devastating episodes of violence that Sri Lankans have experienced in recent years, I can note the importance of both considering the kind and quality of violence under investigation, and also the importance of work that would locate other kinds of violence at their analytical centre. In this regard I have found Malathi de Alwis' work (1997) on the southern Mother's Front inspiring.

5 I will, throughout this chapter, operate with the dual categories of Tamil[nes]s in 'Southern Sri Lanka'. While this usage is primarily geographical, it can also mark a political distinction between 'southern Tamils' and 'north-eastern Tamils', in the logic of contemporary Tamil nationalism itself. My understanding of this distinction is indebted to a categorically acute argument produced recently by Qadri Ismail (1997). Ismail's own reading of southern Tamil identity, in relation to the logic of Tamil nationalism, is an important complement to my efforts here.

6 There is, of course, sophisticated and multi-faceted literature that has advanced our understanding considerably. A comprehensive overview is available in Stanley Tambiah (1986). For a reading of the political economy of the violence see Newton Gunasinghe (1984) and Sunil Bastian (1990). Important anthropological accounts of the practices of violence at stake can be found in Bruce Kapferer (1988), Roberts (1995) and Jonathan Spencer (1990).

7 See for example, Veena Das' work (1990) which describes the survivors' experience in the wake of the 1984 Delhi riots, and also more generally essays in her recent collection (1995).

8 All proper names relating to and including Patupara are fictitious.

9 A four-lane highway that connects the capital of Colombo, to the southern city of Galle along the south-west coast.

10 Colombo is a colonial city that takes shape in relation to European colonial power during and after the sixteenth century. For a historical account of its spatial organisation, see Michael Roberts (1989), and for a comprehensive demographic account see Bernard Panditharatne (1961). For the historicisation of the construction of space in South Asian cities, see E. Anthony D. King (1976); and on building forms see King (1989).

11 For a sensitively wrought description of capitalisation catalysed by a new road in a Sinhala rural community, see Gunadasa Amarasekere's Sinhala novel *Karumakkarayo* (1953).

12 'Lord', here, will be my gloss for the Sinhala *Hamu*. I see the relationship of 'Lord' to 'servant' here as a modern reactivation of an archaic form. See Newton Gunasinghe's brilliant ethnography (1990) for a theorisation of such relationships; also Tamara Gunesekere's work (1994) for recent ethnographic details in a rural context.

13 I draw here on an argument that I have expanded on in Jeganathan (1997a).

14 I have tried to think through this problem in Jeganathan (1997b).

15 Another paper, Jeganathan(1997b), contains both a detailed ethnographic account, and anthropological argument about this event.

16 There is not a significant literature on any one of these events. But see, on '1958' Tarzi Vittachi (1958) a comprehensive journalistic account which also serves as a preliminary administrative history of the event, and James Manor's essay (1982) which only hints at the sociological complexities at stake. Edmund Leach (1958) is only of incidental interest.

17 After the violence, the Josephs, their house and home in ruins, emigrated to Australia from a refugee camp. As such they joined hundreds of thousands of Tamils who have made their way out of Sri Lanka to metropolitan nations in the last twelve years. For a reading of such migration see Valentine Daniel (1992).

18 For a close reading of debates surrounding these 'mixed' working class marriages, in a different historical period see Jayawardena (1986).

19 James Cartman (1957: 124) has suggested that the Vel festival comes into being in the wake of the regulations and restrictions imposed on the festival held in Kataragama, by colonial authorities, given fear of cholera epidemics in the late nineteenth century. For an account of the ritual relationship between Kataragama and Vel see Don Handelman (1985). For ethnographic accounts of Kataragama see Gananath Obeyesekere (1977) and (1978).

20 I think through such a community in another work: Pradeep Jeganathan (n.d.).

21 Such situations are not uncommon; Kanapathipillai (1990) has also noted an instance of the inflection with violence of a landlord–tenant relationship, as has Sumitra Rahubadha in her Sinhala novel *Sura Asura* (1986).

22 It is not only Ravi who anticipates this possibility. There is more at stake than the desire of Sri Lankan Tamils to migrate seeking a better life for themselves. Immigration itself is part of a globalised circuit of capital with its own logic and imperatives, and large scale migrations of Tamil political refugees to the metropolis from Sri Lanka after 1983 have inserted 'Tamilness' into those circuits. On the one hand are the many hundreds of thousands of Tamils in North America and Europe who live in the 'half-light' of migrancy. They are not quite in yet; so they could be sent back. Every so often bureaucrats will look down at the files, and wonder if Sri Lanka could be re-classified as 'safe'. This would spell disaster for those who have paid tens of thousands to immigration 'brokers' who got them to the West, where they thought the good life was at hand. On the other hand, of course, are the 'brokers', who have a good thing going. There is something to be made off every refugee. They, too, live in anticipation of violence. A consideration of this ethnographic field, however, is beyond the scope of this chapter.

8 At the frontiers of the modern state in post-war Guatemala

Finn Stepputat

Movement and the 'national order of things'

This essay deals with movement, violence and the formation of nation-states. Interest in the nation-state as an object of social science has greatly increased in the 1990s. Several factors have nurtured this interest, such as the demise of the bipolar world system, the proliferation of 'internal' national conflicts and 'humanitarian interventions', the surge of nationalisms, the creation of new nation-states, immigration to Europe and North America, and the formation of new economic and political supranational unions.

While much current writing on nation-states focuses on these as important arenas for the politics of identity, this chapter will have a closer look at the relation between the formation of nation-states and the movement of people across territories. Of course, the politics of identity are integral to this relation. Post-structuralists have for some years engaged in an effort to historicise the otherwise naturalised nation-state by deconstructing how the nation-state is produced as 'real', and as a container of a homogeneous national culture. This production is contingent upon violence and forced displacement as well as strategies of containment, misrecognition and forgetfulness (Shapiro 1996).

Gupta and Ferguson's well coined notion of the 'politics of space' (1992) directs our attention to the struggles and dynamics which feed into the organisation and representation of (national) space. In the twentieth century, the politics of space have resulted in the globalisation of the nation-state as a model for societal organisation. Thus a 'national order of things' has become dominating world-wide (Mallki 1992), although it has been increasingly contested. By contestation we do not refer to nationalist or ethnic challenges to existing nation-states. As the post-war mapping of ex-Yugoslavia illustrates, such challenges draw heavily upon the nation-state repertoire of practices and symbols. Rather, following Appadurai (1993), we refer to 'post-nationalist' practices inherent in, for example, transnational migration and the refugee regime.

The present essay suggests that movement and the control of movement, are important substances for the construction and reproduction of the sovereignty of (territorial) nation-states. Nomads and modern, illegal immigrants have experienced how nation-states inscribe notions of sovereignty on their lives. As Lynn Doty has suggested, nation-states, faced with challenges to their sovereignty by border-transgressors, tend to reinscribe sovereignty through techniques of differentiation, thus creating distinctions between first and second class citizens. Lynn Doty uses the notion of 'internal exclusions' which reconfirm the inside/outside distinction so fundamental to the imagery of nation-state sovereignty (Lynn Doty 1996). Here, I will use a different notion: I will refer to the construction of 'internal boundaries', since this notion directs our analytical attention towards the spatial dimensions of the hierarchies (of gender, age, class, race, ethnicity) through which the 'national order of things' works.

Spatial strategies and the frontier of the modern nation-state

In the following, we will consider a case of threatened sovereignty which differs somewhat from the case of illegal immigration to the North, considered above. The point of departure is the situation of Guatemala in the early 1980s, when a left-wing guerilla movement had the military government on its heels. For a moment the guerillas controlled a good part of the rural districts in the highland, where the basically non-Indian armed groups had won the support of many Indians. In late 1981, the army launched a counter-insurgency programme which in less than one year recuperated military control of most of the national territory.

In the present analysis, however, we will not consider the case as one of territorial recuperation only. Rather we regard it as a process of nation-state formation in regions where the nation-state has been non-existent, or at least strongly contested. In this sense we are dealing with the 'frontiers' of the modern state, i.e. areas where the political authority and administrative capacity of the state apparatus is diffuse and limited (Prescott 1978). In Foucauldian terms, the modern techniques of government, based on individualising systems of surveillance and control, have not yet been installed and legitimised.

A paradigmatic example of what we are talking about is the practice of forced conscription as utilised in Guatemala until the early 1990s. In the absence of an administrative system that would enable state representatives to identify, locate and draft young male individuals at their home address or in their place of work, the military used other techniques. Basically these techniques have relied on the physical control of movement, such as road blocks or raids on market days, when many people gather in the rural towns. Pre-war conscriptions are described as round-ups of young males who desperately try to escape the soldiers, 'running away like rabbits'.[1] This practice is predetermined by the colonial system of administration (resettling the subjects in 'Indian towns') and the system of market places and market days which channel movement in certain time-space patterns. These systems enable the state representatives to predict when and where to find and stop 'people' but not specific individuals.

In contrast to these momentous encounters between representatives and subjects of predatory states, 'grids of modern rationality' are seen as embedding the individual in a permanent system of disciplinary power which obliterates violence as a means of government (e.g. Giddens 1985).[2] This form of power is contingent upon specific organisations of space which circumscribe property relations, work relations and entitlements. Thus, the liberal land reforms in nineteenth-century Latin America could be interpreted as one technique of government that contributed to such spatial organisation (Ronsbo 1997).

De Certeau uses the notion of 'strategies' for the kind of (panoptic) techniques which organise space so as to render residence and movement permanently predictable and controllable (de Certeau 1984). 'Strategy' is a model which is inherent in military, political, scientific and economic rationality: the institution or actor in question delimits a place of its own (a 'proper place'), from where it can generate relations with an exterior of targets, enemies, clients or objects distinct from itself. 'A Cartesian attitude, if you wish: it is an effort to delimit one's own place in a world bewitched by the invisible powers of the Other' (*ibid*: 36). This would be the situation at the frontier of the modern state that we will consider below.

In modern nation-states this 'proper place' of strategies comprises the whole territory. There is no more externality, nowhere to escape surveillance and mapped out space. The subjects have to 'make use' of this spatial organisation; they consume (and produce) it through everyday practices which are pragmatic in nature, or 'tactical', in de Certeau's terminology. 'Strategies' are to 'tactics' what maps are to tours, or movement, which cannot be reduced to the trajectory because of the time sequence involved. Thus strategies may be seen as attempts to channel, predict and control movement across territories. Shapiro, inspired by de Certeau, has noted that states are often represented as the 'stasis' which is challenged by (social) 'movements'.... 'Yet, states themselves resist these challenges through perpetual movement' (Shapiro 1996: 52).

Frontiers are not just a question of the management of movement by violent means in the absence of a grid through which modern techniques of power can work. As de Certeau's 'strategic' distinction between the 'proper place' and 'a world bewitched by the invisible powers of the Other' indicates, representations are very much at stake as well. For most people, the (Anglo-Saxon) notion of the frontier conveys images of encounters between civilisation and savageness, settlements and wilderness, settlers and wanderers, known and unknown. This is no coincidence. These images have been constructed in historically and geographically specific processes of colonisation and state formation that, more often than not, involve acts of violence. Thus, in her study of frontier violence in the Andes, Deborah Poole notes that the polarising logic of ethnic, racial and cultural oppositions dominates at the level of discourse; 'Yet what renders it dominant (i.e. what authorises its universality) is the fact that in everyday life and in popular memory, such oppositions [...] are inscribed in both individual memories and the social imaginary as labels inscribed on the body through concrete acts of physical violence' (Poole 1994: 208).

Examples are numerous. Gerald Sider shows how, at the extremely violent and dangerous seventeenth and eighteenth-century frontier in the south-east of North America, native agricultural producers and merchants were transformed into 'Indians', represented as tribes of savage warriors (Sider 1994: 112). Likewise, Ana Maria Alonso has traced how Mexican state formation intertwined with identity formation at the northern frontier, where the 'placeless' Apache epitomised the barbaric 'Indian'. At the frontier, the subsequent civilising projects of King and State opened an opportunity for people of varying colours and social status to 'whiten' if they settled at the frontier as agents of the civilising state project (Alonso 1995). The most important index of the civilised *gente de razón* (people of reason) was their belonging to and settlement in a bounded place, as opposed to the perceived placelessness and unbounded livelihood of the Apache. The lack of place and territory was, on one hand, an asset in the struggle at the frontier. As an observer noted in a report from 1776: 'They are not obliged to defend, protect, nor maintain any Stopping Place, Site or Population' (*ibid*: 60). On the other hand, this very placelessness (and hence savageness) legitimised the colonisation and ultimate inclusion of the Apache area.

De Certeau's 'strategy' and 'tactics' pop up again when we consider the frontier in terms of relations of violence, movement and state formation. Colonisation and territorial conquest is concerned with the production of places, or points of control. In this move, which according to Deborah Poole usually involves violence, objects are excluded and an exterior is produced. This move of exclusion marks the frontier, which in Poole's words refers to 'any socially constructed relation of social difference, and specifically to the ways in which this imagined relation of (hierarchical) difference or exclusion is encoded into the territorial or geographic identity of a group of people' (Poole 1988: 369).

The question is how the modern nation-state is produced. How is the 'savage' exterior brought under control, encapsulated, integrated, or extinguished, and a uniform national territory produced? How is the nation-state extended beyond the 'civilised' points of control? Our contention is that current 'humanitarian interventions' and 'post-war reconstructions' can be meaningfully addressed as problematic of 'the frontier'. Below, I will describe three encounters in contemporary Guatemala in terms of violence, movement and state formation at the frontier.

Violence and displacement at the Guatemalan frontier

The province of Huehuetenango in north-western Guatemala was indeed a frontier in 1982. The guerillas controlled many rural townships and had won substantial support in the villages. Some were actively engaged, others were just 'listening at the meetings', but everybody was organised in order to channel their 'contributions' to the guerillas (food, sons, *tortillas*, money, scrap iron). The guerillas were cleaning up the area, threatening the rich and people associated with the state to leave, and executing those who were accused of being collaborators of the army. They were undoing the infrastructure of the state by blocking roads, destroying bridges, impeding road construction and tearing down village prisons. They killed large land-owners and even representatives of groups of peasants who were in the process of acquiring landed property, since they claimed 'the land is free, the land belongs to everybody'.

But the situation was ambiguous. The army was not totally absent. Patrols visited the villages on occasions. People fed the soldiers as well as possible, and complied to some degree when they were ordered to organise themselves in civil patrols for self-defence, the 'PACs'. In the villages, people seemed to manage the situation in pragmatic ways by resorting to 'humility and compliance'. 'We had two masters', explained one woman.

When the army started their counter-insurgency offensive, the people were told to stay in the villages; 'there was a law, that we should stay in our houses'. The guerillas wanted people to leave for camps in the wilderness when army patrols approached the villages. Three weeks before the massacre in San Francisco, the army had told the villagers that 'the most important thing is that you stay in your houses, that you don't leave. If you are not here in your houses, we will have to kill you, because it's you who are doing damage to Guatemala' (Falla 1983: 20).

So, people stayed in the village – and were killed. The army surrounded the village and gathered the men in the office of the deputy mayor and the women and children in the church. Until then, according to one of the survivors, people had been tranquil. But after plundering the houses, the soldiers took the women to their houses, one by one, violated them and shot them. Afterwards they killed the children, cutting open their bellies or crushing their heads. Next, the old men had their throats cut with a 'blunt and rusty knife', before the rest of the men were shot or burned in the *juzgado*. In total more than 300 were killed.

The systematic form of the massacre – the killing was organised in terms of age and gender categories – is disturbing in itself; yet this disturbance may be a product of the modern relegation of violence to the realm of the irrational or pre-modern. Nevertheless, the form itself was not meant for public consumption.[3] Its objective was to strengthen the perpetrators' ability to carry out the task. For public consumption was the exhibition of the man who was accused of being the leader of the guerillas in San Francisco. According to a young, female refugee from a village in the region, the army patrol 'brought him along, put a pole up his ass, and showed him to villagers in the area to warn them what would happen if they supported the guerillas. He was a stout man and his head was rolling like this (...). Soon he died.' The symbolism of the act is too obvious.

Even without surviving witnesses to tell the story, or the spectacle of the man–with–a–pole–up–his–ass, the massacre could be considered a theatrical rather than a secluded act of violence (Foucault 1979). The massacre as such was meant for public consumption, but unlike medieval executions no audience was invited. However, neighbours saw the smoke from the burned houses; the smell of burnt flesh was in the air for days. There were no dead or mutilated bodies to be seen, but empty villages produce a significant absence in the same way as do *desaparecidos*, the disappeared: *Hubo silencio*. 'There was silence'. This is how people in the area in general depict abandoned villages, although some accounts describe how the abandoned animals would howl and growl.

Indeed, the massacre produced a distinct sense of disorder, which gave impetus to the flight of more than a thousand families from neighbouring villages. Two facts seemed to influence their decision to flee. First, they could no longer rely on pragmatic tactics (compliance and humility), since they could be killed even if they stayed in the villages and did what the army told them to do. The villagers lost confidence in their ability to manage the situation. Second, San Francisco was killed *in toto*, including army as well as guerilla supporters, women and children as well as men. As one of the survivors commented on the act: 'How could the government give orders to kill women and children who were innocent? How many weapons did the women hand in, how many did the children hand in? The Government is crazy' (Falla 1983: 82). Thus, violence had transgressed the habitual boundaries between the public and the private, through which politics and warfare have been constructed as men's business; it is within the limits of the predictable that men become targeted by the state. But women and children?

Such violence is not meaningless; on the contrary, it is structured by the meaning of the habitual frames and boundaries which are broken and transgressed. I contend that the massacre in San Francisco was planned and designed so as to produce a 'space of death', and to provoke a massive displacement of people in this strategically important border region. The effect was a dichotomisation of these areas between a network of armed villages under army control, and a space beyond control, represented as *el monte*, the wilderness.

The organisation of space during counter-insurgency became politically effective through the representation of spaces and the subjected bodies within. Once divided, more or less arbitrarily, between those who stayed and those who ran away when the army arrived in a village, the bodies were defined according to space: subjects of the Guatemalan state were in the armed villages, and subversives were in the 'wilderness', or in the refugee camps in Mexico. Once organised, the villages made up an almost perfect system of social surveillance and information. Through the system all inhabitants surveilled each other. 'We did nothing in hidden ways (*a escondidos*). What one did, everybody did'. The system generated information on every movement in and out of villages and detected people out of place – the dangerous 'unknown' (*desconocidos*).

Since space defined identities, even 'known' people with written permission were treated with suspicion if encountered in 'the wilderness'. When somebody passed from a residence in 'the wilderness' or in Mexico, to the space of the villages, the passage was represented and orchestrated by the army as a *rite de passage*: from savagery, vagrancy, poverty, danger and irresponsibility to civilisation, family, fatherland, work and a certain degree of prosperity: in short, as a representation of the well-known dualisms of nation-building.

The army succeeded in producing a claustrophobic space in which the rural population was tied to well-defined places, mobility firmly controlled, and the guerillas and their social base were contained in circumscribed, strategically less important areas. As noted by Feldman, in the case of Northern Ireland, spatial reconfigurations during armed conflict can be interpreted as efforts to 'concentrate violence in manageable and exchangeable forms' (Feldman 1991: 37). Indeed, armed confrontations in many areas were reduced to almost ritualised exchanges in specific locations, which became renowned for these encounters between the guerillas and the army (Stoll 1993; Stepputat 1996).

In this interpretation of armed conflict, displacement is not just an unintended effect of violent acts. Displacement is provoked so as to introduce a spatial organisation which facilitates the control (and reduction) of movement and reduces ambiguity. For the 'displaced' population in the 'wilderness', mobility within the delineated areas was the ultimate tactic of survival in the face of bombings and army raids. The Communities of Population in Resistance, CPRs, were nomadic villages.

For those in the Guatemalan zones of conflict who stayed, control of movement amounted to a displacement of sorts. Movement is an important element of 'peasant' livelihoods, although they are usually depicted as place-bound. But the impossibility of commercial relations, migrant labour, cultivation of land at different altitudes, and other activities involving movement outside the village, amounts to a serious problem of survival. Thus, 'displaced persons' may not be the most adequate category for prioritising post-war entitlements.

Mimicry and state surrogates

Twelve years after the massacre in San Francisco, I was driving a white off-roader belonging to the UN human rights mission in Guatemala,

MINUGUA, down a worn out dirt-road leading to an army outpost, 10km from the Mexican border. My task was to 'verify' a denunciation we had received from a neighbour in the village of La Ceiba, where village authorities presumably had violated the peace agreement over human rights. The neighbour claimed that the deputy of the village had threatened and intimidated him, forcing him to leave the village, an act which might be classified as a violation of the right to physical integrity.

Apparently, the neighbour had refused to accept an appointment as third police officer in the village, where appointed deputies and police officers had to take turns for a one-year period. Such appointments are regarded as 'voluntary' community services, which, nevertheless, entitle the holder to (continued) membership of the community and constitute steps in the customary hierarchy of Mayan communities. The neighbour in question, a man from a different county who had married a woman from the village, wanted the community to pay him for the service. To him, MINUGUA was a resource for fighting the village authorities.

Close to the village, a group of young men from La Ceiba were working on the road. They had blocked the road with a few sticks and stones so I had to stop. A man approached me asking for a 'contribution' (*una colaboración*) because they were 'working voluntarily' on the maintenance of the miserable road. The army had constructed the road as part of the counter-insurgency programme in the mid-1980s, but since the guerillas had destroyed the machinery of the construction company, the army had never felt encouraged to maintain the road. Now, a private bus company, merchants, army trucks in disguise, and *coyotes* with their loads of US-bound 'wetbacks' use the road. Since a large group of refugees have returned, 'organised and collectively', from the camps in Mexico to a nearby settlement, an increasing number of development organisations have also used the road.

On the initiative of a group of returned refugees, a regional committee of fifteen villages has been formed to put pressure on the authorities to introduce electricity to the region and undertake road maintenance. But the mayor has answered that the road still belongs to the army, so the government can do nothing. The young man on the road block explains that in his village, at the roadside, many people wanted to do something about the problem, but had been unable to agree on a general, communal work turn-out. They undertook the job, therefore, on a volunteer basis, 'taking turns'. After a long conversation, I paid and continued.

Five hundred metres down the road there was a new road block and a new group of workers. 'This is not fair, I have paid once' was my first reaction. 'But we're a different group', they insisted. After a while I managed to negotiate and pay my way through the road block, and continued, wondering about the state of the modern, civil state in post-war Guatemala. Seen from a former conflict area, where schools, clinics, water supplies and credit schemes are being constructed mainly by the EU, UNHCR and international NGOs, and where the National Guard rarely leave their offices in the town, the modern state appears to be very distant in institutional terms.

But does the absence of the modern state make room for other features in the landscape? Talking in concrete terms, the incident urges us to consider a number of past and current practices related to road construction/maintenance, or to road blocks which may have informed the action of the young men. Of course, they had invented a kind of local wage labour that was at least as profitable as work on the plantations on the southern coast or in Mexico, which the young men mentioned as unfavourable choices. But in their discourse they apparently felt compelled to refer to systems of community service and general labour turn-outs. These systems have, of course, been produced and reproduced in relations between Indians and the government during past centuries.

In many communities, road maintenance is an obligation which confirms membership and entitles the member to land, water, firewood or the like. But other authorities have obliged the communities to give away their labour (*regalado*) in road construction. The grandfathers of the young men had to work two–four weeks every year, constructing the roads of President Ubico in the 1930s. And their fathers had to work for the army in the same way on occasions during the 1980s.

Today, the idea is emerging that road maintenance is an obligation of the state. In this region, the returning refugees in particular have endorsed this idea, as expressed in the regional committee. But the state does not acknowledge this. Hence, the (unauthorised) practice of blocking the road appears as an alternative that turns road maintenance into free enterprise. After all, road blocks became commonplace during the conflict. The guerillas blocked the road when they wanted to attract the attention of the army and the public media or extract war taxes, the civil patrols did it, the army does it. And today the National Guard and Treasury Guard (*Guardia de Hacienda*) block the roads in strategic locations in order to extort bribes from the *coyotes* ($4 per wetback per road block) and other smugglers.

Thus, this incident shows us what may happen when the institutions of the civil state do not take responsibility for the territory at the frontier. As in many other regions of Latin America, the frontiers in Guatemala have seen state authority delegated to hacienda owners or other surrogates of the state. Mimicking government techniques, which basically consist of taxing movement by coercive means, the young men act as state surrogates. In their discourse, the lack of communal, as well as government action, legitimises their actions.

Unmaking the frontier: settlement and new entitlements

Next to the border with Mexico we find three villages located on three of five *fincas* or large farms, which belong to an absentee landlord. He bought his

10,000 hectares before the war broke out but has never worked the land 'because of the subversives', he states. Now, when peace is approaching, he, and the rules of private property, are becoming ever more present. During the conflict, the danger, rather than any formal entitlements, defined the access to land and other resources.

The residents have grown corn on the land for generations, especially since the former landlord left the land idle because of meagre results. In the late 1980s, the peasants heard rumours that the landlord intended to sell the land to a mining corporation or to groups of refugees in Mexico. They investi- gated the possibility of buying the land, but found no source of credit for its purchase. Meanwhile, a small group of refugees who had left the same cluster of villages in 1982, managed to locate the landowner and buy one of the *fincas* next to the villages. The price was high, but the leader of the refugees had established a good relation to CEAR (the Guatemalan Commission for Repatriates and Refugees) and to the credit institution for refugees, FORELAP. The pine trees on the land made the credit feasible, according to the technical report. The institutions on their part saw this as a chance to launch an 'organised and individual repatriation' scheme under the 'Permanent Commissions', the politically informed answer of government to the success of the 'organised and collective return' of Guatemalan refugees from Mexico. The government considered this organisation to have some relations with the guerillas.

The villagers, in particular those who had been working the *finca* land in question during the armed conflict, expressed their discontent publicly: they claimed a share of the land, arguing that the land had the only forest reserve for house construction in the villages. The dispute escalated, and upon repatriation, a large group of the 'locals' presented themselves in the repatriates' settlement launching threats and displaying violent attitudes, according to present government employees. UNHCR and several govern- mental organisations involved themselves in the case and sought to reconcile the parties.

The villagers based their claim on their status as *mozos-colonos*, a Hispano- American notion of occupation and residence (tenant) which implies a reciprocal relationship between tenants and the *patrón*. According to the tenants, when he left the *finca*, the former landlord – the good '*patrón*' – had told them to 'work the land as if it were yours, but never let strangers onto the land'. During the armed conflict, they had indeed 'defended the land' as good patriots and tenants. At least twenty members of the civil patrol had died in battle with guerillas on this piece of land. These PACs had constituted the centre-piece of the army's intent to control the frontier. The refugees, on the other hand, based their claim on their status as rightful owners of a private property. Of their opponents, the villagers, of whom many spent weeks, months and years with them in Mexico, they said 'they were refugees with us, they know very well that in Mexico you have to pay for everything, land, water, firewood. They are just *posados* on the property of others'. *Posado* refers to the condition of having access to land on the grace of others.

After the incident between the repatriates and the tenants, the army and CEAR were called to a meeting of reconciliation. The director of CEAR, arriving by helicopter from the capital, made his speech of national reconciliation in which he said:

> We, from CEAR, represent the authority of the government. We are committed to peace in our country and do not side with one party or the other. We work for a Guatemala without rich or poor, without *indigeno* or *ladino*, where we're all Guatemalans (...) The refugees are as Guatemalan as we are, this is important to understand. We have a problem here with some violent attitudes. This is what we do not want. We want to bury every violent solution to problems, this belongs to the past. Before, people killed each other with the *machete* every day, but not now. Seek dialogue! There are many national and international institutions now. Ask them to mediate instead of using the *machete*.

The general from *Zona Militar No. 19* closed the meeting congratulating the participants for 'this exhibition of civilised behaviour'. The myth of authority feeds on representations of savagery. Thus, the villagers, the former civil patrollers, are confronted with a drastic change in discourse. Before, they were encouraged to cross the border and kidnap and kill refugees – 'guerillas', 'savages' and 'non-Guatemalans' – in order to become legitimate members of the national community. Now, they, themselves are deemed savages because of their violent attitudes and their lack of respect for private property, while the repatriates are represented as civilised Guatemalans, who are entitled to land.

The former commander of the civil patrol finds himself in a difficult situation. As an influential community leader and ex-soldier, he, like many others did not endure the hardships of exile for long but returned to the village in order to 'seek the protection of the army'. He obeyed the orders of the army on behalf of the village, and is therefore held responsible by the widows for the twenty men who died in combat. Today, he is seeking 'projects' for these widows, and has, unsuccessfully, been leading the struggle for land. Meanwhile his leadership is seriously contested by younger men who have not been compromised by the conflict.

Finally, the present conflict over land has an additional irony. When these villages sided with the guerillas at the beginning of the armed conflict, the present leader of the group of repatriates propagated the view that land cannot be owned because it belongs to everybody, a view generally held by the guerillas. Today, he is returning as the owner of land which members of the civil patrol 'defended', while their *patrón*, very un-patriotically as it were, sold part of it to the refugees.

When former members of the civil patrol confront army officers with this seemingly unjust outcome of an armed conflict which they won, the army officers tell them that international organisations, not government, are paying for the land for the repatriates. This coincides with a view held by some sectors in Guatemala that the peace negotiations and process of reconciliation are illegitimate and unconstitutional. The guerillas should not be in a position to negotiate anything without the intervention of the international community.

Nevertheless, repatriation, including the conflicts which it may cause, is an opportunity for the state to 'recuperate' the territory and the people. In the case at hand, representatives of government organisations are authorising and supervising the resettlement scheme. They have involved themselves in the process of reconciliation and are organising the negotiation and technical delimitation of the land of the repatriates. They are also introducing and administering credit schemes for land and production, and they have been involved in the design and organisation of production activities that supposedly will enable the repatriates to reimburse the credit.

Intervention and the 'men of the frontier'

The delegation of state authority to a particular class of persons is a common feature of the frontier, where otherwise the state would not have a permanent, personified presence. In Latin America, authority is often delegated to the *patrón* of economic units such as *haciendas*, mining corporations, or logging companies. These persons are able to monopolise relations and access to the state apparatus, which, in turn, sees them as a medium for the extension of sovereignty to (bewitched) regions of weak state presence. The use of violence at the frontier is therefore not monopolised by the state apparatus; but by extra-legal or 'private' forms of justice and coercion that are tolerated or even encouraged by the state (cf. Fowerraker 1981;Taussig 1987; Poole 1988; Alonso 1995).

At the frontiers of the armed conflict in Guatemala, *hacienda* owners, entrepreneurs, and other influential non-Indians left in numbers. The authority of state was delegated to the commanders of the civil patrols (the PACs) and the (civil) military commissioners in towns and villages, who used their authority in different ways, with or without the consent of the army. The PACs were engaged in a civilising mission that, as Ana Maria Alonso notes for Chihuahua, involved a gendered ethic (Alonso 1995). To stay and defend the land at the Guatemalan frontier is represented in terms of male virtues. As a PAC commander said about the repatriates: 'They were the ones who ran, they were the most frightened (*miedosos*). We who stayed thought we were very brave and courageous, We did what we did for the fatherland (*la patria*)' (fieldnotes 1996).

But what happens to these 'men of the frontier' when the frontier is closed or undone, when the 'civilising' project is well under way? In spatial terms we are talking about the extension of de Certeau's strategic 'proper place' to the whole territory. By means of violence, displacement, civil patrols, and the delegation of authority to militarised civil leaders of the villages, the army succeeded in extending control from the level of towns (where colonial forms of power were focused) to the village level. But the army was not able to extend permanent control beyond the space of the villages. It did not 'homogenise' national space.

We may interpret the present wave of intervention as an intent to establish a proper organisation of space, a grid of modernity, through which power can work within the totality of the territory. Legal regulation and individualisation of access to land is one feature of the intervention. This is not a new form of regulation, and the individualisation of land tenure is not (yet) complete.[4] But legal regulation was partly suspended during the armed conflict, and legal regulation of the 1990s is complemented by a whole range of other interventions which link the subject and the state, such as land credits, credit schemes for production, productive projects, etc.

Post-war interventions in the social landscape work through a number of objectifying categories which are essentialised in terms of national reconciliation and repair: repatriates, the displaced, returnees, widows, victims of human rights violations etc. The land conflict in this case was accentuated by the use of the category of 'repatriate', which, in the present context, gives entitlement and legitimises interventions in the name of reintegration and reconciliation. In the national press, the conflict was represented as a conflict between 'repatriates' and 'locals', categories which nurture an imagery of antagonistically opposed parties of the national conflict, i.e. civil patrollers and guerilla supporters. But the trajectories of livelihood and survival are more complex than that. All of the 'locals' sought refuge in Mexico in 1982. Some returned 'on their own account' (i.e. without the UNHCR support for resettlement) and had to pass through the army's amnesty ritual. Others were repatriated during the late 1980s under a tripartite agreement between Mexico, Guatemala and UNHCR. And the families on both sides of the border had been in more or less continuous contact during the conflict. As we have seen, the lack of coincidence between the categories of intervention and the social identities of people has the potential to create much conflict.

For men of the frontier, the regulation and closing of the frontier changes their position in the national hierarchies. Alonso describes how peasant warriors at the northern frontier with Mexico lost their privileges and emblems of honour and civilisation, as the ever-more present authorities of state sought a reduction of their now 'wild and threatening masculinity' (Alonso 1995: 118). At the end of the last century, the new buzz words were 'order and progress'. At the end of the twentieth century, 'peace and development' discourse has taken their place, including human rights, democracy and sustainability. But the former patrollers, the PACs, who may or may not resort to threats of violence, are nonetheless seen more as an obstacle to development than their northern precursors. In the discourse of the repatriates, the patrollers, whom they are now in conflict with over land, are people who 'want to see blood, who will only destroy, while we daily try to improve ourselves and create development. They are not conventional people (*gente formales*) like us' (fieldnotes 1994).

Contrary to these dichotomising representations, we see the former men of the frontier, the patrollers, as standing between resistance to the introduction of the new organisation of space, which reduces the former liberties in the 'wilderness', and the quest for a 'government that takes us into account, that respects people rather than killing them, a government that gives its contribution', as a patrol commander expressed it. Thus, in the aforementioned conflict, the ex-patrollers followed two strategies: they solicited support from the government in order to purchase the land they were working; and they demonstrated their potential force in a way that told everybody in Guatemala that 'there will be trouble if they buy our land'.

The context of this chapter is a wave of international interventions which comprise a large repertoire of techniques for nation-state formation encompassing human rights institutions, democratic institutions and procedures, institutions for the management of cultural difference, decentralisation, environmental protection and development measures. One of the logics at work here is the preoccupation in the North with the problems that migration may produce. Migration has increasingly been interpreted in terms of security issues (Weiner 1993), and aid to the South is increasingly being regarded as a measure against migration (cf. Böhling & Schloeter-Paredes 1994). Thus, intervention may be interpreted as measures to consolidate a national order of things in which movement can be controlled without recurrence to coercive means of control.

This essay is a warning against the de-subjectification of people through dichotomising interventions which may recreate the barbary of the frontier.

Notes

1   Since the 1930s, a resident 'military commissioner' has organised conscription in many towns, but the system did not produce sufficient numbers without the organised coercion.
2   However, as Poulantzas (1978) argues, monopoly of the legitimised use of force is a premise for the absence of violence.
3   Three witnesses escaped, which was apparently not meant to happen.
4   This fact is deplored by many of the intervening, international agencies.

9 Vital force, avenging spirits and zombies

Discourses on drug addiction among Surinamese Creole migrants in Amsterdam

Ineke van Wetering and Paul van Gelder

Introduction[1]

Since the early 1970s, the traffic in drugs has put some segments of the African Surinamese or Creole community in Dutch cities under great pressure. Members of some groups make energetic moves to maintain ethnic solidarity and control tensions arising from participation in these pursuits, but the problems caused by addicts in particular, put solidarity to severe trial. In general, no means, secular or ritual, are left unturned to effect reintegration of those whose norms have gradually deviated from those of 'traditional' group culture. However, there is also a tendency to abandon some members as hopeless, primarily the addicted, and to exclude them from community life. Such matters are rarely discussed directly, but are often referred to obliquely, in symbolic language derived from the Afro-Surinamese cultural heritage, called *Winti*, *Akodrey* or *Kulturu*.[2] The labels attached to drug addiction are an indication of a programme of rehabilitation or ritual action. Although a 'traditional' world-view has lost its hold on many Creoles, it is striking that a highly modern phenomenon such as drug addiction has caused a multifarious replication of old concepts. For traditionalists, this has acted as an incentive to apply some time-hallowed interpretations of misfortune to a new situation, whereas it proved a stimulus for modernists in an emergent new middle class to reconstruct the cultural heritage to suit new experiences. Here, we will discuss the discourses current among the addicted, their friends and relations, kinsmen, partners and social workers, including volunteers in churches and sects.

This is a difficult field of research among any group, but is especially so among minorities. Neither drug addiction nor *winti* is freely discussed, and regarding both issues, ambivalence is pervasive. Traffic in drugs is one of the few avenues to short-term financial success in a period of economic decline and lack of job opportunities for young migrants. But involvement in the drug scene also poses a threat to respectability, one of the cardinal values in Creole culture.

Financial matters are shrouded in secrecy under normal circumstances, and this is even more true of illegal earnings. Though 'hustling' is an accepted practice among Surinamese Creoles (van Gelder 1990b), theft and 'scoring' behaviours attendant upon addiction, are considered disgraceful. Involvement in problematic pursuits that cause a public loss of face is held characteristic of the lower classes. The same is true of *winti*. While the African heritage is a source of pride, an expression of a collective identity, its practices are closely associated in the public mind with social problems. At best, *winti* is a family affair, under the firm control of the elderly and responsible.

Discourse and ethnicity

Here, it is neither the drugs scene nor popular religion that is the topic of discussion per se, but their reflection in the discourses produced by those involved. 'Discourse' is understood here as the specific way social issues are stated and tackled. Any discourse only partially assumes a verbal form, with what is left unsaid assuming equal importance. It is also our assumption that more than one discourse is current within the ranks of a group commonly referred to as one ethnic group.[3] Different social strata have specific ways of defining and dealing with matters regarded as problematic. Open discussion is favoured by the middle class. There is also discourse considered suitable for public debate and another for inner circles. Discourse that takes place in Dutch is different from discourse in *Sranan Tongo*, Surinam's lingua franca, and there is a differentiation within both categories, though as discourses are not isolated, there tends to be an interplay. As MacDonell (1986: 33, 47) has stressed, thoughts expressed in one discourse are related to thoughts not surfacing there, but noticeable in other discourses. Drawing on Althusser, MacDonell points out that discourses tend to take form in a struggle with other complexes of thought or ideologies. And all varieties of discourse among Surinamese or other ethnic groups and subgroups are in some way related to the discourses current in mainstream society. As will be noted, for instance, colonial oppression and exploitation forms a manifest part of the addicts' discourse, whereas this does not figure in the same way in public discourse or among kinsmen. Likewise, applying the notion of 'illness' – borrowed from a medical regime – to their condition is not supported without ambivalence by other parties. Both differentiation and overlap in discourses are of interest to us here.

Janssen and Swierstra (1982), two criminologists, first introduced the concept of discourse in Dutch studies of drug addiction, hoping thus to bridge a gap between micro- and macro-level studies and between political and symbolic anthropology. They interviewed addicts, starting from assumptions current among students of subcultures, life styles, marginalisation and survival strategies. The method implied a restriction to a discourse of one party in the social field, the addicts, and to only one of their discourses, namely that in a modern Western language. The views of other parties, of non-using Creoles in some socially significant ways related to the users, and discourses in the native vernacular, were not considered.

Anthropologists rarely have access to complete versions of discourses: parts are often missing and a cacophony of messages may flood listeners simultaneously. Here, we will try to sketch some communications, including some noticeable silences, in public meetings, in privately-managed but public places such as churches, in the semi-private sphere of associations, and in interviews. Written texts on drug addiction do not figure. The advantages of noting reactions from audiences to statements, speeches and other performances are patent.

Surinamese Creoles and illegal drugs in Amsterdam

Although the use of hash and marihuana was common in Surinam in the 1960s, the use and traffic in cocaine was negligible and heroin was completely unknown. The use of the latter suddenly expanded enormously in Europe in the early 1970s. Within a short span of time the Surinamese had wrested control of the market in the Netherlands from the Chinese who had previously dominated this field. Thus, a segment of the ethnic group developed vested interests in this 'niche'. Around 1975, when Surinam gained political independence, the number of migrants increased greatly. Many were young and unskilled, and unable to find employment (van Gelder 1990a). The traffic in drugs was one of the few prospects for quickly gaining a considerable income (cf. Buiks 1983: 44). Drug dealers met the fully packed planes arriving at Schiphol from Paramaribo, Surinam's capital, and recruited middlemen and street-dealers among the newcomers. The news spread in Paramaribo, where unemployment was rising fast, and many wished to try their luck. Research has borne out that most addicts drifted into the drugs scene for economic and social reasons (Biervliet 1975; Janssen & Swierstra 1982; Buiks 1983; van Gelder & Sijtsma 1988: 1). They were also keen for adventure: they experimented with drugs and some ended up as addicts.

Some quarters in Amsterdam are centres of illegal drug traffic and use. In spite of the administration's attempts at control, illegal drugs remain a tricky problem. Bijlmermeer, in the south-eastern part of Amsterdam, offered shelter to many Surinam migrants in the mid-1970s. The traffic in drugs gained a firm footing there and many jobless young migrants became involved. Bijlmermeer is second only to the city's red light district as a focus of attraction for both addicts and dealers. The reception centre for addicts there has been functioning for longer than anywhere else in the city, and its inmates have close relations with the inhabitants of the surrounding apartment buildings. Although Bijlmermeer is usually referred to as a disadvantaged area, the influence there of black money is patent.

The administration opted for an integrated approach (Ahmed *et al.* 1988) to reduce inconvenience and simultaneously create conditions favourable to a decent life for addicts. Relief centres were created, some managed by Dutch institutions, others by ethnic organisations subsidised by the administration, but they were often short-lived as it proved impossible to keep drug dealers away. Attempts to open new centres invariably met with opposition from the neighbourhood's inhabitants because of nuisance and violence. The free supply of methadone since 1980 has proved to be viable only in cases of heroin addiction, the use of which in Amsterdam appears to have stabilised since then. However, this is not true of cocaine (van Gelder & Sijtsma 1988 I: 152).

The inadequacies and vicissitudes of government policies, coupled with the failures of organised social case-work have left scope for private initiatives. Some such initiatives aim to control drug use or help individuals kick the habit. The field is also open to volunteers. The lack of clear-cut policies in the public domain has left the neighbourhood and kinsmen to fend for themselves and addicts who are not interested in rehabilitation programmes to fall back on informal networks. Those who choose not to remain aloof from the addicts have to rely on their personal resources and guidelines. Where social distance is smallest, in the case of partners and kinsfolk, the risks are highest. Theft, burglary and violence are the 'costs' to be reckoned with. We will see in what way those personally involved react and try to cope.

Shadows on the wall: public discourse

No one in the Surinamese Creole community is interested in an open discussion about the impact of the drug scene, which for many has been traumatic. Abolishing social case-work within ethnic organisations also caused unrest. Drug use and traffic are interconnected and because addicts attracted dealers, the addicted could no longer be admitted to the centres and youth clubs (Buiks 1983: 211; van Gemert 1988: 15, 25, 46).

In Bijlmermeer, an unsuspecting visitor will notice at a glance that differences in living standards are great. Some Surinamese inhabitants have been hit by cut-backs in pensions and hover at subsistence levels, while for others this obviously does not apply. The sizes and types of cars, the quality of clothes and abundance of gold jewellery show that money is freely spent. Among women this mostly applies to the younger ones. Buiks' (1983: 208) observation that dealers or *wakaman* channel funds to disco girls seems to apply here. Upon further acquaintance it is evident that gambling – an obvious means of spending black money (*ibid*: 17) – is also very popular. It is striking also that all kinds of entertainment in the neighbourhood are expensive and beyond the reach of people living off welfare allowances or old-age pensions. Posters announce the costs of nightly dances and boat trips: 25–35 guilders is a common price, and the costs of refreshments are correspondingly high.

A star goes down

By the end of 1983 a plan was made by volunteers to improve the social climate in the ward. For a long time it had been a source of discontent that the cultural centre in the neighbourhood, *Ganzenhoef*, designed as a showpiece of multi-functional, cultural activities in Bijlmermeer, was mostly disused. The principal activities going on there were dances organised by sponsors of renowned Surinamese bands. But its alleged purpose was to serve all groups living in Bijlmermeer. For the elderly there was little to do and they rarely left their apartments at night for fear of being mugged. The foundation *Sitara* (Star) hoped to overcome the deadlock, bring people together from all ethnic groups, and foster goodwill and mutual understanding. The committee's composition was mixed: the initiative was taken by a Dutch 'cultural broker' who had been active in stimulating amateur theatre in Surinam. He had the support of a Hindustani from that time and a few deputees from a Creole club interested in the performing arts. They asked the community organisation for a grant and suitable persons were approached and invited. However, difficulties soon arose that thwarted this rather common-place plan. An assistant manager of the Ganzenhoef complex, a young Dutch woman who was to be the contact person, refused to enter the premises after nightfall. She was afraid to walk the half-mile distance from the underground station to the Ganzenhoef building, as she had been threatened with robbery and rape. This caused some confusion among the committee members: where had the threat come from, from outside or inside the complex? The junkies hanging out in and around the building were apparently not involved, but the bands might have been. The latter would brook no rivals to their lucrative festivals that would provide less expensive amusements. They feared they might lose clients. As things stood people went there because there was nothing else to do, and the elderly stayed at home. Things had reached such a point that the management refused to lease the halls to organisations for cultural purposes. Acquiescence was the rule; and the building would be empty but for the nights of the dances.

The committee's meeting passed off rather chaotically, with tall stories told of threats and violence. A social occasion for the elderly was organised in the daytime, but few turned up. And *Sitara* quietly expired.

The impact of the drug traffic is obviously at play here. Even when 'the scene' is not involved directly, radiation from a world where money and violence loom large is palpable. Music and bands are not directly related to illegal pursuits and, objectively, there is no reason for musicians to behave like drug dealers. But the example is there, opportunities are open, money is at stake, and norms change. On the surface the situation seems to be accepted. Neither community workers nor representatives of voices from any other formal organisation protest. In public discourse about the Ganzenhoef's malfunctioning the issue is not even raised (cf. Verhagen 1987: 96). Neighbourhood organisations that should rally the inhabitants for participation in community matters have been immobilised. Things have come to such a head that sometimes even drug dealers take part in public deliberations about the ward's problems.

Halting consultations

An information meeting had been organised in the Ganzenhoef concerning hard drugs. However, it attracted few ward residents. Whether native Dutch or immigrants, they obviously felt in no need of information or did not want to be involved in public discussions about policies. In retrospect, the absentees seem to have been right. As the meeting drew to a close, it became transparent that no clear views or propositions had been presented. With an impressive show of indignation and rhetorical fervour a group of young Creole men inveighed against maladministration. They protested against what they referred to as a treatment of symptoms and the dismantling of ethnic organisations. The latter had made sound plans for specific projects, they argued; if grants had only been supplied concrete results would have been forthcoming. This evoked loud applause from the backbenches. The speakers' style was truly Surinamese; one party that felt slighted eloquently brought a charge, to be countered by a second party, whereupon a third, neutral party, judged the case and proposed a settlement. The other parties kept silent. Behind a small table some delegates of Surinamese organisations were seated, and two policemen. In a circle around the group that was letting off steam a number of representatives of political parties and community workers could be observed. Gauging from their looks and outfit, their views would be leftish and progressive. Some deputies from a Surinamese welfare organisation active in the city centre were also in attendance. At the side, some figures in black leather and sunglasses were leaning against pillars. A Surinamese friend, better acquainted with the neighbourhood than I, indicated to me in a soft whisper that they were drug dealers. Now and then they took part in the discussions, but mostly they stood by passively. The caseworkers, administrators and managers plainly demonstrated disinterest, sniggering among themselves. The local policeman, tired of the harangues, advised the company to apply to the municipal centre where policies are made. By that time, people had started to leave and the meeting closed.

But passivity or laughter does not prevail in all parts of the neighbourhood. Elderly Surinamese inhabitants who suffer the consequences of addiction in the family circle are not to be found at information meetings, but in the churches. The public and secular fields of discussion have been virtually deserted by those directly involved. Discourses current there have not assumed a clear form, nor are they acknowledged and sustained by any demarcated social category.

Discourses within privately-managed public spaces

The denominations that have publicly endorsed specific views on the subject can be subdivided into two main categories. First, the established churches or denominations: Roman Catholic and Protestant. Among the latter, the Moravians or Community of Evangelical Brethren are mostly of concern here, since they count many adherents among the Creole population.[4] Second, religious sects have made headway in recent decades among Creoles, both in the mother country and in the Netherlands. The Pentecostals probably rank first among them, although accurate figures are hard to give.

As might be expected, the attitudes of the established churches come closest to the discourse of mainstream society. The Roman Catholic parish in Bijlmermeer, for example, has taken a public stand, whereas the Community of Evangelical Brethren, to our knowledge, has not. The Pentecostals regard Amsterdam as a mission area, and take an unambiguous stand against all forms of addiction. Bijlmermeer's Roman Catholic parish has initiated a study group to extend pastoral care to the many addicts roaming there (Rapport 1973: 58; IBVR 1988). The group organises special services, for instance at Christmas time. The addicts are not overly interested in the messages; in particular not in the testimonials of those who have kicked the habit, nor in the singing of Christmas carols. Gospel singing is more to their taste, but even an accommodation to black culture and 'roots' hardly has any effect.

A special church service

January 1984. A religious service has been announced in 'De Nieuwe Stad' (The New City), a hall within the Ganzenhoef community centre reserved for religious worship and related activities. The sponsors are the Roman Catholic parish '*De Granaatappel*', the Pomegranate, and a foundation for the prevention and combat of drug addiction '*De Regenboog*', the Rainbow, an initiative taken by a Surinamese study group. Information and refreshments are being offered. The aim is to encourage open discussion. The service is not going to be a mass in the proper sense, although there is occasion to receive communion, and many churchgoers do in fact take part. A choir of Franciscans sings modern hymns composed for a post-war generation, and the parish priest has given the floor to two church members, a man and a woman. They read a letter written by a drug addict and a real-life story about the distress and dilemmas of the user's parents. The tenor is that we cannot turn our backs on the problem or the addicts, but neither will the much-discussed policy of free distribution of drugs or drug substitutes do. Thus, the attitude taken is rather conservative, and is an explicit repudiation of the policies advocated by a progressive, secular lobby that does much to control the discourse on the topic in town. It is puzzling that so few Surinamese or Antilleans are present. The building is full, but, apart from a few light-coloured young women and a Chinese family, the audience is middle class and autochthonous. The migrant population, though well-represented among the

Catholics, has not turned up. After the meeting in the church hall, a smaller group withdraws to the consistory. The first question that arises there is why the stricter view of forced rehabilitation has not been taken. The answer is that experiences abroad have not been encouraging. One Surinamese spokesman recapitulates the current views about joblessness, disadvantages and lack of prospects in the formal social and economic sector. He adds that young migrants, fresh from Surinam, have been welcomed at Schiphol airport with offers to earn 500 guilders a week. What can one expect? the spokesman asks rhetorically. A proposal is made to open a consultation room for parents of addicted children. The same speaker instantly dismisses the idea, 'Placards will be immediately torn down', he predicts, 'by people uttering the most abominable curses. The dealers offer money, don't they, and people want it badly.' A general sense of powerlessness prevails.

Strict views are held by the Pentecostals. They offer less liberal, but time-hallowed Christian remedies. Since the influx of Caribbean migrants, the ranks of some native groups have swelled, and new, Caribbean-controlled groups have mushroomed, particularly in Amsterdam's Western outskirts. Surinamese members living in Bijlmermeer often prefer to attend services there. It is made clear in many ways, directly and indirectly, what the community hopes to do, and it is also obvious that these meet the needs of those present. Whenever a preacher touches on the problem, in prayers and also in hymn-singing, intensity of feeling is almost palpable. It is clear that many parents and grandparents of the addicted are present here. Sermons are replete with testimonies of those involved in drugs who found their way back to a godly life. Prayers are offered up for particular needs. God's omnipresence is stressed for all those who feel insecure and threatened; particularly the elderly in Bijlmermeer, as they are a target for addicted robbers. Sins, illness and idolatry are driven out by the laying-on of hands; problems are treated as demons or foul fiends that must be cast out. In fact, in some cases, rituals of exorcism are performed. Some of the leaders are in fact young and apparently upwardly mobile. The whole congregation is rather young and carefully dressed. Families attend as units with many children present. People seem relaxed and out-going. There is a tendency to intensify group life; activities are announced for weekdays. Social control can be tight (Caffé 1987), but on the whole, the outlook seems optimistic.

Between public and private: case-workers and therapeutic agents

Both case-workers and traditional healers confronted with drug addiction construct their own discourses around the phenomenon. Many social workers employed by Surinamese or general welfare institutions belong to the Creole group and are to some extent familiar with the African heritage and world-view of their clients. Sometimes they use cultural resources to mobilise the young in the struggle against addiction and all its concomitant behaviours. In

Bijlmermeer, within the Ganzenhoef complex, the organisation *Jongeren Overleg Bijlmer* is actively engaged in promoting ethnicity. The popularity among the young of 'roots' and 'Africa' suits the purpose very well. Groups are formed that play drums, instruments vital in ritual practice. Lectures and discussion meetings are organised to provide information for the general public and to fight negative stereotypes: lift a taboo on *winti*. To this end, youth workers keep in contact with traditional healers knowledgeable about 'traditional' culture. When the occasion presents itself, the specialists can be of help. It is not exceptional for persons not regularly involved with 'traditional' religion to fall into a trance upon hearing *winti* rhythms and tunes. This often happens at feasts or other occasions that purportedly have only secular goals.

Processes of 'bricolage' are occurring among the young in such clubs. Traditional culture is reproduced according to personal situations, needs and inclinations. This could hardly be otherwise, and is true of any cultural tradition. For *winti* this holds in particular, as there are few formal institutions or written documents that individuals can resort to which might canonise lore. Also, the fact that one's own personal guiding spirits impart and legitimise religious knowledge, ensures that there is a wide scope for individualism. Although books are now available to the general public about *winti*, overtly for information, but which equally standardise a religious code, this is unlikely to keep individuals from making their own interpretations or combining ideas in novel ways. Moreover, many Creoles who regard themselves as belonging to this ethnic group are in fact of mixed descent, and draw upon more than one tradition.

An Amerindian cigar

Iwan was eight years old when he migrated to the Netherlands with his parents. In the working-class neighbourhood in which they then lived, Dutch boys were his playmates. But soon he found himself getting into closer contact with boys from Surinam. He felt more at ease among them. He also discovered that more was going on in his new home, and certainly more money was circulating among his new friends. As one of them remarked, 'Dutch boys had only mopeds, chips, and a greased quiff. Nearly all the Surinamese guys I met had a brother or a friend who dealt in coke. I figured out all kinds of things for myself, and I wanted to make some cash. I started to deal a little, to use some. I don't remember what came first.' Thinking back, he attributes his current addiction, and that of a brother and a sister, to their Amerindian grandfather: 'it is a case of *famiri siki* (family illness),' he claims. His grandfather had lived in Surinam's interior and had probably smoked cigars the way Indian healers used to do: 'So it was my grandfather who used drugs first.'

Social workers belong predominantly to a new middle class (cf. Haakmat 1978). In the social background of traditional healers there is a great diversity. To some extent, the discourse of persons active in this sector coincides with that of the addicts and their kin. This is only to be expected, as they all belong to an ethnic category and are often in personal contact. Networks among Creoles are actively maintained. The therapeutic elite mediates contacts between all parties concerned and shares ideas with all.

Spirit help in rehabilitation

One traditional healer confesses that he has indeed prompted two young men to cultivate their cultural heritage. Their mother had called in his help; her sons' life style worried her deeply and she felt quite powerless. The boys needed a lot of money and this caused many conflicts and problems. He reported that he had asked the two of them whether they knew anything about *winti*. Not much, was the reply. He had then looked at them knowingly and said: 'But you truly do entertain important *winti*, although you do not realise it. I see a *Kromanti* from your father's side and an Amerindian spirit from your mother's. These spirits are angry with you now, because of the way you lead your lives.' One of the boys was a really nice kid he said, but was quite depressed and slept for days. It had been necessary to get him interested in something, and his heritage, for the time being, had been a start. The boys had been really scared and had thrown away all their drugs. 'I have shown them how to make ritual ablutions, but how this will work out, I cannot say. It is wait and see', he said.

These views, minus the overt psychologising, are part of a shared cultural heritage. Case-workers and the healers co-operating with them generate versions specific for their subgroup that are not heard among the addicts' kinsfolk. One traditional healer, for instance, starts from the shared conviction that the condition is caused by bad powers, and claims, 'the evil manifests itself in a tendency to make its victims wander around'. He refers to the *djumbi* concept taken up in the whole complex of collective representations (Herskovits & Herskovits 1969: 106; Wooding 1973: 135). A *djumbi* is described as a spectre, a nebulous appearance of a human being. However, the concept is not often mentioned spontaneously by traditionalists; the notion of *yorka* has far wider currency. A *yorka* is a 'shade' or ancestral spirit of a particular deceased person. Case-workers often compare their addicted clients to zombies or mummies, living ghosts, apparently or partly dead. The use of these terms seems to have been derived from Haitian popular beliefs rather than from those current in Surinam. There, the term was more or less loosely applied as a synonym of *yorka*. The drug users are also familiar with the term, but they will not apply it to their own persons; it is intended for those worse off than themselves. It is advanced as a negative point of reference; a bad example of what might happen. The healer referred to previously is of the belief that a purification ritual is a proper remedy against the affliction. In this way, he classifies the evil as part of a field of forces to be potentially controlled. He will not turn his back on the addicts. Another healer attributes a heavy case of addiction to a *bakru,* a sprite from the wilds. Theologically speaking, this was an apt choice, as *bakru* induce a tendency to steal in their victims (Stephen 1983: 59; Wooding 1973: 195–6). In such a case, therapy is thought of as potentially effective.

Among case-workers, allusions bordering on reification are current.[5] Janssen & Swierstra (1982) note these among the addicts, and we discuss them below. The interpretations are translated back into a quasi-traditional vernacular. Heroin is represented as a spirit that gets the user in its power in an inscrutable way and thus causes addiction: 'It is a very hard, and unruly spirit'. The striking element here is not the fact that this view has evolved; it is hardly a far-fetched idea, and can be regarded as either an extrapolation of secular metaphors or of sacred notions. What is worthy of note is that those who can maintain some distance from the addicts by their professional and social position, entertain ideas about addiction that stress 'otherness'. These are not found among the addicts' kinsfolk, who, as we will see below, stick to interpretations which stress a shared fate.

The private world of addicts

A key notion stressed in sociological analysis (Janssen & Swierstra 1982: 18ff, 65) is the autonomy or *verzelfstandiging* of the drug scene. This has been an unintended result of various processes, such as the market, democratisation, extension of compulsory education, welfare allowances, scholarships, increased leisure time and development of youth cultures, and the interests of drug dealers and social workers. Those involved may not know much about these processes or newly-evolved structures, but they are aware of the opportunities they open up for them. The addicted make good use, for example, of prison and relief systems; Janssen & Swierstra (1982: 19) refer to this as adapting the system to their own ends, *omfunctionaliseren.* Biervliet (1975: 199), Buiks (1983: 184), van Gelder & Sijtsma (1988 I: 47,131) and van Gemert (1988: 53) have likewise found the addicted to be quite knowledgeable about the ways of the welfare state. The discourse created involves legitimation: as victims of colonial exploitation they now have a right to benefit from such openings (cf. Sansone 1992: 137–41). Such discourses offer a collective solution for the predicaments within a social system that is unable to live up to their expectations, observe Janssen & Swierstra (1982: 56) but, according to them, the solution can only be symbolic.

In most studies of drug addiction among Surinamese Creoles the notion of marginalisation is central, and it is commonly assumed that solidarity among kinsmen is waning (Janssen & Swierstra 1982: 395). Also, it is readily accepted that kinsmen will disown addicted family members (Buiks 1983: 142). While this may be true occasionally, it would not do to presume that all Creoles who start living independently organise their lives in a modern Western and individualistic way. There are various forms of symbiosis between most households. Also, it would be hard to make a clear-cut distinction between a category of addicts and one of dealers (Biervliet 1975: 197; Buiks 1983: 141, 151; van Gemert 1988: 25, 46, 100). For dealers, relations with kin are extremely important as relations of trust (van Gemert 1988: 47–8). Addicts also make an effort to keep relations with kinsfolk intact (van Gelder & Sijtsma 1988: 139,142; Ligeon, van Roekel & van de Wijngaart 1990: 60; Janssen & Swierstra 1982: 435). All sorts of problems may be involved, but a radical severing of ties is rare.

Addicts complain of misunderstanding and a panic fear of any form of drug use: 'My mother will not make a distinction between a joint, hash, and heroin. Whenever I look somewhat disoriented she immediately assumes I am stoned', one of them said in an interview. They object to the controls imposed by family life and try to escape them, but they also look to kinsmen for support and a refuge when the need might arise. The result is ambivalence and insecurity. The young of the first generation of migrants may be ready, willy-nilly, to accept the pattern of traditional authority and show respect to older people, for those in between and for the second generation this is not self-evident.

The category 'kinsmen' means primarily 'mothers'. By tradition, mothers and grandmothers are key figures in lower-class households. In the Netherlands the pattern of female-headed households has been re-established (Hoolt 1986). The mother figure has a great emotional and culturally acknowledged significance, which is brought out in proverbs, for instance: '*Mama na sribi krosi, a no tapu dede ma a tapu shin*' (Mother is a cloak, she cannot protect one from death but she will shield one from shame). This is important for the addicted. Fathers are less dependable and they tend to be stricter over maintaining formal group norms. Many fathers and brothers emphasise an enforced kicking of the habit. Often the father is not part of the household, and a stepfather is present who is less concerned about the current partner's offspring. Other relatives assume the mother's role: sisters and cousins bring messages from kinsfolk in Surinam and watch the addicted with concern. The latter often try to hide from them from fear of losing face. A reputation of respectability keeps its meaning within a migrant community. The elderly may act as guardians of morality towards the younger generation. The addicted tell of being accosted in the streets by Creole seniors who point out the risks of addiction to them. Partners of addicts are manoeuvred into a mother role, but offering a refuge and haranguing are the limited repertoire open to them. Drug use intensifies a pattern of separated domicile that was current in Surinam. The addicted will explain this separation by a concern to save their wife/partner the nuisance. The latter will look after the children and visit them in jail should the occasion arise.

The mother role influences drug use in female addicts who will try, because of their children, to show restraint or kick the habit. They are afraid to lose the children to Child Welfare or to relatives (Ligeon, van Roekel & van de Wijngaart 1990: 60–1, 72). Some are sensitive to the children's anger for neglecting them. Neglect brings them a loss of prestige in the eyes of their kin, which is a touchy subject.

Parents may strive to send an addicted child back to Surinam, in the hope that opportunities and temptations will be less there. But the hope seems less and less warranted now that drug use has gained a firm foothold in the mother country, and the chances of gainful employment there have declined. Most striking is the impotence of kin to take meaningful action. In fact they have little grip on the addicted. Older people complain that their authority has been undermined by state welfare allowances and other provisions. This element is new for Surinamese; the informal pressures they rely on, are effective only as long as interdependence lasts. The autonomy of youth is noted by all and regarded as a problem by elders (cf. Lenders & van de Rhoer 1984: 18, 81, 158). Nevertheless, the self respect of most Creoles, including the addicts, has been formed in social conditions other than those in which they now live. It struck Janssen & Swierstra (1982: 391) for instance, that Surinamese addicts have kept their footing in a better way than their Dutch counterparts who, as a consequence, are looked down on by their Surinamese peers as pitiable.

Van Gelder & Sijtsma (1988: 27, 96) observe that Surinamese addicts do not apply the term 'junkie' to themselves. Instead they borrow their identity from the *wakaman* ideal, the successful dealer. Although the outside world, social workers included, looks down upon them (Buiks 1983: 142; van Gelder & Sijtsma 1988: 27), they derive satisfaction and a sense of power from the notion that they belong to an ethnic group that has firm control of the drugs traffic (Janssen & Swierstra 1982: 402). They pin the blame for their addiction on the dealers, and on colonialism (Buiks 1983: 142, 149; van Gelder & Sijtsma 1988: 47; Sansone 1992: 138–9). Although there is a hierarchy within the drug scene with patent differences in power, in which their position is low and where 'dealing' has greater status than the hustling they engage in (van Gelder & Sijtsma 1988), they do not regard themselves as problem cases. The fault is not theirs; it is 'beyond'.

Janssen & Swierstra (1982: 15) found that addicts are inclined to split their self-image into two egos; one intended for the outside world and one that is valid within the drug scene. This corresponds to comments made earlier with reference to Surinamese Creoles. Due to colonialism, it has been argued, there has been a long tradition in this group of splitting egos: one for the oppressor and one for the peer group (Budike & Mungra 1986: 137). A sense of powerlessness, of an inability to live up to the norms held by dominant groups, led to *fromu* (deceit), an accepted strategy within the subgroup. Conceivably, this strategy has coloured the outlook on addiction, that is, that they will fail to live up to the demands of the outside world is within an accepted range of expectations, and often regarded as inevitable. Moravians, as Jones (1981: 48–9) noted, may have also contributed to a Creole tolerance for personal weakness, with the image, stressed in religious tradition, of men as *potiman, zwakaman* and *mofinawan* (poor, weak and deprived). This view, however, is counterbalanced by other images current among the addicted, and if we compare the views of the addicted with those of their relatives, we discover a common ground.

In contacts with outsiders, the addicts are highly strategic in presenting a self-image. They borrow notions from mainstream society that fit their purpose. They classify abstention and withdrawal symptoms as 'illness' (van Gemert 1988: *passim*; van Gelder & Sijtsma 1988: 122), confirming an image of themselves as in need of assistance. In their own culture the accent is different. Around two-thirds of the hard drug users of Creole or mixed descent are involved in traditional or popular religion and its practices. This does not imply that a direct connection between drug use and religion is made, nor is there consensus over the issue of whether *winti* is of use as a means of countering drug addiction (cf. Lenders & van de Rhoer 1984: 115). Women in particular have ideas about *winti* and are willing to discuss them. Most suggest that there is a tension between drug use and *winti*. One woman said that if spirits were involved at all, they would be very bad spirits, for drug use 'is something that carries one away ... only a very bad *winti* can prompt one to spend one's money in such a way'. Another is convinced that her drug use has saddled her with a heavy religious problem, a *hebi*. There is a consensus that drug use impairs vital force. Protracted use will dissolve the protective shield that a pure self or soul offers, a strong *kra* or *yeye*. Someone suffused by drugs will be deaf to messages received in dreams from protective *winti*. Dreaming keeps a human being in contact with his or her true self, and the addicted get out of touch with this potential. In this manner, protection against black magic or witchcraft (*wisi*) equally wears out. Who lives by stealing is under the influence of a very dangerous *winti*. Who persists in such a life style for too long runs the risk of estrangement from self and gods. Also, one's children run the risk of confrontation, with dire consequences.

In the discourse shared by addicts and kinsmen another side surfaces: human beings have responsibilities. Those who get involved with drugs play with dangerous forces, which can turn the user into an asocial, unthinking being. Asocial dealings may be thought of as inevitable or justified in some situations, yet, on behalf of sheer survival, some restraint is required. These ideas are not expressed in a straightforwardly moralistic idiom, but in the language of pollution, ritual purity and supernatural danger.

Addicts, kin and neighbours

Relations between addicts, their kinsfolk and neighbours who live within the same subcultural orbit are highly charged. They emphasise the value of solidarity; the idea that a mother, and all classificatory 'mothers', would disown the young is foreign and unacceptable. But they experience the burden as unbearable. Many of the apartments' inhabitants are terrified of thieves and burglars and refuse to open their doors after nightfall. There is not a single family that cannot tell a story about house-breaking and robbery. The addicts have to 'score' each day and often try their luck where access is easiest: among kinsmen and friends. The day after a successful break-in the family that is despoiled of its valuables will often point to 'a cousin who had called and noticed that we had just bought a video'. Stories are told about older brothers carrying away the TV set in front of crying younger sisters – 'the addicted are not really people, you see'. Fear of robbery thus discourages sociability: 'There is no need to let all and sundry into one's house to see what one has there'.

But prevention is difficult. Apartment buildings may share one entrance hall, there will be friends there, and there will be a 'nest' on another floor. A father of grown-up boys, unable to cope with them, moves out and joins one of his former wives in another building, leaving the youngsters in the care of a grandmother who cannot control them even if she wished to. They have the keys to the recently made burglar-proof walkway. Even when they cannot enter this way, they often succeed because addicted girlfriends living on other galleries will open the doors for them. The neighbours grumble, but do not see what action can be taken.

There is hardly a trace of sentimentality, however, when some notorious type is arrested or dies. As a rule, they have a record of violence and here sympathy clearly stops. Aggression, or rather mismanagement of assertiveness, worries the women. Self-assertion rates high in lower-class Creole culture, but when things clearly run out of hand they deplore this deeply and take an uncompromising stand on such matters in public. More than is common in a generalised Western culture, Creole women feel responsible for the maintenance of norms and behaviour in public. Thus, it is not so much addiction that is feared but its unforeseen consequences.

As a rule, the kinsmen of the addicted will endorse the views discussed above about the dangers inherent in a weakened and defiled soul. Many mothers try to muster the funds necessary for a ritual ablution to heal and fortify the *kra* or *yeye* (van Wetering 1995). They may perform the ritual themselves, or request an older relative to do so. Such remedies are not classified as *winti* but rather as *oso sani*, home rituals. They form so much a part of daily life that even staunch supporters of the Christian faith will acknowledge to performing them. In their view, it is merely a traditional way of praying. Nevertheless, some women feel so estranged from their cultural heritage that they will enlist the help of a traditional healer. They may also do so because they consider the case too serious to be dealt with by simple remedies. But on the whole, most of these rituals are intra-family affairs.

Ritual for the soul varies in complexity. Its basis is the ablution to get rid of the effect of all negative experiences, crowned by a bath which fortifies and seals out any lurking evil. If the situation is believed to demand this, a *luku* may be performed to see what the wishes of the soul are. As this type of divination has been described extensively in the ethnographic literature (Herskovits 1936: 47–9; Schoonheym 1980: 61–3; Wooding 1973: 129) and has basically not changed much, there is little reason to repeat it here. The soul is expected to wish for a feast, a festive dinner or a jewel. Either the afflicted person whose soul is weakened, or the kinsmen, will try to oblige. In fact, the *kra tafra*, the dinner for the soul, is a highly popular ritual among *winti* adepts in the Netherlands, far more so than the famous *winti prey*. Perhaps this is because home-bound rituals are more easily performed by a city-dwelling population in a cold country, but it is also conceivable that the discreet and respectable character of the ritual makes it a favourite in the mother country as well. All the women known to us, whose sons are drug addicts, have performed rituals of this type.

When ritual action does not lead to the desired result – re-socialisation – other supernatural agencies are called upon to account for the failure. The soul is regarded as an arena where various forces struggle for supremacy, and, particularly when in a state of weakness or defilement, protective 'high' *winti*. may lose out against an overpowering vindictive spirit. Often, a bad or unappeased shade or ancestor spirit (*yorka*) is singled out for blame. Ritual action of a more complicated nature has then to be taken, which often involves a trip to the mother country. If matters run to such a head, willingness to discuss the case diminishes considerably. Here, an anthropologist touches upon a family's best-kept secrets, the *oso tori* (house stories).

A belief in cause and effect, coupled with the notion of a kin group's collective liability, implies that one can fall victim to other people's failures and misdeeds. In a number of cases, addiction was attributed to a past neglect of ritual duties by kin. This is a recurrent theme; almost a standard interpretation. In the case of one addicted young man, confined to an institution, reference was made to a deceased grandfather who was a traditional healer in his lifetime, and who had courted powerful spirits. After the healer's demise, the spirits should have been appeased, and such counsel was given by elder members of the family, only to be disregarded by a younger generation who do not care about old beliefs. Whenever a kin group fails to take ritual precautions, an angered *winti* can turn into an avenging spirit, a *kunu*. Such a case is regarded as practically hopeless (cf. Stephen 1983: 109).

At first glance, it seems that in endorsing such interpretations, people are shying away from accepting liability, the way they do in secular discourse. But this is misleading. Accepting ritual obligations means that one has to invest time, energy and money to expiate sins, and in identifying with the failures and trespasses of forebears, one can vicariously experience and come to terms with one's own.

As to the effectiveness of ritual acts, some doubts are warranted. Boys such as those discussed here will prefer to stay in their mothers' good books, so they will be ready to support them and hide them from the police if need be. If their commitment to rituals is not strong, they may consider acceptance to please their mothers. Some healers believe that men are deeply afraid of supernatural dangers and quickly feel threatened, perhaps even more so than women, but are less willing to perform simple rituals. They are more inclined to let things run out of hand and then take to drastic and costly action. Also, the willingness to keep the taboos inherent in the cult of the high-ranking *winti* is diminishing. Interest in the pursuit of these forces has been on the decline for some time.

Conclusion

Although public discourse may be inconclusive, perhaps chaotic, this does not equally hold for the discourse of other segments of the groups involved with Creole life-worlds and the drug scene. In churches and sects, views have to a greater extent crystallised, although the former show the same awareness of a lack of control that is manifest in public debate. As to the Creole group as an assumed ethnic unity, no formal or informal organisation that might try and bring some uniformity in the 'definitions of the situation', has sufficient recruiting power to span the entire group in the Netherlands. Churches and sects, social workers and kin groups have their own specific ways of con-structing reality and of shaping policies. Social workers, who mainly belong to an educated middle class and are in a relatively independent position towards clients, can afford a different outlook to that of the relatives of dealers and addicts. In reproducing the notion of zombies in connection with addicted clients, they stress distance and 'otherness'. Class allegiance demonstrably carries weight. The discourse produced by each of the groups and categories in close contact with the drugs scene plainly shows its roots in the social stratum to which it belongs. Among kinsmen, interdependence surfaces in a discourse emphasising close relationships, symbolised in the ancestors, figureheads of a shared past and a common fate. There is thus an emergent disparity in the cultural heritage as it is reproduced over time.

Nevertheless, there is a shared element in Creole thought regarding ideas about the dangers that beset the soul. Although there are different viewpoints as to the financial aspects of ritual practice, the symbolism is shared by those who belong to the middle and lower classes and presents a common idiom in which the threats to group life can be discussed. This discourse forms part of 'covert culture' and is rarely brought into the open, let alone politicised. The tendency to keep this discourse safely tucked away in the intimacy of the family circle, *winti*'s epicentre, and to withstand any attempts to produce shared meanings with outsiders is part of a power game characteristic of ethnic relations in a stratified society.

Notes

1   This paper is an abridged and revised version of an article published in Dutch (van Gelder & van Wetering 1991). The ethnographic data were gathered from different angles. Paul van Gelder, who wrote a PhD thesis on the informal sector in Surinam, has interviewed young Surinamese addicted to hard drugs, as well as social workers and traditional healers. The Amsterdam Municipal Administration sponsored this research project in 1986 and 1987. Ineke van Wetering has pursued Afro-Surinamese studies for many years, notably in Surinam's interior. In 1982 she joined a Creole women's club which has the preservation of Creole culture as an

aim, and she lived in Bijlmermeer. Research, almost exclusively by way of partici-
pant observation, was subsidised from 1984 to 1987 by ZWO, now NWO (the
Netherlands' Organisation for Scientific Research), The Hague.

2   Different terms are current for 'traditional' religion, often used interchangeably.
The term *Winti*, literally meaning 'winds' refers to invading spirits causing possession trances which loom large in religious life. The term *Afkodrey* literally means
idolatry, but has no negative connotations for the believers. The young and
intellectually oriented who want to enhance the reputation of the Creole cultural
heritage prefer the term *Kulturu*.

3   The term 'ethnic group' is used in a naive way here, as a synonym for 'migrant
group'. At the outset, no assumptions about 'belonging', boundaries or shared
meanings are implied. As the argument unfolds, such meanings will emerge which
are characteristic of a whole immigrant population or specific sub-groups or -
sections.

4   In 1986, the south-eastern part of Amsterdam had 16,249 registered Surinamese
inhabitants, of whom 4,910 were Roman Catholics and 3,420 members of the
Evangelische Broedergemeente.

5   It has struck Janssen & Swierstra (1982: 391) that Creole addicts refer to heroin in
a reifying way: they spoke of 'the thing' ('*a sani*' in *Sranan Tongo*). Buiks (1983:
122) and van Gelder & Sijtsma (1988: 55) have also noted this. Janssen & Swierstra regard this as an indication that the addicted acknowledge the power of
heroin in their lives, and they see this way of speaking as a form of fetishism.
Other powers can be manipulated, this seems to convey, but heroin has an absolute hold over them. This appears to be a fact which determines their position in
relation to kinsmen and freelance social workers. They seem to have been prised
loose from all social networks and turned over to heroin. This view is interesting,
but raises some doubts. Surinamese Creoles often refer to 'things' or 'the thing'
without any intent to reify. Often this is no more than a means of mystification, of
screening-off, and evoking a suggestion of intimacy between conversation partners. For the time being, we will regard the idea as a hypothesis which needs
further investigation.

10 Consuming modernity

Mutational processes of change

Alberto Arce and Norman Long

Introduction

This chapter takes the view that the realities of inequality, poverty, hunger and marginalisation cannot be understood in terms of the assumed 'unequal' exchanges that exist between different economic and political orders and epistemologies; but rather should be seen as the outcome of social processes that are contingently located in ongoing struggles over meanings, values and resources. This entails a description and analysis of the complex interfaces that lie at the heart of 'the manufacture of society'. We are all of us the architects of 'modernity' and cannibals of social order. Viewed in this way, modernity is as salient in present-day 'Third World' scenarios, where globalisation and decivilisation processes are part and parcel of the application of instrumental and scientific rationalities as in the more industrialised societies of the West.

Improved transportation and media communication on a world scale and extensive trade liberalisation imply globalisation of local competitive advantage, regulation of possible development options and a redefinition of policy instruments. On the other hand, local practices and heterogeneous social relations generate a great diversity in institutional responses and new political conjunctures involving contestations over values and renegotiation of the meanings of 'development' and the role of the national state. Some have argued that this marks the beginnings of a search for new forms of identity (or new class struggles?) leading to 'new' trajectories of change, whilst others, such as Giddens (1991) and Beck (1992), consider these reorganising processes as characteristic of the dilemma of 'late-modernity' or of the 'risk society'. The critical issue, however, is that all these positions assume, without question, that what we are witnessing is the unfolding of the 'final stage' of modernity.

Our view rests upon the simple assertion that we should not engage in a reworking of old dichotomies based upon variations of the modern/traditional type, with globalisation thrown in, but rather grasp the nettle of the emerging complexities by seeking to understand the encounters between multiple and divergent modernities. After all, witchcraft trials by poison ordeal can be interpreted in terms of instrumental rationality, cost/benefit calculations, as well as notions of 'supernatural' intervention. In a similar vein, science-based development programmes are not only shot through with techniques of control and the use of logical frameworks, but they also entail individual interests and desires based upon utopian rediscoveries of notions of 'primordial' democracy or modernity and the prevalence of 'new' languages of participation.

Global studies may help us to conceptualise issues and types of social ordering, but the latter cannot be comprehended in terms of the confrontation between 'modern' and 'traditional' systems, nor between the administrative domains of 'the state' and regulatory mechanisms of 'the market', nor in terms of 'scientific' versus 'magical' beliefs. Instead we need to identify the processes by which heterogeneous social forms are constructed or mutate out of the interplay of specific practices, commodities and values of modernity, which populate the spheres and interstices of the globe.

We insist that 'we have always been modern', and argue that all societies contain within them a multiplicity of rationalities and values, but guided by their own historical pasts and their visions of the future. Thus one can always identify ingredients of modernity/tradition, including expressions of extreme forms of instrumental rationality and decivilisation. In short, there is no fixed and clearly defined 'modernity', since such properties, ideas and practices are constantly dismembered, consumed, recycled or excreted through the processes of everyday life and experiences. In this way, the properties of modernity are constantly constituted and refashioned in their interaction with diverse other modes of organisation, rationalities and artefacts. Clearly, in the understanding of these processes, we must give attention to situations in which meanings and values are contested, allocated and constantly reappraised. Yet, having identified some ingredients of modernity – in the form of practices, discourses and rituals – we should guard against assuming that those labelled as 'modern' are more relevant for understanding the shaping of the ensembles of people, ideas and things than other value repertoires. Furthermore, we need to explore how the internal rearrangement or re-assembling takes precedent over so-called 'externalities'. Mutated forms represent a range of unstable values and meanings, such that commodities, for instance, embody simultaneously both commoditised and non-commoditised values and relations.

In the discussion that follows, we intend to examine aspects of situated modernity, representations of development, and the globalised commoditisation of coca/cocaine production in the El Chapare area of the Cochabamba region of Bolivia.

The social construction of a region and the social characteristics of a crop

El Chapare is a tropical forest area in the Department of Cochabamba in Bolivia. At the beginning of this century the area was only sparsely populated, and was regarded as culturally insignificant for the national development and culture of Bolivia. In the imagination of Bolivians it is the Andean peaks and mountain valleys that have been seen from time immemorial as the cultural cradle of national identity. However, nowadays one of the most modern and economically active cities of Bolivia is located in the tropical zone. This city, Santa Cruz de la Sierra, since the second half of the twentieth century, has been a constant competitor to Cochabamba (the cultural capital) and La Paz (the administrative capital). More recently, Santa Cruz was characterised as the metropolis of the coca industry.

The tropics are perceived from Cochabamba as an area in which life is hard, unhealthy and made up of a large floating population. A popular image for those who go there to farm and work is that it is possible to make money through engaging in illegal activities. Coca production accounts for 85 per cent of the monetary income generated in the El Chapare area (Hoffman 1994). El Chapare exists within people's popular representations as an 'unknown', harsh physical space. For instance, Rivera (1991) suggests that the area is, from a demographic perspective, 'impossible or beyond planning'. It has as many people as the city of Cochabamba, some statistics indicating that more than 100,000 people constitute its floating population. Rumours circulate that the wealth and fertility of the soils is such that people who live there (*colonos*), although momentarily poor, are sitting on a pot of gold. The isolation of some areas, the absence of infrastructure, and the minimal presence of the state, present the zone as constantly entangled in civil violence that is part of the present illegal reality of the Bolivian tropical regions. It is therefore considered the new 'wild west' – a wilderness, rich in natural resources, difficult to control, develop and modernise. In administrative terms, El Chapare is part of Cochabamba, but its regional and economic importance is because it functions as an active economic corridor linking the cities of Cochabamba and Santa Cruz.

El Chapare is made up of the lower part of the three Amazonian provinces of the Department of Cochabamba (Chapare, Carrasco and Tiraque), usually known as the Cochabamba tropics. Its natural limits in the east are with the Santa Cruz Department (Ichilo River), and in the north with the Beni Department (River Securé). The area has a territory of 24,500 square kilometres.

Landscapes of modernity in Cochabamba

Representing development in El Valle Bajo: the presence of El Chapare

In 1995, I[1] was invited by the Cochabamba University (UMSS) to give a series of lectures on rural development, during which I experienced an interesting encounter with a Bolivian colleague who was conducting local research. The next day he picked me up from my hotel and we went in the direction of the Valle Bajo of Cochabamba. Knowing of my interest in local markets, he said he wanted me to see one of the most important markets for vegetables, after which we would continue on to visit his community.

Indeed, the market of Quillacollo was impressive. A constant combination of modern and apparently traditional icons occupied the physical space: private trucks, public transport, and the market organised according to different products and trades; people moving around wearing Western clothes of their traditional colours, ponchos and different village hats; vegetables and grains transacted in bulk, sometimes for cash and sometimes bartered for other goods. The people in the market were particularly active, exchanging tropical fruits and vegetables. According to my student informant, the main interactions occurred between local producers and middlemen who moved the produce to Cochabamba's markets for sale. We found a *trufi*, a small minibus, carrying passengers and cargo to and fro between local communities, markets and central places. I could not but admire the efficiency of the driver when accommodating passengers and cargo, while negotiating obstacles and delivering passengers along the route. This was an excellent way to get to know people and gain a general idea of the situation in the Valle Bajo. The area was extremely well cultivated. Small agricultural plots were in full production of vegetables and flowers. Small irrigation systems constituted an articulated network of highly commercialised agriculture. There was a clear contrast between the plots having access to irrigation and those supported by rain-fed agriculture. The houses and the layout of the settlement space clearly pointed to processes of urbanisation and close integration with the nearby city of Cochabamba. I relate what my student told me.

> Ten years ago this area was countryside. Today it is part of the outskirts of Cochabamba. We have progressed a lot. People from the city are buying land here to build their houses. I see this as a problem because this is very good agricultural land and it is irreplaceable. But the construction of the new orbital road has made it possible for people to live here and work in Cochabamba. Five or six years ago we used to come here to try the *chicha* (maize beer) and have a good day in the countryside. Nowadays the situation has changed. If you look around the area it is full of fitness centres. People from Cochabamba usually come here to play sports, particularly *fronton*. Private clubs and fitness centres are one of the new types of commercial ventures for the Cochabamba middle

class. During the weekends this road is extremely dangerous. People still come here for chicha, but because they drink too much and then drive back to Cochabamba a lot of accidents take place during the weekends. I think before, when we did not have this highway, it was much more relaxing and safe to visit the Valle Bajo. This area has been transformed in the last few years and can no longer be considered as part of the countryside. These people are not peasants, they are city farmers. They have extensive experience as migrant labourers in Argentina and El Chapare. Their communities are examples of development and transformation. Their agricultural specialisation provides them with excellent economic opportunities. The onions and shalottes you observed in the markets come from here. The only dilemma for people is whether they are going to be able to keep their rights to water and resist the temptation of selling their agricultural land to urban developers.

Several of the producers here obtained access to land as the result of the agrarian reform implemented in the country after 1952. This reform distributed land to communities, and in this area all the landowners were affected, but since communities did not exist, miners were transported by the political parties from 'La Paz' and 'Siglo Veinte and Catare' to create them. Some of these communities were made up of people who did not know how to farm. Two generations ago these people had been miners and builders. Such skills enabled them to migrate to Argentina where they were considered very good construction workers. Some have now finally retired to their own communities and receive their pensions from Argentina. This is a good contribution to the community, because these people are investing in their locality. The new generation has continued with the same pattern of migration, but now they prefer to try their luck in El Chapare.

Eventually and after helping some of the women to take down their cargo from the roof of the minibus, we arrived in the student's research community. I was immediately introduced to some of the people. The first surprise was realising that the majority had an Argentinian accent, even when they were speaking in Quechua among themselves. One of them told me that he had been coming and going from Argentina for twenty years. He said that Argentina was a difficult place. The existence of racism and the fact that they were just seen as cheap labour, meant it was difficult for them to stay there. The Bolivians were organised through networks starting at the community level and expanding into specific regions and cities in Argentina. These networks took time to form and consolidate, and are the backbone of the provision of information about when and what kind of labour is needed and how people can claim their rights as 'guest' workers in Argentina. He said that today it was easier to travel to Argentina. In the past he went only by bus, but now he travels by plane. According to him, today it was more difficult to find jobs. He attributed this to a deteriorating economic situation in Argentina which has dramatically affected the construction sector, although he added that people from the community have continued to work there because their building skills are far superior to those of the local Argentinians.

I toured the community. My student explained how the houses have changed in their physical appearance since people came back with money. In front of me were three huge lorries, one of them being repaired by a young man. I asked my informant if he knew how the family had acquired these lorries. He looked a little worried and said, 'I don't know much about that family. They have been lucky. The father and the son have spent years working in El Chapare and now they are in the transport business. They have organised a family enterprise. They are well off'.

The beauty of the valley is outstanding. The Andes with their impressive conservation of nature overwhelm any feeling one might have for transformation. But these people have overcome such sentiments in their construction of viable livelihood strategies and initiatives. They have created a landscape of scattered modernities. Cacti along the road are covered in delicate white dust, standing, semi-desiccated, as green statues, like lonely Scottish pipers evoking a lament to the silent monument of tradition. I asked about the cacti. The answer was short, unproblematic and uneventful: 'They are the result of the Cochinilla project. The bacteria escaped from the research station and now every single cactus in Cochabamba is infected. They have as yet found no solution to the problem'. The cacti of El Valle Alto have thus also become part and parcel of modernity.

We ended up again in the central market. Activities were quietening. My student asked me if I wanted to see the Cross. This is the Catholic symbol of every town in Bolivia. It was located at the end of the main street on the top of a hill. I negotiated myself out of this situation and we ended up visiting the village church, a colonial building in front of a square resplendent with old trees and a sense of tranquillity and freshness in the middle of the day, an old provincial oasis. We entered the church and I was taken to see the Virgin of Urkupina, adorned in a host of white flowers, a beautiful material representation of religion. I was reflecting on the beauty of this scene when my student said to me:

> Well you know, I am a member of the Bolivian army. I have been a soldier for years, working in the area of communications, and then I decided that the only way forward in my military career was through the study of development. I have participated in various military insurrections but now I am proud of being part of the democratic process, although the situation is presently not so exciting as before. Between you and me, I think the government should say no to the intervention of the gringos. After all coca is the only product that makes money.

This brief account attempts to depict how reality is perceived as a constant amalgam of so-called modernities and traditional forms. The guide for the tour of the valley expressed a mixture of intentions, opinions and projects that could not but be defined as somehow modern. He was a 'mutant', a provider of deletion, translocation and transduction of properties conceptualised as 'modern' and 'local custom', who was generating connections with his companion that went well beyond any kind of simple typology. He was indicating that processes of change had been initiated by the people themselves and that it was difficult to understand how external influences could not but be mediated by the experiences and practices of these people. It was for this reason that the Cochinilla project was unable to prevent the escape of bacteria; that migrant flows to Argentina and El Chapare constituted some of the veins of modernisation, whose blood was thickened by local customs to stem the pace of external development, resulting in unstable, constant mutation. Throughout, the guide wanted to identify progress. In doing so he was making a series of statements that, in the end, led him to underline the importance of coca/cocaine production for the region.

Corpses and buildings: another image of modernity

Images of modernity, like those above, are much more nakedly represented in Bolivia in the 'arch-figure of the devil' (Nash 1979), which compares with the accounts of Taussig (1980, 1995) concerning practices of transgression and pacts with the devil and more generally with the evidence of the close associations of death and modernity (see Scheper-Hughes 1992 on *Death Without Weeping*). Each of these situations illustrates the processes of deletion, translocation and transfiguration in the ritualisation of modernities.[1]

During my visit to Bolivia I was told that the success of the construction industry demands corpses. This is related to the beliefs of the labour force, namely that before *Pachamama* (mother earth, i.e. land), can be used in constructing multi-storey buildings and shopping centres, she needs a human sacrifice. The demand for corpses has generated a semi-legal institution able to respond to this demand. In the shantytowns there are special houses where people suffering the extremes of alcoholism or emotional disorders can go to end their days. The only activity performed in these usually dark and suffocating places is to drink until one drops dead. This results from the 'heavy and free alcohol' supply in such locales. The corpses are then taken and recycled as offerings at the building sites. No intimacy is allowed in this 'gateway of hell'. The 'arch-figure' of the devil is probably the only explanation to illuminate the metamorphosis of emotionally and physically tortured bodies into significant icons for the modern construction industry in Bolivia. The wounds of modernity, as well as the attraction of describing these 'real' transgressions of 'modern morality', take us to the limits of human experience and toll the end of any Protestant ethic based on the diffusion of civilising processes around the world, or in waiting for the unfolding promises of a 'safe road' to modernity. It is clear, therefore, that in each street, in the documents from the colonial past, in the urban and rural landscapes, there rests a success story of Bolivian modernisation, as well as the presence of sacrifice emanating from the seduction that popular religion offers and from the sacred evocation of a Spanish God. The issue of how different social groups and actors have fended off continual crises of legitimacy from the increasingly 'aware' international community concerning the problems of drug-trafficking, fiscal disaster, external debt, the 'failures' of grass-roots development and the impotency of measures of social control, leads one to suggest that Bolivia is now in her finest hour of modernity. This situation, without any doubt, has generated an intensification of politically and economically contested processes, one of which concerns the production and commercialisation of illegal crops.

That thing called coca

According to Canelas & Canelas (1983), the production of coca for cocaine became an issue during the 1950s, but it was not a contested issue until the government of Banzer (1979) used it to generate the 'coca dollars' that the state administration used to finance the national debt. According to the *Carta de Información Politica y Economica*, the production of cocaine produces more foreign earnings than the whole of the rest of the Bolivian economy. This economically profitable activity led to the formation of the first association between state politicians and those involved in narco-trafficking on Monday 30 November 1981. These innovative, although problematic, tendencies of the Bolivian state, aimed at avoiding its total collapse, came to the fore between 1980–85 when the coca boom began dramatically to transform the present and the future of the El Chapare region. This area became a monocrop producer of coca leaves. This crop specialisation transformed the character of the family unit and demanded an ever-increasing number of temporary wage labourers.

From the mid-1970s, a huge wave of people migrated from different parts of the country into the region. Increased impoverishment and land degradation in the highland areas combined with the international demand for cocaine accounts for the decision of farmers to move into the crop, which they could cultivate and easily sell. The crop became the icon that linked local producers, entrepreneurs and an ever-increasing market of consumers in the United States and Europe.

In-migration brought increased cultivation of the coca leaf. During this period, the customary cultivation of coca rapidly changed its cultural value and it become a highly contested issue. Since the cultivation of coca was linked to the global narco-traffic network, the region became more dependent on responding to the forces of supply and demand emanating from the international market. It is no exaggeration to suggest that in Bolivia market-led development has been extremely effective in generating the production of illegal crops.

The pre-conditions for the development of coca production are linked to the following contingencies:

1   a severe drought in 1983 that added to the general economic deterioration of the Bolivian urban economy;
2   a large national debt which consumed up to 30 per cent of its total export earnings and an inflation rate reaching the astronomical figure of 11,750 per cent in 1985; and
3   the total collapse and disintegration of tin mining, one of the main industrial activities of the country. The tin industry declined 30 per cent between 1980 and 1984, due to the decline in international tin prices that dropped 27 per cent during that period.

These three contingencies led to the final breakdown of the formal economy and, in turn, created favourable conditions for the development of an informal economy engaged in the production of illegal crops. The cultivation of coca for cocaine attracted and engaged a great number of people struggling to secure a meagre, if vulnerable, livelihood.

The illicit activities of coca cultivation and cocaine production were an extension of the activities of the informal sector. Some idea of the increase of coca cultivation in El Chapare is provided by a 1973 survey that recorded 7,160 hectares of coca; five years later there were 18,860, and in 1983 this had reached 44,661 hectares. By 1988, coca was calculated to cover 61,000 hectares, producing annually 147,608 tons of dried coca leaf. El Chapare became the new sourcing region and it is estimated that 80 per cent of the total Bolivian coca leaf originates from this area. Government sources argue that 90 per cent of the coca cultivated in El Chapare ends up as raw material for cocaine production (Lohman 1992). By 1985, the Chapare region had become the target for the drug eradication policy. The control of El Chapare followed two strategies: the first aimed to replace coca through the implementation of the so-called 'alternative development' programme; the other consisted of repressive military measures to eradicate coca production. Increased military intervention was supported by the continuation of the 'War on Drugs' policy which was re-launched at the beginning of the 1980s by the then American President, Ronald Reagan. In the Departments of El Beni and Santa Cruz, which, together with Cochabamba, share the production and processing of coca for cocaine, some 1,500 illegal airstrips were estimated to exist, and between 1985 and 1989 the army and police destroyed 4,200 cocaine processing factories (Vasquez 1989: 70).

The demand side of coca/cocaine production

Drug taking is an important practice in contemporary society. In England alone, more than half a million ecstasy pills are consumed during weekends by young people as a new form of recreation. According to the American Department of State, between 10–22 thousand million dollars (i.e. 0.5 per cent of GNP) are spent on the importation of drugs. It is estimated that 50 per cent of these resources remain within US financial circuits. The US is the main market for cocaine, consuming 40 per cent of the production from Peru, Bolivia and Colombia. In present-day America, every major transport accident enquiry starts by removing mechanical parts for inspection and drug testing the people involved. According to Hanson (1993):

> Drug abuse, it seems, currently plays a role in American thinking similar to witchcraft a few centuries ago: it is insidious, pervasive, but not easily recognisable, an evil that infuses social life and is responsible for many of the ills that beset us. At the end of the 1980s, before many Americans had even heard of Saddam Hussein, the big war in America was the War on Drugs. Drugs were a major issue in the presidential election of 1988. A *New York Times*/CBS News poll in late 1989 found that some 65 per cent of Americans considered drugs to be the number one problem facing the nation. Excepting only a time in early 1991, when just over 25 per cent pointed to the economy, this is more than triple the number who, in polls taken between 1985 and late 1991, identified any other single issue as 'America's greatest problem'.
>
> (Hanson 1993: 123)

It seems that drug testing in workplaces since 1985 has become a common phenomenon in America. Twenty-one per cent of 1,090 companies responding to an American Management Association survey in November 1986, reported testing applicants and/or current employees for drugs. Ninety per cent of them had instituted their programmes in 1985 or 1986. Hence drug testing programmes are a commonplace in contemporary America.

It is calculated that some 20 million Americans consume marihuana, another 20 million use cocaine and 5 million use opium. In 1989, the commercialisation of illegal drugs amounted to 150 million US dollars a year. This activity contributed 5.3 per cent of the GNP of the US and generated 20 million jobs. It is calculated that the banking system alone receives 300 million US dollars per year, with approximately 60 per cent of all capital gains being generated by this illegal activity. According to Suarez Salazar, this activity contributed significantly during the 1980s to the re-structuring of the US economy.

Coca farmers in Bolivia protest against the way the 'external world', especially the US, is intervening in their region. Militarisation of every human settlement, violation of human rights and the implementation of 'alternative development' constitute a trilogy of policies favouring the condemnation of

El Chapare coca production. Obviously coca farmers disagree with the criminalisation of their crop practices, since for them coca production is part of their cultural heritage, and presently constitutes the only profitable crop on which producers can build their regional livelihoods and political identities. The unwillingness of local producers to give up their coca bushes is based upon the fact that coca leaves remain the main income-generating crop. There are guaranteed legal and illegal markets and the yields are reliable in comparison with other crops, such as citrus, pineapples and other tropical fruit. In a meeting with producers one of them commented,

> I do not know how the government can expect us to stop producing coca when we are living far from the main roads, deep in the forest, and we need to carry oranges for hours, after which we have to seek public transport to reach the markets. With coca we do not have these problems. It has a good price and we can easily sell it in our local market. We want a policy of crop substitution and not eradication, that means that only when we have roads and good markets for our produce can we stop cultivating coca. So far coca is the only crop that produces a decent income. Until now we have observed the failures of the alternative development plan and the government has not kept its promises of providing alternatives for us.

Farmers interpret the policy of coca eradication as a direct attack on their decision-making power:

> If the coca growers accept the policy of coca eradication, we will surrender our only card for negotiating with the government. We are only important for the government because we are coca growers. They know that if we do not collaborate we can put the state under threat of withdrawal of economic help from the gringos.

El Chapare is not a stranger to fatal incidents between coca growers and the Bolivian anti-drug force (*Umopar*). The military patrol the roads in their lorries, ready to raid the hundreds of clandestine cocaine factories and airstrips that exist in the area. It is no secret that some *sindicatos* (producer associations) have struck bargains with the drug traffickers. A producer explained:

> Sometimes we build and take care of the airstrips. For using them we claim taxes for our community from every plane that takes off or lands there. We know that *Umopar* cannot cover the whole area. While the army can own three or four helicopters, the narcos could own up to 20 private planes. We have to exist and we accept reality as it is. We have learned to load and unload a plane of cargo in no more than ten minutes.

In recent years, after a long interruption due to military intervention between the years 1980–2, the USAID project for El Chapare was reactivated, through the implementation of the Alternative Development Plan (1987), but concurrently, the region has been declared a red area, a military zone, and Bolivian troops have been engaged in the implementation of the forced eradication of coca plants, and have attempted to regain control of the area on behalf of the central government.

The Alternative Development Plan in El Chapare (1987) was shaped by the strategy of USAID. The policy aimed to stop migration to the tropical region through pumping financial resources into the communities from which these people were migrating. Zones such as Arani, Mizque and Aiquile of the highlands of the central valley of Cochabamba received generous financial aid.

In El Chapare itself, I made a brief visit to some of the communities which had been targeted to receive some of these alternative projects. I wanted to see whether producers had tried to find alternatives to coca production. Producers were extremely disappointed with the results of these projects and, as a result, had lost trust in them.

> They [the project experts] arrived here and offered us a pig rearing project. They built this piggery. You can see it is very sophisticated, each animal had its own water tap, and concrete everywhere to avoid disease. According to the experts, it was based on a Japanese design. The only problem was that the experts introduced a very difficult animal to manage, you know, the 'white pig'. These animals are not adapted to the tropics. They are more demanding than a baby (*huahua*), you need to feed them with a lot of milk and special food pellets which were not available locally. The pigs began to develop diseases and parasites. Furthermore, the vampire bat used to feast on the animals. These pigs have no hair protection. Keeping and managing them was not a good idea. In the end the project failed. Some of us sold the animals, others died and what remains here is merely the building. This empty piggery is the final memory we have of alternative development projects. As you can see, it is now used by our free-range chickens. The experts of alternative development never asked us what we wanted here. They simply imposed on us the livestock project and then dictated a type of animal we did not know how to manage. In the end these projects are not to our benefit but only provide jobs for foreign experts who have their own interests. The political issue is that because these projects failed we are blamed and billed for them and the government claims that the failure is proof that we don't want to give up the cultivation of coca leaves. The truth is that what we want here is 'real development' and not just experiments that finally burn up a lot of money and achieve nothing for us.[2] Until we have 'real development' we will continue producing coca leaves.

Lanza (1995) argues that of the 48 million US dollars used on the programme for alternative development, 21 million dollars were spent on direct salaries to USAID and its consultants, 7 million on the operations within the national and regional bureaucracies, and of the remaining 20 million, approximately 50 per cent was invested in the Cochabamba valleys to halt migration. Only 25 per cent was invested in projects in El Chapare itself.

In terms of agricultural research, investment in Chapare has been concentrated in the Institute of Agriculture and Livestock Technology (IBTA). This institution has received around 14 million dollars for adapting some economically viable 'export crops' to the difficult tropical conditions. Products such as macadamia nuts and spices are the laughing stock of local producers. The more successful programme – perhaps not for accidental reasons – was the construction of roads. These attracted 15 million dollars and were implemented by the Bolivian National Road Service (SNC). Such projects receive strong support from the local population. The other main agency supporting alternative development is the United Nations through UNCP. These projects have been concentrated in agro-industry, an example being the milk-processing factory in the zone of Ivirgarzama. This factory has a daily capacity to process 50,000 litres of milk, but the problem is that milk production in the area does not reach 5,000 litres per day. Obviously, these projects have also had very limited impact in El Chapare. It is a similar story with factories set up to process bananas for vinegar and sun-dried varieties.

The failures and loss of trust in any sort of alternative development have generated political problems in El Chapare between the local producer associations (*sindicatos*) and the Bolivian State. This critical situation has placed the NGOs in the middle of this battlefield, with local producers believing that European NGOs are nothing more than collaborators with the state. One of the more important leaders of the cocalero movement, Evo Morales, said:

> Some NGOs are trying to bury us alive and others do not give us any help. Some of them do not want to be associated with us and deny any help even when we need funds to publish our leaflets.

There is in fact a real fear among the Chapare local population that NGOs may end up supporting a policy of forced re-settlement to locations outside of El Chapare. This has been called the 'zero option' and, according to some, is the only solution to the coca/cocaine issue. The local sindicatos believe that they are under attack from the NGOs. They accuse some of these organisations of being paternalistic and of not recognising the importance of local organisations. They mentioned the case of the Swedish Development Agency in Bolivia, which, according to local producers, is too close to official government policies and lacks the resources or interest to implement an integrated rural development programme in El Chapare. In the end, producers argue that they are tired of being experimented upon like guinea pigs. They are frustrated because the experts cannot increase the productivity of alternative crops and because there are no markets for these commodities. In this vein, Chapare producers want to hold on to processes of change that they know they can manage and control.

Before I left the settlement I was visiting, I was taken by one of the local leaders to see what the local syndicate had achieved. Extremely proud, this young man pointed to an abandoned building and said:

> That over there is the state school. As you can see we don't use it. The syndicate has built its own private school: it is that over there. We contract the teacher and we control how our sons and daughters are educated. The state school has never operated here and it will never do so. The government wanted to force us to use the official graveyard, but we do not use that since we have created our own cemetery in a plot that the syndicate was able to obtain. In this colonia (settlement) – from that bridge to that tree – we have total dominion. Here I am a king. This is the syndicate's area of control. Here there is no government, no state. We control everything. This is possible because we have established the coca market. This market is very active among local producers and from this we can collect taxes that eventually we use for the improvement of the colonia. We have learned by experience that we cannot trust anyone to come here to teach us how to achieve development. This is something we have to do for ourselves.

The body, agency and the embodiment of social action

El Chapare is not just any region. Not only does it exude tropical and exuberant varieties of green vegetables, but the humidity and red tropical soils are not easy to domesticate for agricultural production. The landscape is criss-crossed by huge rivers. The army and police are constantly checking people and vehicles at road blocks. This is a normal feature of policing the area in order to stop people smuggling in chemicals for the preparation of coca paste. Smuggling chemicals is one of the most profitable activities in El Chapare. Alongside the main road near the military depot, it is sometimes possible to observe their confiscation. Clearly, some chemicals are discovered fortuitously, but the network that starts in Colombia, passes through La Paz, Cochabamba or Santa Cruz de la Sierra and ends up in El Chapare where it disappears into the jungle, is never completely disrupted. Buses and lorries are systematically stopped and passengers have to wait for the police, military and often the US advisers and their dogs to examine the cargo. They are constantly looking for unusual amounts of coca leaves, chemicals or coca paste. The police and experts attempt to inspect every bag or sack, but these are large loads of merchandise and foodstuffs of all sorts, displaying a variety of international brands, originating from Chile, Argentina, or Peru. The majority are contraband. Chemicals for the production of coca paste are simply one type of contraband commodity among many that fuel small-scale trade and fan the life of hundreds of markets in Bolivia. It has been calculated that, due to the coca/cocaine economy, there are in the tropics of La Paz and Cochabamba around 50,000 small traders who find a ready market for their commodities among the population that live there (Alem 1989: 80).

At road blocks, one sees members of the police and army at work. Farmers are stopped and searched to see if they are transporting the illegal cocaine paste. But how long can they spend identifying the enormous diversity of commodities and contents of the many large sacks of merchandise? How can they penetrate the external display of factory packaging? Chemicals and coca paste are disguised as many other commodities so that such controls fail. Buses have no regular timetables, nobody has a proper ticket, and the names of passengers are not registered or listed. Passengers usually know each other, but travel anonymously. The buses are modern and comfortable but run in an undisciplined, impersonalised manner. Is this lack of organisation or the best form of organisation? Bus enterprises are one of the more profitable forms of economic activity. They constitute the backbone for the transportation of commodities and people.

Such a style of transport operation – with no exactly routed timetabling and no registration of passengers – provides a secure medium for the movement of contraband commodities and for the illegal activities implicated in coca production and commercialisation. The interconnections of buses, the lack of itineraries, the difficulties of checking passenger lists, people's local knowledge and experience of different markets, and the way in which the military and police authorities attempt to control the flow of goods without moving from their sentry boxes, combine to construct a series of situational contingencies that are constantly being disconnected and reshaped. The networks that provide the threads through which these movements and encounters take place can be interrupted at any moment, yet they can never be dismantled completely. It is calculated that more than 4,000 jobs in the transport sector are linked to coca/cocaine activities (Alem 1989: 81).

The movement of chemicals and coca paste does not take place only in motorised vehicles. At different points in the journey, mules, donkeys, and humans (especially their backs) will be used to transport these commodities. The lack of roads in the region means that this is the only way to penetrate deep into the jungle. Animals and humans are more mobile and cunning in the face of police and military control. It takes longer to transport delicate commodities such as chemicals, but it is often the only way. In this situation, knowledge concerning the care of unstable chemicals in changeable weather conditions or unanticipated delays in deliveries is critical.

The network of interconnections does not end with the way in which people practice trade and transport in Bolivia, since it depends crucially on how they utilise various modern artefacts and technology to promote their activities. For instance, at moments of great scarcity, some cocaine manufacturers will cannibalise their and others' car batteries for sulphuric acid. Hence, any motorised vehicle, cargo, or person is not only under threat from the police or army controls but also from competing manufacturers and their group. This makes it difficult to regulate the traffic of people and commodities. Bribes are offered but corruption is not the only factor. Coca is the single most important crop to produce a specific ensemble of organising processes in El Chapare.

Coca cultivators are at the bottom of the cocaine global trade network. They practise a varied cropping strategy, of which the production of coca leaves constitutes approximately 60 per cent of their portfolio of crops. The others are bananas amounting to 15.7 per cent, rice 9.5 per cent, yucca 5 per cent and oranges 3.5 per cent. According to some studies, resident families in the tropics of Bolivia obtain around 515 US dollars per month and require as a minimum 330 US dollars to meet their basic needs. Of this, the cultivation of the coca provides about 55 per cent of the minimal income required to survive in the tropics.

It has been calculated that the investment made by coca producers in Bolivia amounts to some 58 million dollars (equivalent to $US 1.056 per hectare). If we include what producers have invested in opening up and bringing into production new land, then the investment increases to 80 million dollars. This capital has been invested by 48,000 Bolivian small-scale rural producers.

Coca leaves are grown on a small scale and are successful because the production is linked to the global cocaine economy. It is estimated that the Bolivian agricultural frontier has increased by 20,000 hectares in the last 10–15 years, of which it is assumed 70 per cent are related to coca leaf production. Opening up this new agricultural land in the tropics has generated 5,000 new jobs within the Departments of La Paz and Cochabamba.

Coca bushes are well adapted to tropical conditions. They are pest-resistant and can grow on slopes as well as on less fertile soils of the tropical rainforest. Hardly any external inputs are needed. A producer can obtain two or three crops a year for a period of 15–20 years. In El Chapare, the producers have in their *chacos* at least one hectare of coca, as a way of ensuring their economic survival. The harvest of coca is labour-intensive and the leaves have to be picked carefully without damaging them. During the coca harvest many temporary migrants come to work in El Chapare. Coca enters the market as dry leaves. At this time, travelling through El Chapare one observes in front of every house a long green carpet of leaves. This is the customary way of drying them. The drying process helps with transportation, storage and with the concentration of the alkaloid content that eventually will react to chemicals such as sulphuric acid. The drying process is important and requires individual care and local knowledge.

To transform coca leaves into cocaine is a lengthy process that starts with making the alkaloid contents of the leaf react with sulphuric acid and water in a pit. The PH (acidity) for the maceration of the coca leaves is an individual formula, perfected through the experience of individuals working in this field.

It is the secret of the mixer. These 'local experts' constantly use their own body as a referential and biographical source for calculating and controlling the processes of acidity. At first, experts use their hand to inspect the consistency of the mixture, and later they progress to sample the aroma and tang of the blend. It is through expert tongues and tastes that finally the PH for leaf soaking is perfected. After a process of exudation of 18–20 hours when the sulphuric acid and leaves interact, a brown coloured concoction emerges. Into this blend of cocaine, resins, tar and acid, the temporary labourers jump and tread the floating bundles of leaves for about two hours. At this stage the result is a highly concentrated brew that needs to be decanted into another pit. In this second process, the alkaloid is stabilised through the neutralisation of the acid fluid. This is done by incorporating into the concoction sodium carbonate, lime, or cement. After half an hour or so, this becomes a sort of liquid cocaine. It is then combined with kerosene to further the purging and transmutation of the liquid, which after 20–30 minutes becomes a mellifluent liquid to be combined again with a 'formula' of sulphuric acid and water. Finally, sodium carbonate is added and coca paste begins to appear at the bottom of the container. This substance is carefully wrapped in a cloth and squeezed to expel the water. Then it is left to dry in the sun. It is assumed that 80 per cent of the alkaloid present in coca leaves is recovered with this technique for the elaboration of cocaine. The same technique is repeated two or three times and the amount of alkaloid reduced on the second time to 20 per cent and in the third round it consists more of chemicals than anything else. The second and third rounds provide extremely low-quality coca paste.

To produce bad quality cocaine is not an unusual event. There are a lot of elements, knowledge and practices that need to be assembled by a skilful and able 'local-mixer' in order to produce a good quality commodity. In this process a combination of customary and modern knowledge and the use of chemical technology are embodied, sometimes literally, through the agency and practices of the local mixer. Bad quality cocaine is produced by miscalculations of the proportion of sulphuric acid. At any step in the process something can go wrong. This can be the result of circumstances inherent in the leaves or due to the inability of the local mixer to deal with these variations. Factors that can affect the process are: the specific genotype of coca leaves; the region from which the leaves came; the time when they were picked; the humidity content of the leaves; and last, but not least, the chemical 'body' constituting the sulphuric acid in actual use, namely whether it is considered lighter or heavier in quality, which is related to the dilution levels of acid to water.

The local mixer, usually called '*el quimico*' (the chemist) is constantly mastering the chemical processes and increasing his detailed knowledge of types of coca leaf in relation to localities of production. For the chemist it is important to know the origin of the leaves, the climatic conditions of the region and the dates when they were picked. The agency of the local mixer is constantly changing as he incorporates new knowledge and experience and applies it to his craft. He is the alchemist of the tropics, producing a commodity that incorporates monetary, pleasurable and desirable values. The practices he develops arise out of the ongoing history and dynamics of the coca/cocaine industry and from existing political contingencies, but most specifically they are the outcome of his own abilities and experience in connecting and combining his knowledge of substances and techniques with local/global consumption needs. In so doing he produces a material commodity, which is engraved with specific qualities and meanings that facilitate its circulation from the tropics of Cochabamba to various consumption places in Europe and the USA. In this way the provision of the commodity contributes to the establishment of an important global niche economy.

This is a remarkable achievement by any standard. These social actors control spaces in the almost impenetrable jungle of South America, where they practise their transmutational skills. From this base they participate globally in the economic and social re-shaping of contemporary industrial societies. In addition, their association with this remote and unfamiliar kind of 'nature' also contributes to the creation of Western representations of this 'cocaine world'. These representations resemble the European aversion and fear of witchcraft in earlier centuries when the latter was seen as an uncontrollable force disseminating chaos and social disorder. But, unlike that medieval witch who dabbled in magical concoctions and occult powers, the cocaine chemist is a specialist in modern forms of instrumental rationality which is adapted to operate in the far-flung corners of the globe. This is his 'modernity'.

The social practices involved in cocaine production and trading therefore emerge out of a set of contingencies that materialise rapidly in relation to existing experiences and capacities, many of which derive from previous work histories in the mines and the small-scale enterprise sector, as well as from what are seen as the ecological and political possibilities of the Chapare region. Hence, the process entails a re-positioning of individual and group skills, knowledge and resources in the embodiment of new production activities. These reorganised experiences and experiments have given birth to a complex ensemble in which the figure and the distinctive skills of the chemist epitomised the new age of the coca/cocaine economy. The local mixer is comparable to other mythical or real actors in European cultural history, when during the industrial revolution they sought to control and profit from the combination of air, fire and water in the pursuit of progress. These actors have mastered, from within the tropics, the properties of sulphuric acid for the benefit of themselves and a substantial global group of producers and consumers.

This new ensemble of knowledge, technologies and social relations may have emerged from the dynamics of previous experience, but what is new is the accelerated pace by which internal re-arrangements take place and reposition themselves, thus acquiring new properties, meanings, practices and thus agency. It is now the chemist who constitutes the nexus around which a whole series of new connections, values and counter-values cohere and materialise. These newly emergent social forms entail distinctive life styles and social and cultural arrangements. In characterising this rapid transformational process the idea of social mutation is apposite, since mutations are self-organising, internally generated changes that involve the reassembling of properties and the repositioning of actors in such a way that new forms emerge. The forms (or mutants) that emerge are never fully predictable nor are they dependent on a constant infusion of new stock or elements from some external source. One advantage in using this concept is that it avoids the current metaphor of hybridisation which, as suggested in Chapter 1, characterises the process by which new cultures or social forms are created in terms of a process of stitching together the patches and pieces of existing cultures to create hybrid varieties.

This process of social change has entailed the development of other sets of relations constituting a series of interconnected life worlds. The people who work alongside these chemists, and who literally have to throw their bodies into the acid and leaves to release the alkaloids, are *los pisacocas*, coca-treaders. They are temporary labourers who work for wages and coca paste. They earn good money, but their bodies reflect how effectively the chemicals attack their human flesh. Boots made of rubber and leather are not strong enough to protect the feet of the '*pisacocas*', which progressively rot as the acid perforates their bones. For customary reasons there are '*pisacocas*' who tread without any sort of protection and who, according to some reports (Equipo Pastoral del Chapare), after one week of working in El Chapare are unable to walk. By the end of the season the soles of their feet are totally destroyed and with the high levels of sulphuric acid that their bodies absorb they also end up with damaged kidneys leading to the passing of blood in their urine and faeces. The production of cocaine is certainly not without tears.

One of the first striking observations in the region is the intense activity that takes place along the road from Cochabamba to El Chapare. The movement of people and constant trade provides an image of a tropical space that is being conquered by the 'modern' economics of social life. One of the more dynamic activities in El Chapare is the growth of restaurants and bars. Food and drink is a translocation of commercial activities for women in this area, who come from the highlands and valleys of Bolivia. Local people actively link friendship with consuming beer, good food and ostentatiously flashing around their money. In this vein, the bars and restaurants are significant social centres for the tropics. Their red lights, plastic tables and the constant coming and going of cars and buses make one associate everyday life here with a constant bustle that bears some resemblance to Chaplin's film *Modern Times*. Modernity has opened the door to the Cochabamba tropics and generated a fear of American and European legislators, who propagate the view that the people who live and work in the Bolivian tropics are dangerous 'global' enemies, whom they hope to release from their 'criminal' condition through the introduction of alternative development.

In reality, people in the tropics see themselves as neither criminals nor victims in need of the help of moral legislators and development experts. They have simply taken stock of their situation and are following the most viable livelihood options. In so doing, coca/cocaine producers have generated 5,000 new jobs in the area; 60,000 cultivators and harvesters of coca leaves today depend on this form of agriculture; some 50,000 small-scale traders depend on this activity to generate a market; a further 4,000 are related to the transport sector and 6,300 temporary labourers are directly involved in the production of coca paste. In summary, the reality is that the coca/cocaine economy has provided viable and diversified livelihoods for 125,000 families, representing 4.2 per cent of the economically active population in Bolivia.

Criminality is ever present in the social centres. Coca paste is transported via restaurants and bars on its way to the international processing and consumption markets. Each social centre is potentially a strategic location for moving the valuable coca/paste further on its journey. A number of small traders are involved in local trafficking. All have one single property in common, that is, their hunger for cash. They are the actors described in Taussig's stories (1995). They have mastered the art of transgression and discovered the significance of an economy of consumption. Disposable income and the dynamics of spending in the affluent areas of the globe have set in motion extreme paradoxes of social discontinuity in areas like the Cochabamba tropics. In these remote areas, we observe the extremes of social life. Here, we see the interplay of autonomy and freedom, but this discards in practice the associated puritanical values of modernity, to reveal the unfolding of instrumental rationality in its most blatant and vital form. This causes us to doubt whether it is possible to conceive of a future role for, let alone control, planned development and modernisation by the state or other outside bodies for the region.

Is this a case of cosmetic development, the development of excesses, or distorted and perverted development? Perhaps 'modernity' entails all of this! Yet the fact is that the income and consumption levels of the local population, in relative terms, have risen enormously. Commodities in abundance have arrived here attracted by the inflow of dollars and the economic boom. Local markets, like mushrooms, burgeon everywhere. Durable consumption goods are bought and luxury items procured. Food, for which El Chapare is not self-sufficient, is imported from other regions. There is an active, although semi-legal, market for land. There is still a need for people to improve basic health services and the supply of drinking water and electricity. But in all these ways the dramatic commoditisation of the tropical areas of Bolivia has transformed local producers into agricultural exporters, in rhythm with the desire and dreams of cocaine and 'modern' ways of life.

Impressions from El Chapare

Late in the day. The eradication campaign has been in full swing for more than four weeks. The army was mobilised in full and the Bolivian TV reported every hour the number of hectares eradicated in El Chapare. The American Ambassador was clearly saying that if the target for eradication was not achieved by the end of that week, the US would not authorise the transfer of promised financial loans to the government. I could see people cutting down coca bushes, and military trucks in constant movement. With Bolivian colleagues, I went to one of the local bars for a beer. We sat and talked about the consequences of the eradication policy. A producer joined us, listened and then said,

> Yes, sometimes I cannot understand these Americans. They force this eradication of coca bushes. But then, according to me, what is going to happen is something very simple. The price of coca leaves will increase because there will be more demand and less supply. Then people will go into the jungle and they will start new chacos. I don't understand these politicians.

A person who was acting as 'agronomist' for one of the eradication teams said:

> We've been working hard to achieve our targets. We are being paid for achieving them. We leave the centre here at five o'clock in the morning and don't come back until six or seven at night. We are really pushing forward with the eradication programme, but I will tell you how we do it. The government said that the programme is a voluntary one; well, that policy worked until two weeks ago, when some producers who were in need of cash came to ask us for eradication. You know when we eradicate coca bushes the producers are paid compensation. The producers were happy when we gave them US dollars. In the last two weeks we have been paying with Bolivianos and the people are not that happy. We have practically finished with the really small coca producers, so now to achieve our targets we have to go after the medium producers, and here the policy of voluntary eradication no longer applies. What I do to achieve my target is to arrive at a community, look for a 'good area' and then go to the sindicato to say that the area has been targeted for eradication. Sometimes they get angry and don't want me to do my job. So then what I do is call the army. They arrive with their trucks and machine guns and start cutting down the bushes. The producers complain but, in the end, they are forced to accept the compensation money. After that we move to a different sector. I know this is not the proper way, and I know the producers are going to go tomorrow into the jungle and open up a

new 'chaco', but I am not being paid to solve the problem, just to achieve my target. I have to do it, it's my job.

The discussion progressed to the techniques that the eradication team use in the area and more interesting information emerged. We continued to drink and I could see three women scouring the place. They looked nervous. One of my Bolivian colleagues called me to his side and said 'be careful, those women are "mules".' 'Mules?'

> Yes, they are carriers of the 'basic paste'. They're always looking for transport. They've seen our jeep and will probably approach us. They usually pay with sex. When police discover the drug in orifices of their bodies or hidden among their clothes, they always negotiate their freedom by offering sex to the police. They generally conceal their cargo in their bodies, using false breasts or presenting themselves as pregnant. Some of them have managed to establish good and lasting relationships with the local authority representatives. They are experts in how to use their bodies. Some even implant cocaine paste inside their bodies. There are cases where people have died when the plastic bags inside them break open and the overdose kills them. They can carry from 100 to 200 grammes in their bodies. They deliver the illegal paste to refining laboratories and consumer markets. It's not unusual for some of these women to carry as much as five kilos of paste. A carrier will make a few trips a month and their aspiration is to be employed as an international carrier, for which they are paid three to four thousand dollars per trip.

In the Chapare region moving the basic paste is very much in tune with how the body is used. This can generate a variety of strategies that transgress any notion one might have about how commodities should travel and be transported. A producer explained that 'the best way to move paste is inside the corpse of a small child. This is a very safe and reliable way for a mule to smuggle coca paste.' This method of carrying cocaine is mentioned also by Taussig's report on Colombia (1995). According to him, the bodies of dead babies were cut open and filled with paste. According to my informant, this was the most effective way in Bolivia for women to move the basic paste without being detected by the police.

Memories

A normal day in June 1987. The government had not respected certain agreements and the coca producers were extremely angry. They wanted the implementation of the Alternative Development Programme and to discuss the effects of Law 1008 relating to the criminalisation of coca/cocaine production. After one year, on 6 June 1988, in Cochabamba 30,000 coca producers blocked the roads in protest against the implementation of the law concerning dangerous substances. The heat increased until on 27 June, in Villa Tunares, some 185 kms from Cochabamba, 5,000 local coca producers came together to assert their rights as Bolivian citizens. After speeches emphasising that the eradication programme had used dangerous pesticides that would affect not only plants, trees and animals, but the genetic constitution and health of children (rumour had it that the famous orange herbicide used in Vietnam by the Americans had been used in El Chapare), a group of producers headed to the offices of the agency in charge of the eradication programme (DIRECO) to enquire about this. The guards became agitated and nervous and fired into the crowd. The bullets continued for 15 to 20 minutes. After half an hour, helicopters arrived from Parotani and Chimore with American troops from the DEA agency and from UMOPAR who continued firing at the producers. As a result, this incident left eight dead coca producers, ten wounded by bullets and seven who were never seen again.

Conclusions

This chapter proposes an analysis of modernity from the perspective of coming to terms with the scale and excesses of human endeavour in a remote region of Bolivia. It is not a fanciful option, since issues of modernity should be situated in all their beauty and ugliness at the limits of the meaningful, the possible and the obscene of human experience. We argue for a positive analysis of all expressions of situated modernities that contribute to a vision of life in tune with a systematic delineation of practices and their command of competence and efficiency. Hence, the emphasis on the technical and organisational character of a network of actors who are striving to build their own modernities.

This, we believe, provides us with a variety of constructed modernities, which are neither permeated with traditional or post-modern features but which exist within the present scenario of local/global spaces. They constitute ongoing processes, 'discovered', presented and constructed by 'specialised' actors and observers such as commercial middlemen, politicians, scientists, engineers, medical doctors, drug-traffickers, World Bank economists, priests, NGO workers, development experts, military personnel, ethnographers, consumers of nature and tradition, and good Samaritans.

As objects of knowledge such social configurations come to be perceived as threatening the institutional and normative field of the state and other forms of authority. They are seen as generating potential problems for trade, research, spiritual salvation, de-criminalisation, policing, development policy and even 'civilisation'. In this way, local actors and their modes of organisation are often represented as deviant forms, though replete with both Western romanticism and the hidden fears of that which cannot be possessed or consumed. Local people are seen as inert objects of the desires of experts who aim to purify the perverse messages that emanate from the world of coca/cocaine, in an exhibition of counter-values that challenge notions of 'clean' nature and 'progressive' culture. These representations legitimise our 'right(ness)' to speak for 'others' and this blinds us to observing the appropriateness of situated modernities as reflected in the realities of the contemporary global scene.

During this research we entered into conversations with actors who are searching for modernity. We neither questioned nor depicted them as madcaps or oddballs of that modernity. We did not assume that because they wanted such modernity they were acting rationally in the Western sense. We accepted modernity as a contingency, that is, as a way in which locally situated actors had arrived at 'modernity' by experiencing it, by listening and questioning politicians and development experts, by experimenting or balancing up uncertainties and weighing them, in favour of their individual projects and expectations.

Hence, Bolivian people can, and do, respond when confronted with modernity. What is more significant, however, is that their responses sometimes deliberately challenge the aims and objectives of development projects that were so perfectly designed. In other words, local actors often deliberately follow a course of action that runs counter to what development experts assume to be optional. The acquisition of local knowledge and experience is revealed as a constant property of situated organisational networks. These actors, with their production of coca/cocaine, are constantly redefining boundaries between 'nature', 'culture' and the so-called 'economic world'. In the end, they design, produce and distribute a commodity whose properties are outside the control of experts or those who represent social order. Their practice and experiences, as well as the commodities produced, generate livelihoods that are fully part of the 'modern' world.

In summary then, we have tried to portray how the constant transgression of the limits of human experience and the re-assertion of social and political boundaries have very real, material and often unexpected effects in broader processes of development. As a result, one loses one's optimism in externally promoted and sponsored development projects, and comes to respect how local actors are, or may become, independent of our representations of modernisation and the notion of progress. The Cochabamba case brings out the mutational character of the processes rather than the hybridity of the actors. These actors are in charge of their physical and social space and generate the bases of their own meaningful knowledge. Here we argue for, an anthropology of mutation that emphasises the importance of documenting the diffusion, refraction, and internal production of processes of modernity – a focus that can complement the concern for reflexivity and recursiveness in industrialised societies by writers such as Latour, Beck & Giddens.

In addition, we place the understanding of local knowledges and modernities on an epistemological par with the discussion of the relationship between 'subjectivity' and 'objectivity' as dilemmas inherent in the doing ethnography.

The dissolving of modernity into a sea of modernities does not imply the loss of actors' agency or their capacities to experience and exercise power or weakness. Indeed, the Chapare case amply demonstrates the creativity, self-reliance and organisational capacities of local actors to take care of their own destinies.

Notes

1 Though co-authored, the ethnographic impressions of this chapter derive from a visit by Alberto Arce to the region during the summer of 1995. In order to conserve the original tenor of the observations, we have retained the first person singular throughout the ethnographic account of this section of the paper. For this reason the text fluctuates between the first person singular and the plural.

2 According to Lanza (1995), up to December 1993, the Alternative Development Programme had invested U$42 million, with an average of U$4.2 million per year. This development aid was distributed in the following manner: 1) Commercialisation projects: 0.1 per cent; 2) Agricultural and livestock projects: 18 per cent; 3) Basic infrastructure for increasing productivity: 9.0 per cent; 4) Social infrastructure: 8.0 per cent; 5) Support for productive projects: 6.0 per cent; 6) Operational costs of projects: 14.0 per cent; 7) USAID salaries and other related costs: 45.0 per cent. These figures are found on pages 121 and 123 of *La Coca Prohibida* of Gregorio Lanza 1995, edited by SNV Bolivia (Dutch Cooperation Service for Development) and CEDIB.

11 Exploring local/global transformations[1]

A view from anthropology

Norman Long

Many contemporary scholars and observers have stressed that we are now living in an era of radical change – a turning point in history, and the end of industrial society and the Third World as we have known them over the past century. The signs seem clear. Electronic and satellite communication technologies have made it possible for the rapid dissemination and application of scientific knowledge and advanced technologies, as well as the diffusion and blending of newly created or 'reinvented' cultural life styles and art forms. Economies have been restructured around more flexible and diversified production systems and economic enterprise, while commodity markets and financial institutions have become more global and, at the same time, more volatile. Governments are less interventionist (at least in their rhetoric if not in practice) in their regulation and management of human affairs, preferring instead to depend on the 'laws of the market' and to devolve or delegate certain state powers to civic or private organisations at regional, national or international levels.

Such technological and institutional change has undoubtedly liberated many people from certain arduous everyday reproduction tasks, has dramatically improved long-distance transport systems, and has increased the space for self-organisation and individual or collective initiatives and entrepreneurship. But the down side is the fact that much of this has been achieved at the cost of those in the low-paid, work-less, or resource-scarce sectors of society, whose livelihoods and relative living standards remain extremely low and highly vulnerable to economic and political pressures. In the face of this, new forms of conflict and alliance have emerged, involving not only struggles against the national state and international institutions, but also within and between social groups mobilised on the basis of ethnicity, family and clan affiliation, gender difference, and membership of movements focusing upon specific concerns, such as environmental conservation, human rights and food risks. All sorts of sectional interests are now finding a vociferous voice, leading, in some cases, to violent confrontations. Although orientated to the improvement of material and social conditions, such struggles entail contests of values, meanings and rights, and thus raise critical questions of a symbolic, cultural, epistemological, ethical and sometimes ontological nature.

While many of the characteristics of these 'new', non-hegemonic counter-tendencies and voices may be rooted in earlier scenarios, recent commentators have emphasised the extent to which the so-called 'Global Age' (Albrow 1996, 1997) has shaped them. Hence, it is argued that much of what we now witness is essentially 'global' in scope due to the accelerated flows of various commodities, people, capital, technologies, sound-bites, images and knowledge via heterogeneous networks that criss-cross national frontiers.

On the other hand, we should not be seduced into believing that global relations and ideas have a uniform impact everywhere. To do so would be to fall into the same trap as previous attempts at theorising social change, namely that of formulating a general (or universal) theory that seeks to identify certain 'driving forces' (e.g. the 'laws' of capitalist development or the 'imperatives' of modern bureaucratic organisation), 'prime movers' (e.g. technological or economic factors), or 'cultural facilitators' (e.g. religious asceticism or entrepreneurial rationalities). Hence, it is crucial that we stand back from essentialist and reified interpretations of global change, which *assume* rather than demonstrate the force and uniformity of such change. It is also necessary to reject centrist and hegemonic modes of analysis, since there is plenty of solid evidence that seemingly 'peripheral' or 'subordinate' groups may also have a major impact on the trajectories of global change itself. Indeed, the predicaments encountered by so-called 'weaker' parties or nations within a global context can have a domino effect on the stronger members of the pack.

Discerning and interpreting these complex and interrelated processes is a daunting task which will certainly constitute the core of any new research agenda for well into the new millennium. In this chapter, I limit myself to identifying certain key substantive and theoretical issues that will continue to present a major challenge to anthropologists involved in studies of local/global development.

Globalisation: diversity not uniformity

As I emphasised above, we must not overlook issues of social heterogeneity. We are in fact living in an increasingly diversified world which only has the trappings of homogeneity. The revolution in information and communication technologies has made the world look more uniform and interconnected. Yet even the most sophisticated modern communication and media systems and the development of integrated international commodity markets have not destroyed cultural, ethnic, economic and political diversity. Indeed globalisation has generated a whole new diversified pattern of responses at national, regional and local levels.

Awareness of such heterogeneity is reflected in the questioning, in certain policy circles, of standardised solutions to problems of economic development, employment and welfare, in favour of what are described as more flexible, localised and 'sustainable' strategies. This shift implies, at least in public rhetoric, a greater recognition of the strategic contribution that local knowledge, organisation and participation can make to development. Concomitant with this is an apparent decline of hierarchical and corporativist forms of organisation and the emergence of new groupings and coalitions that delegitimise centralised political control and authority, thus reshaping power relations; although, at the same time, we must remember that so-called 'decentralised' patterns of government may often mask 'top-down' measures aimed at reducing the administrative and financial burdens of central government.

Alongside these trends is the swing back to 'market-led' development where the language of 'free enterprise', 'competition' and 'deregulation' prevails, with the consequent 'pulling back' or 'withdrawal' of state institutions. Once again, though, we should not assume that liberalising and privatising strategies, spearheaded by international bodies such as the World Bank and IMF, imply the end of interventionist measures undertaken by the state. Indeed, the very implementation of liberalisation policies requires a framework of state regulation, resources and legitimacy, and the use of a persuasive political rhetoric aimed at mobilising people and enrolling them in this new type of strategic thinking, seen dramatically in recent events in Russia. Moreover, policy measures that address themselves to the 'solution' of pressing economic problems, often fall short precisely because they fail to come to grips with the everyday practicalities and diverse modes of making and defending a living. Thus strategic planning by government is always difficult to realise successfully when faced by a myriad of local and regional adaptations, but especially so when the political conditions militate against the state being able to govern effectively and steer change. Many domains of state activity in fact increasingly require international backing to function at all.

This problem of state 'governability' arises in part from the increased global character of the relationships affecting various domains of human practice. Present day geo-political transformations (such as the break-up of the Soviet Union and Eastern Bloc countries and the establishment of new regions of co-operation like the European Union and NAFTA, as well as the new agreements or 'conditionalities' concerning Third World development aid and trade) question the sovereignty of nation-states, since their rights and obligations, their powers and autonomy, are clearly challenged and redefined. Yet, the immense flows of capital, goods, services, people, information, technologies, policies, ideas, images and regulations that these changes imply are not organised from a few centres or blocs of power, as World Systems theory might suggest (see Sklair 1991: 33–4). Transnational enterprises may have localised sites of operation (e.g. London, New York, Tokyo and Hollywood) but they do not dominate their spheres of influence and investment. Rather they must contest them with their competitors.

It is equally difficult then to think of the nation-state or the transnational corporation as the appropriate power-container of important economic and social relationships in the global political economy. Instead we must replace such a model with that of global orders whose building blocks are groups and associations set within multiple and overlapping networks of power. These various networks are constantly reordering themselves in the face of changing global conditions. In doing so they draw upon diverse local and extra-local resources and values, frequently appealing to images of some new kind of 'global' scenario and 'cosmopolitan' civil society.

Such groups and associations include, not only international trade organisations, financial corporations and newly emerging inter-state political alliances, but also social movements where people group around pressing problems of a global nature. The latter manifest themselves in the growing commitment to new 'causes' which bring people together across the world – people of different nation-states and cultures. For example, there are 'green' movements that address the issues of world-wide pollution, degradation of the environment, depletion of natural resources and the loss of genetic diversity among animal and plant populations. Social movements have also sprung up around issues of health threats affecting the world population at large (and especially vulnerable groups), such as the HIV/AIDS associations and pressure groups; 'alternative development' associations; and groups that have launched campaigns against transnational companies that have introduced what are considered to be nutritionally 'inappropriate' products such as baby bottle-feed formulas and Coca Cola to the poorer nations, as well as 'inappropriate' technologies promoting non-sustainable production methods and systems of labour control that are oppressive.

Other examples include consumers' associations (mostly based in the richer countries) that try to protect consumer interests by pressing for better quality or organically grown produce and more favourable prices; and farmers' organisations that seek to advance their own particular interests – sometimes at loggerheads with each other (such as the French and British producers who have for a number of years been locked into a pitched battle over European Union agricultural export quotas, which led in one instance to the slaughtering of imported British sheep in France), and occasionally mobilising across national boundaries in order to pursue more global issues. Here, the problem of the modern food chain is a critical factor, with transnationals and increasingly supermarkets making direct deals with producer groups in Third World production zones in order to avoid state control and standards (see Marsden & Arce 1993).

Other cases highlight certain shifts in the character of agrarian movements. Latin America in particular has a long history of struggles by small producers and agricultural labourers against landlords and local political bosses who monopolise access to the most productive land and to crucial marketing and servicing channels. But now we witness massive mobilisations of indigenous peoples. For example, around the Amazonian rim we find several different groups fighting aggressively, not just for rights to land (i.e. plots for cultivation or livestock rearing), but for habitat rights (i.e. the right not to be disturbed by transnationals or ravaged by land speculators, and the right to determine how natural resources should be utilised and by whom). This struggle, of course, has a strong ethnic and human rights dimension to it, which prompted the International Labour Organisation to become involved in providing logistical support for the co-ordination of these Amazonian groups. It also sparked off protest marches directed towards the national governments of Bolivia and Ecuador by indigenous peoples who walked from the eastern tropical lowlands to La Paz and Quito to present their cases. The 1994 outburst in Chiapas, which focused upon resistance to the Mexican State and its free trade policies, took place on the day NAFTA was inaugurated and presents a similar mix of issues embracing land, ethnicity, political repression and human rights. This case is also notable for the rapidity with which the leaders of the uprising were able to disseminate their manifesto detailing their complaints and demands: almost as soon as they had taken their first offensive a statement from them appeared on e-mail throughout the global electronic network.

Another interesting global initiative concerns the expansion of women's and feminist associations, to include women of diverse cultural and socio-political backgrounds, leading in recent years to the holding of World Summits to share experiences and to identity problems and areas for future strategic debate and action. Finally, of course, we should not forget the example of the long-standing Esperanto Association, which has been promoting Esperanto as a world language, though somewhat unsuccessfully in the face of the accelerating spread of English.

As we stressed above, at the same time as these movements have been evolving and flexing their muscles, so we have witnessed a re-ordering of power relations due to a decline of hierarchical and corporativist modes of control. The interplay of these two processes has generated a variety of dynamic and contingent situations, which contain both the organisational potentials for the creation of new globally-oriented coalitions of interest, as well as the possibilities of a fragmentation of existing power domains. While the latter may lead to the opening up of new political spaces, at least for some social groups, it may also heighten cultural and political confrontation, resulting (in the worst of scenarios such as the Balkans, and Rwanda-Zaire) in ethnic strife, civil war and societal breakdown.

Clearly, then, globalisation processes generate a whole new range of conditions and socio-political responses at national, regional and local levels. These changes, however, are not dictated by some supranational hegemonic power or simply driven by international capitalist interests. Changing global conditions – whether economic, political, cultural or environmental – are, as it were, 'relocalised' within national, regional or local frameworks of knowledge and organisation which, in turn, are constantly being reworked in interaction with the wider context. It is for this reason that we need to study in detail the disembedding of localised ideas and relations as they acquire global significance, and their re-embedding in specific locales (cf. van der Ploeg 1992 who uses the notions of 'internalisation' and 'relocalisation' to describe this process). Such processes entail the emergence of new identifications, alliances and struggles for space and power within specific arenas.

People develop their own strategies to solve the problems they face through the use of interpersonal networks, community or neighbourhood ties, church or NGOs, and through an appeal to certain widely-accepted value positions, and they may do this either individually or in groups. They do not merely respond to programmes or services provided by 'outside' public or private interests; nor do they simply react to distant market conditions. On the basis of 'local' knowledge, organisation and values, they actively attempt to come to grips cognitively and organisationally with 'external' circumstances, and in so doing the latter are mediated or transformed in some way (Long 1984, 1989; Long & Long 1992). And in this manner, 'states', 'transnationals', 'markets', 'technologies' and 'global images' themselves become endowed with highly diverse and 'localised' sets of meanings and practices.

Global transformations then present us with a range of heterogeneous processes for analysis. These processes involve multiple levels, values and realities, and span diverse local patterns of organisation and management of resources, regional economic, political and cultural phenomena, intervening state and non-state institutions, development programmes and representations, and global market, political and cultural scenarios. At the core lie central issues concerning livelihoods, organisational capacities and discourses, intervention measures and ideology. In short, this is a complex drama about human needs, desires, organising practices, power relations, skills and knowledge, authoritative discourses and institutions, and the clash of different ways of attempting to order and transform the world.

The principal challenge for the researcher is to devise an analytical approach that allows us to elucidate and analyse the construction of these many complex discursive and social forms. Although one must recognise the need for topic-specific concepts and methods, work at Wageningen has focused on elaborating an actor-oriented approach to development, modernity and local/global issues.

In the sections that follow I outline some of the main concepts of this approach and where possible show its relevance to the theme of local/global relations and representations.

The centrality of actors' perceptions and representations

An actor-oriented approach must begin with actor-defined issues or critical events, whether defined by policy makers, researchers, intervening private or public agents or local actors, and whatever the spatial, cultural, institutional and power domains and arenas implicated. Such issues or events are, of course, often perceived, and their implications interpreted, very differently by the various parties/actors involved. Hence, from the outset one faces the dilemma of how to represent problematic situations when there are multiple voices and contested 'realities'. A field of development is of course discursively constructed and delimited practically by the language use and strategic actions of the various actors. How far consensus is achieved over the definition of such a field or arena of contestation requires empirical evidence. One should not assume a shared vision. Actors must work towards such a common interpretation and there are always possibilities for dissenting from it.[2]

It is assumed that all actors work – mostly implicitly rather than explicitly – with beliefs about agency, that is, they articulate notions about relevant acting units and the kinds of knowledgeability and capability they have vis-à-vis the world they live in. This raises the question of how people's perceptions of the actions and agency of others shape their own behaviour. For example, local farmers may have reified views about 'the state' or 'the market' as actors, which, irrespective of their dealings with individual government officials or market traders, may influence their expectations of the outcomes of particular interventions. The same applies to the attribution of motives to local actors, such as political bosses and village authorities.

The issue is how actors struggle to give meaning to their experiences through an array of representations, images, cognitive understandings and emotional responses. Though the repertoire of 'sense-making' filters and antennae will vary considerably, such processes are to a degree framed by 'shared' cultural perceptions, which are subject to reconstitution or transformation. Locally-situated cultures are always, as it were, 'put to the test' as they encounter the less familiar or the strange. An actor analysis must therefore address itself to the intricacies and dynamics of relations between differing life-worlds and to processes of cultural construction. In this way one aims to understand the production of heterogeneous cultural phenomena and the outcomes of interaction between different representational and discursive domains, thus mapping out what we might describe as a cartography of cultural difference, power and authority.

But, since social life is composed of multiple realities, which are, as it were, constructed and confirmed primarily through experience, this interest in culture must be grounded methodologically in the detailed study of everyday life, in which actors seek to grapple cognitively and organisationally with the problematic situations they face. Hence, social perceptions, values and classifications must be analysed in relation to interlocking experiences and social practices, not at the level of general cultural schema or value abstractions. For example, the production of commodities for global markets implies a whole range of value transformations, not only in regard to the commodity chain itself (i.e. the analysis of 'added value' at the points of product transformation, commercialisation and consumption) but also in terms of how such commoditisation impacts on the social values attributed to other goods, relationships, livelihood activities, and forms of knowledge. In this way, involvement in commodity chains may set off (but not determine) a number of significant cultural transformations. In order to analyse these dimensions we must reject a homogeneous or unitary concept of 'culture' (often implied when labelling certain behaviour and sentiments as 'tradition') and embrace theoretically the central issues of cultural repertoires, heterogeneity and 'hybridity'. The concept of cultural repertoire points to the ways in which various cultural ingredients (value notions, types and fragments of discourses, organisational ideas, symbols and ritualised procedures) are used and recombined in social practice, consciously or otherwise; heterogeneity points to the generation and co-existence of multiple social forms within the same context or same scenario of problem-solving which offer alternative solutions to similar problems, thus underlining that living cultures are necessarily multiple in the way in which they are enacted (cf. the concept of polymorphic structures in the biological sciences[3]); and hybridity to the mixed end-products that arise out of the combining of different cultural ingredients and repertoires. Of course there are certain inherent difficulties in the use of the term 'hybridity' to characterise contemporary patterns of change since, like bricolage, it suggests the sticking together or strategic combining of cultural fragments rather than the active self-transforming nature of socio-cultural practice. In Chapter 10 of this volume, we have suggested the term 'social mutation' for such internally generated and transforming processes.

Social domains and arenas: the question of constraints and boundaries

In order to get to grips with encounters between life-worlds, we need to develop a methodological approach to the study of domains and arenas in which contestation over values and resources takes place. The concept of 'domains' helps to identify areas of social life that are organised by reference to a central core or cluster of values which, even if they are not perceived in exactly the same way by everybody, are nevertheless recognised as a locus of certain 'rules', norms and values implying a degree of social commitment. Examples include the domains of family, market, state, community, production, and consumption, although, depending upon the situation, particular domains will differ in their prominence, pervasiveness or social significance. In this way 'domains' are central to understanding how social ordering works, and to analysing how social and symbolic boundaries are created and defended. The values and interests associated with particular domains become especially visible and defined at points where domains are seen to impinge on each other or come into conflict, that is, at the points of interface. Hence, domains together with the notion of arenas – and how they are bounded – give us an analytical handle on the kinds of constraints and enabling elements that shape actors' choices and room for manoeuvre. Domains should not be conceptualised a priori as cultural givens but as produced and transformed through the experiences shared and the struggles that take place between actors of various sorts. Like the notion of 'symbolic boundaries' enunciated by Cohen (1986: 16), domains represent for people some shared values that 'absolve them from the need to explain themselves to each other – [but] leaves them free to attach their own meanings to them.'

'Arenas' are social encounters or a series of situations in which contests over issues, resources, values, and representations take place. That is, they are social and spatial locations where actors confront each other, mobilise social relations and deploy discursive and cultural means for the attainment of specific ends, including that of perhaps simply remaining in the game. In the process actors may draw on particular domains to support their interests, aims and dispositions. Arenas therefore are either spaces in which contestation associated with different practices and values of different domains takes place or they are spaces within a single domain where attempts are made to resolve discrepancies in value interpretations and incompatibilities between actors' interests.

The concept of arena is especially important for identifying the actors and mapping out the issues, resources and discourses entailed in particular situations of disagreement or dispute. While the idea of 'arena' has an affinity to that of 'forum', the latter carries with it the implication that the rules for debate are, in a sense, already agreed upon, whereas contestation in an arena denotes discontinuities of values, norms and practices. Arena is especially useful when analysing development projects and programmes since intervention processes consist of a complex set of interlocking arenas of struggle, each characterised by specific constraints and possibilities of manoeuvre (see Elwert & Bierschenk 1988).

We should not, however, assume that an actor analysis is primarily interested in face-to-face confrontations or interactions or only in local situations, interests, values and contests. Quite the opposite, since we are also interested in exploring how 'external' or geographically distant actors, contexts and institutional frames shape social processes, strategies and actions in localised settings. Moreover, local situations, struggles or networks are often stretched out or projected spatially as well as temporally to connect up with other distant, unknown – and sometimes unknowable – social worlds. Very few social arenas in fact are self-contained and separate from other arenas. Here the impact of modern communication and information technologies has been crucial, since these allow for spontaneous, technology-mediated interactions of global proportions, thereby underlining the importance of developing analyses of interlocking arenas that go beyond earlier territorialised conceptions of social space based, for example, on the dichotomies of 'rural-urban', 'centre-periphery', or 'nation-international order'.

From social drama to critical event analysis

These ideas of domain and arena can be extended to embrace the study of critical events and issues. A useful forerunner of critical event analysis, which involves the understanding of complex interlocking arenas, is the early work of Victor Turner on 'social dramas'. Turner first developed the notion of social drama for the analysis of social conflict and dispute settlement in African village politics. This was applied to a wide range of other types of dramatic situations by members of the Manchester School, from struggles between trade unions and mine management to clashes between town and village life styles and values, to larger scale disruptions in socio-political arrangements. And it can also fruitfully be applied to the understanding of critical events entailed in so-called 'natural' and 'man-made' disasters.

A central aspect of Turner's original use of social drama is the disruption of an existing set of social relations or breach of norms which occasions efforts to repair the damage and restore social order or institute some new, negotiated social arrangements. As Turner graphically puts it, focusing upon social dramas makes transparent 'the crucial principles of social structure in their operation, and their relative dominance at successive points in time' (Turner 1957: 93). This enables one to analyse the realignments in power relations consequent upon the struggles that take place between specific individuals and groups (*ibid*: 131). Through careful analysis of the set of ongoing relationships and situations in the conflict he is able to demonstrate its mode of resolution. In this way he limits his study to localised issues pertaining to contests over 'traditional' village headmanship and does not feel the need to explore much the broader implications (in this case the key protagonist's exposure to town values and experience).[4]

Social dramas that are more complex in scale and ramification can best be looked at using a critical event approach. As an instructive example of this type of event, one can consider the explosion at the Union Carbide chemical plant in Bhopal, India, in 1984. The explosion affected many thousands of people who had nothing to do with the industry or the Union Carbide company directly, and who received none of the industry's benefits. The accident and what followed over the short and longer term enrolled a whole range of actors, spanning local, national and international arenas around several normative and ethical domains and issues that the disaster brought to the fore. These involved environmental effects, quality control standards, the freedom of transnationals to flout national and international agreements, the allocation of blame and accountability, the rights of the local labour force, and levels of compensation for affected workers and town and village residents, and a host of political ramifications that put the Indian State, regional government, international bodies, Union Carbide, and the legal profession all, as it were, 'on trial'. In an interesting analysis of the Bhopal disaster, Veena Das (1995) highlights the dynamic interplay of bureaucratic, scientific and judicial discourses and images around the symbolisation of pain, victimisation, healing and compensation.

As Das (1995) argues, this type of social drama can be described as a 'critical event' because people were seriously confronted with the limitations of the set of existing institutions and practices available for dealing with the many problems it raised. Such events are often the result of institutional breakdowns, administrative incompetence and/or a lack of political will to manage problematic or critical situations, arising from a range of man-made and so-called natural calamities. They include extreme forms of exploitation of people and resources, famine, environmental degradation and (as in the recent Indonesian case) the wilful destruction of forest lands, or political and ethnic conflicts that result in the dismantling of the state and civil order.

Another example which I touched on earlier concerns the critical events associated with the 1994 Zapatista uprising in Chiapas, Southern Mexico, and its aftermath, where the Internet was used to propagate Zapatista views, to win wider national and international support and to influence the negotiations taking place between Zapatista leaders and government spokesmen. This complex situation, now in its fifth year, has also generated a series of dramas involving struggles in other social sectors of the Mexican population for better political representation, or aimed at countering the detrimental effects of neoliberal policies.[5] Through the media and Internet many spatially dispersed actors are brought together as 'virtual communities' that clearly exert influence on their members and play an increasingly crucial role in the definition, representation and symbolisation of critical events. International news correspondents, who immediately descended upon Chiapas, and their network of colleagues via portable satellite connections throughout the world, played an important role in profiling the conflict, and developed ploys to keep the story on the front pages. One intriguing case of this was the craze for Zapatista paraphernalia that erupted: they began writing about Zapatista dolls, pens, T-shirts and other souvenirs. It is said that it was the correspondent for the Spanish daily *La Vanguardia* who had suggested to an Indian street hawker selling traditionally dressed dolls that she might sell more if she produced special Zapatista dolls. Two days later the hawker turned up with the new merchandise, complete with black Zapatista army ski masks (Oppenheimer 1996: 29–30). Soon the wearing of the black mask itself took on a wider comico-political significance throughout Mexico as a general, unspoken symbol of protest against government.

The issue of 'collective actors'

Starting with problematic or critical livelihood situations leads to a consideration of the ways in which actors develop social strategies to cope with them. These situated practices involve the management and co-ordination of sets of social relations that carry with them various normative expectations and commitments, as well as the deployment of technologies, resources, discourses, and texts in the form of documents that likewise embody wider sets of meanings and social relations.[6] Also, as I indicated earlier, they frequently draw upon certain so-called 'collective' resources and symbols.

The designation 'collective actor' covers three distinct connotations, each relevant to the understanding of social practice. The first sense is that of a coalition of actors who, at least at a given moment, share some common definition of the situation, or goals, interests, or values, and who agree, tacitly or explicitly, to pursue certain courses of social action. Such a social actor or entity (e.g. networks of actors or some sort of enterprise) can meaningfully be attributed with the power of agency, that is the capacity to process experience, make decisions and to act upon them. These collective actors may be informally or formally constituted and spontaneously or strategically organised. Furthermore, as Adams (1975) has argued, such operating units fall, broadly speaking, under one of two contrasting forms: those that are characterised by a coordinate pattern of relations as against those that are centralised. In the former, there is no central figure of authority, since the individuals grant reciprocal rights to each other, while retaining the prerogative to withdraw from the particular exchange relationships at their will. Here, networks are more symmetrical in form but often have ambiguous and shifting boundaries. On the other hand, in the centralised case, there are imbalances in the exchanges, differences in access to strategic resources, and a degree of centralised control and decision-making exercised by a central body or persons (and sometimes backed by 'higher' authorities) who claim to 'represent' the collectivity in its dealings.

The second sense of collective actor (or rather *collectif*) is that of an assemblage of human, social, material, technical and textual elements that make up what Latour (1994) and Callon & Law (1995) designate a 'heterogeneous actor-network'. This usage attempts to dissolve the 'commonsense' distinction between 'things' and 'people' by arguing that 'purposeful action and intentionality are not properties of objects, but neither are they properties of human actors. Rather, they are properties of institutions, of *collectifs*' (Verschoor 1997: 27). That is, they are emergent effects generated by the interaction of both human and non-human components, not a group of individuals who decide to join together in some common organisation. Hence attempts to define collective social action without acknowledging the constitutive role played by materials, texts and technologies fall short analytically because they assume that collective social arrangements are simply the aggregated outcome of the effective agencies and interests of the participating individuals. The merit of this second interpretation of collective is twofold: it stresses the heterogeneous make-up of organising practices founded upon enrolment strategies; and it warns against individualist/reductionist interpretations of collective forms.[7]

The third meaning of collective actor recognises that social life is replete with images, representations and categorisations of things, people and institutions, that are assumed or pictured as somehow constituting a unitary acting whole, such as 'the state', 'community', 'global markets', and 'the transnationals', which are often endowed with generalised (or collective) modes of agency that shape actors' orientations and actions. But it would be wrong analytically to adopt these reifications or 'black-boxed' entities as representing a primary grid for analysing their complex interactions with each other or with similar collective 'others'. The principal reason for this is that although symbolic representations and categorisations necessarily form part of an understanding of social practice – namely in its discursive and pictorial dimensions – they should not be disconnected from the pragmatics and semiotics of everyday life within which they are embedded and acquire their social significance. Indeed, a major advantage of actor-oriented analysis is that it aims to problematise such conceptions and interpretations through an ethnographic study of how specific actors deal organisationally and cognitively with the problematic situations they encounter.

All three kinds of collective actor – notwithstanding the probable epistemological objections and reservations of Latour – have, I believe, a place in actor-oriented analysis.

Organising processes: livelihoods, networks and social interface

Social life encompasses both face-to-face and more 'distanced' relationships. The types of social relationships range from inter-personal links based upon dyadic ties (such as patron–client relations and involvement in certain types of transactions – buyer–seller, producer–money lender, and client–ritual specialist, farmer–extensionist etc.) to social and exchange networks of various kinds, to more formally constituted groups and organisations where dimensions concerning legal prescriptions, bureaucratic legitimacy and authority, and defined membership criteria assume greater significance.

Central to the idea of networks and organising practices is the concept of 'livelihood'. Livelihood best expresses the idea of individuals and groups striving to make a living, attempting to meet their various consumption and economic necessities, coping with uncertainties, responding to new opportunities, and choosing between different value positions. Studying livelihoods also entails identifying the relevant social units and fields of activity: one should not prejudge the issue, as many studies do, by fixing upon the more conventional anchorage points for an analysis of economic life such as 'the household', 'the local community', 'the production sector' or 'commodity chain'. Indeed in many situations confederations of households and wide-ranging interpersonal networks embracing a wide variety of activities and cross-cutting so-called 'rural' and 'urban' contexts, as well as national frontiers, constitute the social fabric upon which livelihoods and commodity flows are woven. In addition, we need to take account of the normative and cultural dimensions of livelihoods, that is, we need to explore the issue of life styles and the factors that shape them.

In this regard, Sandra Wallman (in her studies of households in Wandsworth, London) makes an interesting contribution when she writes: 'Livelihood is never just a matter of finding or making shelter, transacting money, getting food to put on the family table or to exchange on the market place. It is equally a matter of ownership and circulation of information, the management of skills and relationships, and the affirmation of personal significance [involving issues of self-esteem] and group identity. The tasks of meeting obligations, of security, identity and status, and organising time are as crucial to livelihood as bread and shelter' (Wallman & Associates 1982). Hence, she adds to the three conventional categories of material resources, labour and capital, three additional critical elements, namely 'time', 'information' and 'identity'. The emphasis on the latter brings us to an important, often neglected element, namely, the identity-constructing processes inherent in the pursuit of livelihoods. This is especially relevant since livelihood strategies entail the building of relationships with others whose life-worlds and status may differ markedly.

Livelihood therefore implies value choice, status issues, identification with or distantiation from other modes of living and types of social persons. It implies both a synchronic pattern of relationships existing among a delimited number of persons for solving livelihood problems or sustaining certain types of livelihoods, as well as diachronic processes. The latter cover actors' livelihood trajectories during their life courses, the types of choices they identify and take, and the switches they make between livelihood options. Livelihoods are both individually and jointly constructed and represent patterns of shifting inter-dependencies.

While much organisational analysis focuses on formal rules and administrative procedures, highlighting for example the ways in which state, company and development agency rules and regulations shape the workings of organisations, an actor perspective concentrates, among other things, on delineating everyday organising and symbolising practices and the interlocking of actors' projects. Organisational networks entail overlapping domains and fuzzy boundaries. Thus ordering processes are, as Law suggests, built upon strategic interests and representations of self and other.

These various social and organisational practices function as a nexus of micro and macro relations and representations, and often involve the development of 'interlocking actor projects' that are crucial for understanding the articulation and management of actor interests and life-worlds, as well as for the resolution of conflicts. They constitute, that is, a 'new' or 're-established' field of enablement, constraints and mutual sanctioning within which new embodiments of agency and social action take shape (for further discussion of the concept of interlocking projects and practices, see Long & van der Ploeg (1994, 1995).

In order to explore these issues in more depth it is useful to adopt an analysis of interface situations, that is the critical points of intersection between multiple life-worlds or domains where discontinuities exist based on discrepancies in values, interests, knowledge and power. More concretely, they characterise social situations wherein the relationships between actors become oriented around the problem of devising ways of 'bridging', accommodating to, or contesting each others' different social and cognitive worlds. Interface analysis aims to elucidate the types of social discontinuities present in such situations and to characterise the different kinds of organisational and cultural forms that transform them (Long 1989; Long & Long 1992).

Migration, globalisation and transnational networks[8]

In this final part of the chapter I look briefly at a topic involving local/global issues in which the above actor concepts are central to understanding the social processes involved. The topic centres on the construction and transformation of values, livelihoods, and identities in the context of transnational migration – an increasingly prominent and disquieting phenomenon in global political and economic scenarios.

Previous studies of migration have tended to represent the flows of people to new locations in terms of the adaptation or adjustment of new migrants to their 'host' societies, or they have offered a dualistic analysis of the interrelations of peripheral places of origin and central places of destination. More recently, migration flows have been reinterpreted as an integral feature of the global economy, giving rise to new types of 'nomadic' peoples and to transnational communities. Hence an essential aspect of the social life of 'global nomads' or international migrants is the fact that their networks ('real' and 'imagined') reach out into the wider realm of transnational space linking them not only to their places of origin but also to compatriots living in widely dispersed locations. These networks of persons and places are bound together through 'collective' memories and images of a common place of origin, and possibly of places of migration and having the sense of another identity – of being a nomad having empathy with all other similar nomads.

Though it has been commonplace in much of the literature to depict these migrant flows in terms of the emergence of new international divisions of labour, a more interesting facet concerns the nature and development of particular transnational networks of people and places. This demands an understanding of the interlocking of 'localised', 'transnational', 'nomadic' and 'hybrid' experiences and also of how these constituent elements transmute into a new 'globalised' cultural identity associated with 'migrants on the move'. So far research has accorded only minor attention to the dynamics of these inter-cultural processes and their consequences.

This problematic is related to the broader issue of the emergence of globalised cultures characterised by a continuous flow of ideas, information, values and tastes mediated through mobile individuals, symbolic tokens and often electronic simulations (Waters 1995). Such flows take place in culturally constructed social fields and spaces that make possible new 'imagined communities' (Anderson 1991) that are increasingly detached from fixed locations or territories. This phenomenon indeed constitutes a major challenge for actor-oriented research since it throws into question the implicit assumptions of some formulations – that domains and social arenas coincide with delimited spatial and territorialised settings.

In the case of global migrants and refugees, their social lives are still tied to particular notions of 'place' and 'home community', but these are reworked to include a wide network of individuals and institutions physically located in very different places (e.g. localities in Europe and the US, in city neighbourhoods and villages, as well as in the community of origin). The precise constituency and salience of the particular 'imagined communities' to which people belong, will, of course, vary according to the geographical locations of the groups and individuals involved, the relevant issues at hand, members' accessibility in terms of communication media, their visions of the future etc. Also family members back in the home setting may themselves participate in these practices of constructing 'imagined communities'.

Clearly these elements are central to understanding the life-worlds and orientations of international migrants and refugees, but equally they are relevant for returnees and for those who choose not to migrate, since the latter too are exposed via interpersonal ties and media to such global forms. The flows of 'home-destined' goods (such as taped music, garments, furniture styles, house decorations, 'exotic' posters, foreign mementos, family photographs etc.) carry with them specific meanings and values associated with the migrants' 'global' life-world. In reverse, the flow of 'migrant-destined' goods and messages help keep migrants in touch and for some they provide a strong anchor. This differentiated global space provides a critical field for defining or crystallising new notions of 'community' and 'belongingness' that are now emerging within localities in many parts of the world.

Another way in which migration is linked to globalisation is the diminished capacity of nation-states to control the flow of people and goods across their borders. Here, it is important to take account of the fact that migrant life-worlds include encounters and avoidance of contact with various agencies of migration control that seek to define eligibility of national citizenship and to regulate the movement of 'aliens' in and out of national territories. Hence research on this topic should include a study of those agencies involved in managing (controlling) the in-flow of migrants and refugees seen from an organisational, legal-normative, brokerage and cultural point of view. Linked to this, is the exploration of how precisely migrants enter national spaces illegally and how they find a place to live, find work and establish themselves within an acceptable social environment with which they can to some extent identify.

This has led to an interest in analysing the emergence of so-called transnational migrant communities, and the associated practices of transnationalism (Appadurai and Breckenridge 1988; Gupta 1992; Kearney 1991; Rouse 1991; Basch, Glick & Szanton 1994). Transnationalism, however, should not imply that the nation-state has ceased to be an important referent in the imagination of space or in the situated practices of migrants, returnees and villagers. Instead, as Gupta (1992: 63) argues, the inscription of space in representations of the nation-state now occurs in a de-territorialised way. Hence, notions of belonging and 'citizenship' become harnessed less to the idea of a particular national political system than to ethnic identities that transcend borders and to imagined notions of place and home (such as a specific village or Andean valley); and they often take shape under the influence of global debates (launched by new social and ethnic movements).

The other face of contemporary population movements is the displacement of people due to socio-political violence and the consequent dislocation of economic life and livelihood patterns. In the aftermath of violent conflict, many elements are reconfigured: relations of power, techniques of government, modes of organisation, livelihoods, identities and collective memories, and the relations between people and places. Displaced groups are often reluctant to return to their villages and regions of origin after the cessation of hostilities, and if they do they often reconstruct their lives on the basis of new values, desires and organisational assets or deficits. Frequently they continue to depend on support networks and patterns of aid and resources assembled during their period of exile; and some returnees never in fact fully return. Instead they live within 'multiple realities' where, if they have the necessary strategic skills and knowledge, they can access a wide range of livelihood options, which continue to tie them to both their places of origin and of exile. Other less fortunate individuals or households, of course, may become trapped cognitively and emotionally in the traumas of violence and displacement and be unable effectively to rebuild their lives.

Seen from another point of view, such former conflict-ridden areas become frontiers where new battles are fought out between the engaging parties involved in the reconstruction process, represented by the state, international development agencies, political groupings and various local actors and families. A characteristic of these situations is the emergence of unstable tactical alliances and the continuous clash and transformation of interests, priorities and worldviews. If solutions are to be negotiated between the opposing parties then careful analysis is required to reveal the rhythm and dynamics of the various social, cultural and political reconfigurations that take place.

Given the increasing vulnerabilities of many populations in the face of global economic change and political violence, the analysis of differing scenarios and outcomes of global networks, transnational migration and the movement of displaced persons will continue for the foreseeable future to be major topics for research. These processes raise critical issues concerning the viability of certain types of livelihoods and modes of organisation, and address fundamental questions about people changing their cultural identifications and social relations in what looks like being an increasingly diverse and complex world.

Notes

1 This chapter is an amalgamation and revision of two recent papers: Long 1996 and Long 1997. I would like to thank Alberto Arce and Ann Long for suggesting how I might achieve this, and Ann for helping me to finally edit the version.

2 See Mongbo 1995 for a detailed analysis of this process in a programme of agricultural development in Benin.

3 In biology, polymorphism denotes situations in which two or more variants of a species co-exist. An intriguing example is that of the African *Papilio dardanus* butterfly, whose females mimic in colour and wing patterning several other species. This heterogeneity protects them from certain predators who mistake them for other, nasty-tasting butterflies, giving them a better chance of survival.

4 In fairness to Turner, one should note that he applies a more wide-ranging and historical approach to the analysis of social dramas in his later studies of political and religious movements (see Turner 1974; also Moore 1986).

5 The rising was timed to coincide with the inauguration of the North American Free Trade Agreement (NAFTA) which was the lynch-pin of the new package of neo-liberal measures introduced by the Salinas government.

6 Thus, as both Latour (1987) and Appadurai (1986) argue – though from different theoretical standpoints – a sociology of social action necessitates a sociology and epistemology of things (see also Miller 1987).

7 This Latourian position is not without its conceptual and epistemological shortcomings. See endnote 13, Chapter 1, for a brief account of these.

8 A project on this theme is presently being undertaken in respect to the central highlands of Peru under the co-ordination of myself and Pieter de Vries (Wageningen, the Netherlands), Teófilo Altamirano (Catholic University, Lima, Peru) and Moshe Shokheid (Tel-Aviv University, Israel).

Bibliography

Abdel Metaal, S. (1992) 'The civilizational role of the Islamic movements' (in Arabic) *Manbar al-Sharq*, Vol.1, 33–45, March, Cairo: The Arab Islamic Studies Centre.

Abrahams, R. G. (1967) *The Political Organization of Unyamwezi*, Cambridge: Cambridge University Press.

Abram, S. and J. Waldren, eds (1998) *Anthropological Perspectives on Local Development: Knowledge and Sentiments in Conflict*, London and New York: Routledge.

Adams, R. (1975) *Energy and Structure: a Theory of Social Power*, Austin and London: University of Texas Press.

Adjanohoun, E. (1964) 'Végétation des savanes et des rochers decouverts en Côte d'Ivoire centrale,' Memoire ORSTOM No. 7, Paris.

Ahmed, D. *et al.* (1988) 'Het harddrugsbeleid in Amsterdam 1982–1987,' Faculty of Law, University of Amsterdam: Amsterdam.

Albrow, M. (1996) *The Global Age*, Cambridge: Polity Press.

——(1997) 'Travelling beyond local cultures: socioscapes in a global city,' in *Living the Global City: Globalization as Local Process*, Eade John, ed., London and New York: Routledge.

Alem, J. (1989) 'Nuevos Elementos de Discusion y Accion,' in Coca: Hacia una Estrategia Nacional Reporte de la Comision de Narcoticos y Farmacodependencia al Honorable Senado Nacional, ILDIS-Senado, 73–88, La Paz, Bolivia.

Alexander, J. (1985) *Neofunctionalism*, London: Sage.

Al-Ghanoushi, R. (1992) 'The future of the Islamic movement (in Arabic)', *Manbar Al-Sharq*, Vol. 1, March, 23–32, Cairo: The Arab Islamic Studies Centre.

Alonso, A.-M. (1995) *Thread of Blood. Colonialism, Revolution and Gender on Mexico's Northern Frontier*, Tucson: University of Arizona Press.

Al-Qaradawi, Y. (1994) 'The Arab Islamic culture: between authenticity and modernity (in Arabic),' Cairo: Maktabet Wahba.

Al-Turabi, H. (1992) 'The priorities of the Islamic movement (in Arabic)', *Manbar Al-Sharq*, Vol.1, March, 15–22, Cairo: The Arab Islamic Studies Centre.

Ameresekere, G. (1953) *Karumakkarayo*, Colombo: Gunasems & Sons.

Anderson, Benedict (1991) *Imagined Communities*, 2nd edn, London: Verso.

Anderson, Benjamin (1870) *Narrative of a Journey to Musardu, Capital of the Western Mandingoes*, New York: S.W.Green.

——(1912) *Narrative of the Expedition Despatched to Musahdu by the Liberian Government Under Benjamin K. Anderson, Senior in 1874*, Monrovia College of West Africa Press, Liberia: Freederik Starr.

Appadurai, A. (1986) *The Social Life of Things: Commodities in Cultural Perspective,* Cambridge: Cambridge University Press.

——(1990) 'Disjuncture and difference in the global cultural economy,' *Public Culture* 2 (2): 1 –24.

——(1993) 'Patriotism and its futures,' *Public Culture* 5(3): 411–29.

——(1995) 'The production of locality,' in *Counterworks: Managing the Diversity of Knowledge,* R. Fardon, ed., London and New York: Routledge.

Appadurai, A. and Breckenridge, C. (1988) 'Why public culture,' *Public Culture* 1 (1): 5–9.

Apthorpe, R. (1984) 'Agriculture and strategies: the language of development policy,' in *Room for Manoeuvre: An Exploration of Public Policy in Agriculture and Rural Development,* E. Clay and B. Schaffer, eds London: Heinemann Educational Books.

Apthorpe, R. and D. Gasper, eds (1996) *Arguing Development Policy: Frames and Discourses,* London: Frank Cass.

Arce, A. (1986) 'The administration of agrarian policy in a less developed country: the case of the S.A.M. in Mexico,' unpublished Ph.D. Dissertation, University of Manchester.

——(1989) 'The social construction of agrarian development: a case study of producer-bureaucrat relations in an irrigation unit in Western Mexico,' in N. Long, ed., *Encounters at the Interface: a Perspective on Social Discontinuities in Rural Development,* Wageningen: Wageningen University Press.

——(1990) 'The local effect of export agriculture: a case from Western Mexico,' Hull University Papers in Development Areas, 3 June.

——(1993) *Negotiating Agricultural Development: Entanglements of Bureaucrats and Rural Producers in Western Mexico,* Wageningen Studies in Sociology, Wageningen: PUDOC.

——(1997) 'Globalization and food objects,' in *Images and Realities of Rural Life,* H. de Haan and N. Long, eds, Assen, The Netherlands: Van Gorcum.

Arce, A. and Fisher, E. (1997) 'Global configuration of food objects and commodities: apples, honey & coca,' Paper presented to the Conference Global Commodities, Toronto, 1997.

——(1998) 'The accountability of commodities in a global market place: the case of Bolivian coca and Tanzanian honey,' Paper presented to the International Conference on Globalization, Development and the Making of Consumers: What are Collective Identities For? The Hague, 13–16 March 1997, EIDOS-WOTRO.

Arce, A. and Long, N. (1987) 'The dynamics of knowledge interfaces between Mexican agricultural bureaucrats and peasants: a case from Jalisco,' *Boletin de Estudios Latino Americanos y del Caribe, CEDLA* 43, December: 5–30.

——(1992) 'The dynamic of knowledge: interfaces between bureaucrats and peasants,' in *Battlefields of Knowledge: the Interlocking of Theory and Practice in Social Research and Development,* Long, Norman and Long, Ann, eds, London and New York: Routledge.

——(1993) 'Bridging two worlds: an ethnography of bureaucrat-peasant relations in Western Mexico,' in *An Anthropological Critique of Development: the Growth of Ignorance,* M. Hobart, ed., London and New York: Routledge.

——(1994) 'Re-positioning knowledge in the study of rural development,' in *Agricultural Restructuring and Rural Change in Europe,* David Symes and Anton J. Jansen, ed., Wageningen: Agricultural University Wageningen.

Arce, A. and Marsden, T. (1993) 'The social construction of food: a research agenda,' *Economic Geography* 69 (3): 293–311.

Arce, A. and Mitra, S. (1991) 'Making development relevant: beyond the impasse in development studies,' Occasional Paper 7, Department of Sociology and Social Anthropology, Hull University.

Arce, A., Villarreal, M. and Vries, de P. (1994) 'The social construction of rural development: discourses, practices and power,' in *Rethinking Social Development: Theory, Research and Practice*, Booth, David, ed., London: Longman.

Asad, T. (1993) *Genealogies of Religion: Discipline and Reasons of Power in Christianity and Islam*, Baltimore and London: Johns Hopkins University Press.

Aubreville, A. (1938) *La Fôret Coloniale: Les fôrets de l'Afrique Occidentale Française*, Annales d'Academie des Sciences Coloniales IX edn Paris: Société d'Editions Geographiques, Maritimes et Coloniales.

——(1949) *Climats, fôrets et desertification de l'Afrique tropicale*, Paris: Société d'Edition de Geographie Maritime et Coloniale.

——(1962) 'Savanisation tropicale et glaciation quaternaire,' *Adansonia* II(1): 233–7.

Bacon, E. (1966) *Central Asians under Russian Rule: A Study in Culture Change*, Ithaca, New York: Cornell University Press.

Baker, H. (1753) *Employment for the Microscope (two parts)*, London, Pall Mall: Tully's Head.

Barth, F., ed. (1969) *Ethnic Groups and Boundaries*, Boston, Mass.: Universitetsforlaget and Little Brown.

——(1992) 'Towards greater naturalism in conceptualizing societies,' in *Conceptualizing Society*, A. Kuper, ed., London and New York: Routledge.

Basch, L., Glick, Schille and Szanton, Blanc (1994) *Nations Unbound: Transnational Projects, Post-Colonial Predicaments, and De-Territorialised Nation States*, Basel: Gordon and Breach.

Bastian, S. (1990) 'The political economy of ethnic violence in Sri Lanka: the July 1983 riot,' in *Mirrors of Violence: Communities, Riots and Survivors in South Asia*, Das Veena, ed., Delhi: Oxford University Press.

Baudrillard, J., Poster, M. (eds) and Maclean, M. (trans.) (1988) *The Masses: the Implosion of the Social in the Media: Selected Writings*, Oxford: Polity.

Baum, G.-H. and Weimer, H.-J. (1992) 'Participation et dévélopment socio-economique comme conditions préalables indispensables d'une implication active des populations riveraines dans la conservation de la fôret classée de Ziama,' Deutsche Forst-Consult/Neu-Isenburg/RFA/KfW.

Beck, U. (1992) *Risk Society: Towards a New Modernity*, London: Sage Publications.

Benda-Beckmann, von F. (1994) 'Good governance, law and social reality: problematic relationships,' *Knowledge and Politics* 7(3): 55–67.

Berger, D. (1997) 'Kausachum coca! The case of coca farmers in Bolivia: livelihood and resistance in the shadow of illegality,' unpublished MSc Thesis, Wageningen University.

Bhabha, H. K. (1994) *The Location of Culture*, London and New York: Routledge.

Binns, C. (1979) 'The changing face of power: revolution and accommodation in the development of the Soviet ceremonial system, Parts I and II,' *Man* 14 (4) and 15 (1): 585–606 and 170–87.

Blanes, J. (1983) *De Los Valles al Chapare: Estrategias Familiares en un Contexto de Cambios*, Cochabamba: CERES.

Biervliet, W. E. (1975) 'The hustler culture of young unemployed Surinamese', *Adaptation of Migrants from the Caribbean in the European and American Metropolis*, Amsterdam/Leiden: Cansa Publications.

Böhling, W. R. and Schloeter-Paredes, M-L., eds (1994) 'Aid in place of migration', Selected contributions to an ILO-UNHCR meeting. Geneva: ILO.

Booth, D. (1985) 'Marxism and development sociology: interpreting the impasse,' *World Development* 13(7): 761–87.

—— ed. (1994) *Rethinking Social Development: Theory, Research and Practice*, Essex: Longman Scientific & Technical.

Bouchet, B. (1991–2) 'Tribus d' autrefois, Kolkhozes d'aujourd'hui,' *Revue du Monde Musulman et de la Mediterranée*: 59–60, 55–69.

Bourdieu, P. (1984) *Distinction*, London: Routledge.

Bovill, E.-W. (1921) 'The encroachment of the Sahara on the Sudan,' *Journal of the African Society* 20: 171–85.

Bremmer, I. and Taras, R., eds (1993) *Nations and Politics in the Soviet Successor States*, Cambridge: Cambridge University Press.

Brokensha, D., Warren, D. M. and Werner, O., eds (1980) *Indigenous Knowledge Systems and Development*, New York: University Press of America.

Bromley, Yu (1974) 'The term ethnos and its definition,' in *Soviet Ethnology and Anthropology Today*, Yu Bromley, ed., The Hague and Paris: Mouton.

Brubaker, R. (1994) 'Nationhood and the national question in the Soviet Union and post-Soviet Eurasia: an institutionalist account,' *Theory and Society* 23: 47–8.

Budike, F. and Mungra, B. (1986) *Creolen en Hindostanen*, Houten: Unieboek.

Buiks, P. E. J. (1983) *Surinaamse jongeren op de Kruiskade, overleven in een etnische randgroep*, Deventer: Van Loghum Slaterus.

Caffé, D. (1987) Etniciteit en emancipatie, AWIC-Nieuwsbrief, jrg IV(1): 18–25.

Callon, M. and Law, J. (1995) 'Agency and the hybrid collectif,' *South Atlantic Quarterly* 94(2): 481–507.

Canelas, A. and Canelas, J. (1983) *Bolivia: Coca Cocaina*, Cochabamba, La Paz, Bolivia: Los Amigos del Libro.

Carley, P. M. (1989) 'The price of the plan: perceptions of cotton and health in Uzbekistan and Turkmenistan,' *Central Asia Survey* 8 (4): 1–38.

Carrere-d'Encausse, H. (1979) *Decline of an Empire: The Soviet Socialist Republics in Revolt*, New York: Newsweek Books.

Cartman, J. (1957) *Hinduism in Ceylon*, Colombo: Gunasena & Sons.

Chevalier, A. (1909) 'L'extension et la regression de la fôret vierge de l'Afrique tropicale,' Comptes Rendus des Séances de l'Academie des Sciences, Seance 30 Aout: 458–61.

——(1912) 'Rapport sur une mission scientifique dans l'ouest Africain (1908–1910),' Paris, 12 Janvier 1912, Missions Scientifiques.

Clay, R. S. (1924) 'Some developments of the Hooke Microscope,' *Journal of the Royal Microscopal Society*.

Cohen, A. (1985) *The Symbolic Construction of Community*, Chichester and London: Ellis Horwood Limited and Tavistock Publications.

——(1986) 'Of symbols and boundaries, or, does Ertie's greatcoat hold the key?,' in *Symbolising Boundaries: Identity and Diversity in British Cultures*, Anthony, Cohen ed., Manchester: Manchester University Press.

Colomy, P., ed. (1990) *Neofunctionalist Sociology*, Aldershot, Hants: Edward Elgar.

Comaroff, J. and Comaroff, J. (1993) *Modernity and its Malcontents: Ritual and Power in Post-Colonial Africa*, Chicago: University of Chicago Press.

——(1992) *Ethnography and the Historical Imagination*, Boulder, Col.: Westview Press.

Cooper, F. and Packard, R. eds (1997) *International Development and the Social Sciences: Essays on the History and Politics of Knowledge*, Berkeley, Los Angeles, London: University of California Press.

Corbridge, S. (1992) 'Discipline and punishment: the new right and the policing of the international crisis,' *Geoforum* 23 (3) August: 285–302.

Coronil, F. and Skurski, J. (1991) 'Dismembering and remembering the nation: the semantic of political violence in Venezuela,' *Comparative Studies Society and Culture* 33(2): 289–337.

Croll, E. and Parkin, D., eds (1992) *Bush-Base-Forest-Farm*, London and New York: Routledge.

Crush, J., ed. (1995) *Power of Development*, London: Routledge.

De Alwis, M. (1997) 'Motherhood as a space of protest,' in *Appropriating Gender: Women, the State and Politicized Religion in South Asia*, A. Basu and P. Jeffreys, eds, New York and London: Routledge.

De Certeau, M. (1984) *The Practice of Everyday Life*, Berkeley, Los Angeles and London: University of California Press.

Derrida, J. (1976) *Of Grammatology*, Baltimore: Johns Hopkins University Press.

Dilley, R. (1992) 'A general introduction to market ideology, imagery and discourse,' in *Contesting Markets: Analyses of Ideology, Discourse and Practice*, Roy, Dilley ed., Edinburgh: Edinburgh University Press.

Douglas, M. (1994) *Risk and Blame: Essays in Cultural Theory*, First edn, 1992, London: Routledge.

Dragadze, T. (1980) 'The place of ethnos theory in Soviet anthropology,' in *Soviet and Western Anthropology*, E. Gellner, ed., London: Duckworth.

——(1988) *Rural Families in Soviet Georgia: A Case Study in Ratcha Province*, London: Routledge.

Dunn, E. and Dunn, S. P. (1973) 'Ethnic intermarriage as an indicator of cultural convergence in Soviet Central Asia,' in *The Nationality Question in Soviet Central Asia*, Allworth, ed., New York and London: Praeger.

Edwards, M. (1994) 'Rethinking social development: the search for relevance,' in *Rethinking Social Development: Theory, Research and Practice*, D. Booth, ed., Essex: Longman.

Eickelman, D. E. (1993) 'The other orientalist crisis,' in *Russia's Muslim Frontier*, D. F. Eickelman, ed., Bloomington: Indiana University Press.

Eisenstadt, S. N. (1966) *Modernisation: Protest and Change*, New Jersey: Prentice Hall.

Ekanza, S.-P. (1981) 'Le Moronou à l' époche de l administrateur Marchand: aspects physiques et économiques,' *Annales de l'Université d'Abidjan*, Seri I, Histoire 9: 55–70.

Elias, N. (1939) *Uber den PozeB der Zivilisation: Soziogenetische und psychogenetische Untersuchungen*, Vol. 2, Basel: Haus zum Falken.

——(1983) *The Court Society*, Oxford and New York: Basil Blackwell and Pantheon Books.

——(1994) *The Civilizing Process*, Vol. 1, Oxford: Basil Blackwell.

——(1998) in *On Civilization, Power, and Knowledge: Selected Writings*, S. Mennell and J. Goudsblom, eds, Chicago and London: University Chicago Press.

Elwert, G. and Bierschenk, T. (1988) 'Aid and development (Special Issue),' *Sociologia Ruralis* XXVII 2–3: 100–16.

Engel, P. (1995) 'Facilitating innovation: an action-oriented approach and participatory methodology to improve innovative social practice in agriculture,' unpublished Ph.D. Dissertation, Wageningen Agricultural University.

Escobar, A. (1984) 'Discourse and power in development: Foucault and the relevance of his work to the Third World,' *Alternatives* 10(3): 377–400.

——(1995) *Encountering Development: The Making and Unmaking of the Third World*, Princeton: Princeton University Press.

Evans-Pritchard, E. (1937) *Witchcraft, Oracles and Magic among the Azande of the Anglo-Egyptian Sudan*, Oxford: Clarendon Press.

Evans-Pritchard, E. E. (1940) *The Nuer: A Description of the Modes of Livelihood and Political Institutions of a Nilotic People*, Oxford: Clarendon Press.

Fairbairn, H. (1914) 'The agricultural problems posed by sleeping sickness settlements,' *The East African Agricultural Journal* ix: 1–6.

——(1944) 'Sleeping sickness in Tanganyika,' Medical Pamphlet No.40, Government Printer, Tanganyika.

——(1948) 'Sleeping sickness in Tanganyika Territory: 1922–1946,' *Tropical Diseases Bulletin* 45(1): 1–17.

Fairhead, J. and Leach, M. (1994) 'Contested forests: modern conservation and historical land use in Guinea's Ziama reserve,' *African Affairs* 93: 481–512.

——(1995) 'False forest history, complicit social analysis: rethinking some West African environmental narratives,' *World Development* 23: 1023–36.

——(1996) *Misreading the African Landscape: Society and Ecology in a Forest-Savanna Mosaic*, African Studies Series ed., Cambridge and New York: Cambridge University Press.

——(forthcoming) *Forest of Statistics: Reframing Environmental History in West Africa*, London: Routledge.

Falla, R. (1983) Massacre de la Finca San Francisco, Huehuetenango, Guatemala. Documento IWGIA 1. Copenhagen: IWGIA.

Featherstone, M., ed. (1990) *Global Culture*. London, Newbury Park, New Delhi: Sage.

Feldman, A. (1991) *Formations of Violence. The Narrative of the Body and Political Terror in Northern Ireland*, Chicago: University of Chicago Press.

Ferguson, J. (1990) *The Anti-Politics Machine: Development, Depoliticization, and Bureaucratic Power in Lesotho*, Cambridge and New York: Cambridge University Press.

Fisher, E. (1997) 'What future for the Shamba la Bibi? Livelihoods and local resource use in a Tanzanian game reserve,' unpublished Ph.D. dissertation, University of Hull, England.

Flores, G. and Blandes, J. (1984) *Donde va el Chapare?* Cochabamba, Bolivia: Centro de Estudios de la Realidad Nacional.

Foggie, A. (1958) 'Forestry problems in the closed forest zone of Ghana,' *Journal of the West African Science Association* 3: 141–7.

Ford, J. (1971) *The Role of Trypanosomiasis in Africa Ecology: a Study of the Tsetse Fly Problem*, Oxford: Clarendon Press.

Foucault, M. (1972) *The Archaeology of Knowledge*, New York: Harper Colophon Books.

——(1974) *The Order of Things: an Archaeology of the Human Sciences*, First French edn 1966, English edn 1970, London: Tavistock.

——(1979) *Discipline and Punish: The Birth of the Prison*, New York: Vintage.

——(1980) *Power/Knowledge*, New York: Pantheon Books.

——(1991) 'On governability,' in *The Foucault Effect*, G. Burdell, C. Gorden and P. Miller, eds, London: Harvester Wheatsheaf, .

Fowerraker, J. (1981) *The Struggle for Land: a Political Economy of the Pioneer Frontier in Brazil from 1930 to the Present Day*, Vol. Cambridge Latin American Studies No. 39, Cambridge: Cambridge University Press.

Galjart, B. (1981) 'Counterdevelopment: a position paper,' *Community Development Journal* 16(2): 88–96.

Garcia Canclini, N. (1989) *Culturas Hibridas: Estrategias para entrar y salir de la modernidad*, Mexico, DF: Grijalbo.

Gardner, K. and Lewis, D. (1996) *Anthropology, Development and the Post-modern Challenge*, London, Chicago, Illinois: Pluto Press.

Geertz, C. (1974) 'From the natives' point of view': on the nature of anthropological understanding,' in *Culture Theory*, R. A. Shweder and R. A. LeVine eds, Cambridge: Cambridge University Press.

Gelder, P. van (1990a) 'Tussen leger-groen en oranje boven. De Surinaamse crisis en het gebrek aan ontwikkelingsperspectief,' *Internationale Spectator* 44(3): 184–93.

——(1990b) 'Het Surinaamse begrip 'hosselen',' *Migrantenstudies* 63(3): 31–43.

Gelder, P. van and Sijtsma, J. (1988) 'Horse, coke en kansen. Sociale risico's en kansen onder Surinaamse en Marokkaanse harddruggebruikers in Amsterdam,' Institute of Social Geography, University of Amsterdam, Two Parts, Amsterdam.

Gelder, P. van and van Wetering, I. (1991) 'Zielskracht, wraakgeesten en zombies. Vertogen rond drugverslaving bij Creools-Surinaamse migranten in Amsterdam,' *Medische Anthropologie* 3(1): 3–27.

Gellner, E., ed. (1980) *Soviet and Western Anthropology*, London: Duckworth.

Gemert, F. van (1988) 'Mazen en netwerken,' Instituut voor Sociale Geografie, Universiteit van Amsterdam, Amsterdam.

Geschiere, P. (1997) *The Modernity of Witchcraft: Politics and the Occult in Postcolonial Africa*, French 1995 edn: University of Virginia.

Giblin, J. L. (1990) 'Trypanosomiasis control in Africa history: an evaded issue?', *Journal of African History* 31: 59–80.

Giddens, A. (1985) *The Nation State and Violence*, Cambridge: Polity Press.

Giddens, A. (1991) *The Consequences of Modernity*, Cambridge: Polity Press.

Gleason, G. (1991) 'The political economy of dependency under socialism: the Asian republics in the USSR, studies in comparative communism,' *Comparative Communism* 24(4): 335–53.

——(1993) 'Uzbekistan: from statehood to nationhood?,' in Bremmer and Taras 1993.

Golinski, J. (1998) *Making Natural Knowledge: Constructivism and the History of Science*, Cambridge: Cambridge University Press.

Gray, H. C., ed. (1995) *The Cyborg Handbook*, New York and London: Routledge.

Grillo, D. R. and L. R., Stirrat, eds (1997) *Discourses of Development: Anthropological Perspectives*, Oxford and New York: Berg.

Grindle, M. (1980) *Politics and Policy Implementation in the Third World*, Princeton: Princeton University Press.

——(1986) *State and Countryside: Development Policy and Agrarian Politics in Latin America*, Baltimore: Johns Hopkins University Press.

Gross, J.-A. (1992) *Muslims in Central Asia: Expressions of Identity and Change*, Durham and London: Duke University Press.

Grove, R. (1995) *Green Imperialism: Colonial Expansion, Tropical Island Edens and the Origins of Environmentalism, 1600–1860*, Cambridge: Cambridge University Press.

Gunasinghe, N. (1984) 'The open economy and its impact on ethnic relations in Sri Lanka,' in *Sri Lanka's Ethnic Conflict: Myth, Realities and Perspectives*, Committee on Rational Development, ed., Delhi: Navrang.

——(1990) 'Changing social relations in the Kandyan countryside,' Social Scientists' Association, Colombo.

Gunesekere, T. (1994) 'Hierarchy and egalitarianism: caste, class and power,' in *Sinhalese Peasant Society*, T. Gunesekere, ed., London: Athlone Press.

Gupta, A. (1992) 'The song of the non-aligned world: transnational identities and the re-inscription of space in late capitalism,' *Current Anthropology* 7(1): 63–77.

Gupta, A. and Ferguson, J. (1992) 'Beyond culture,' *Cultural Anthropology* 7(1): 6–23.

Gwassa, G. C. K. (1967) 'History of Buha through Tunze papers,' Unpublished paper Dar es Salaam: University College.

Haakmat, A. (1978) 'Het druggebruik onder jeugdige Surinamers,' *Jeugd en Samenleving* 8(3): 123–35.

Habermas, J. (1983) 'Modernity – an incomplete project,' in *Postmodern Culture*, Foster, Hal, ed., London and Sydney: Pluto Press.

Hall (1987) 'Conservation of forest in Ghana,' *Universitas (University of Legon, Ghana)* 8: 33–42.

Handelman, D. (1985) 'On the dessitude of Kataragama,' in Man(13):157.

Handelman, D. and Leyton, E. eds (1978) *Bureaucracy and World View: Studies in the Logic of Official Interpretation*, St John's Newfoundland: Institute of Social Economic Research: University of Newfoundland.

Hannerz, U. (1992) *Cultural Complexity: Studies in the Social Organization of Meaning*, New York: Columbia University Press.

Hanson, F. A. (1993) *Testing, Testing: Social Consequences of the Examined Life*, Berkeley, Los Angeles, London: University of California Press.

Haraway, D. (1988) 'Situated knowledge: the science question in feminism and the privilege of partial perspective,' *Feminist Studies* 14(3): 575–600.

——(1991) *Simians, Cyborgs, and Women: The Reinvention of Nature*, London: Free Association Books.

Harvey, D. (1989) *The Condition of Post-modernity: An Enquiry into the Origins of Cultural Change*, Oxford: Basil Blackwell.

Harvey, P. (1996) *Hybrids of Modernity: Anthropology, the Nation State and the Universal Exhibition*, London and New York: Routledge.

Hasler, R. (1996) *Agriculture, Foraging and Wildlife Resource Use in Africa*, London: Kegan Paul International.

Hatchell, G. W. (1949) 'An early sleeping sickness settlement,' *Tanzania Notes and Records* (27): 60–4.

——(1956) 'Resettlement in areas reclaimed from Tsetse fly,' *Tanzania Notes and Records* (53): 243–24.

Headrick, R. (1994) *Colonialism, Health, and Illness in French Equatorial Africa, 1885–1935*, Daniel, R. Headrick, ed. , Atlanta, Georgia: African Studies Association Press.

Heelas, P. (1996) 'Introduction: detraditionalization and its rivals,' in *Detraditionalization: Critical Reflections on Authority and Identity*, P. Heelas, S. Lash and P. Morris, eds, Massachusetts and Oxford: Blackwell, 1–20.

Heimstädt, O. (1927) 'Stereoscopic vision with the microscope,' *Journal of the Royal Microscopal Society*.

Herskovits, M. J. and Herskovits, F. S. (1969) *Suriname Folk-lore*, First edn 1936, New York: AMS Press.

Hobart, M., ed. (1993) *An Anthropological Critique of Development: The Growth of Ignorance*, London: Routledge.

——(1995) 'Black umbrellas: the implication of mass media in development,' EIDOS Workshop on Globalization and Decivilization, Agricultural University of Wageningen, November.

Hoffmann, C. (1993) 'Impacto del Credito Agricola en la Unidad Productiva Familiar del Chapare: El Caso del credito condicionado a la erradicacion de cultivos de coca 1988–1991,' Reporte, Cochabamba, Bolivia.

——(1994) 'Diagnostico Socioeconomico del Area Colonizada del Parque Nacional Isiboro-Secure,' Reporte Unidad del Tropico, Equipo de Accion Regional, Cochabamba, Junio, Bolivia.

Hogg, J. (1858) *The Microscope: its History, Construction, and Application*, London: George Routledge & Co.

Hoolt, J. (1986) 'De Amsterdammers in zeven beVolkingscategorien,' Dept. Administrative Information, Municipality of Amsterdam, Amsterdam.

Hoppe, A. K. (1997) 'Lords of the fly: colonial visions and revisions of African sleeping sickness environments on Uganda Lake Victoria, 1906–1961,' *Africa* 67: 86–105.

Howaidi, F. (1991) 'The Quran and the Sultan: modern Islamic preoccupations (in Arabic),' Cairo, Dar Al-Shuruq.

——(1994) 'Bias in the Western Schools of Sociology (in Arabic),' in: *Manbar Al Sharq*, Vol. 2, June, Cairo, The Arab Islamic Studies Centre.

Humphrey, C. (1983) *Karl Marx Collective: Economy, Society and Religion in a Siberian Collective Farm*, Cambridge: Cambridge University Press.

Hutchinson, S. (1996) *Nuer Dilemmas: Coping with Money, War, and the State*, Berkeley, Los Angeles, London: University of California Press.

IBVR (1988) 'Vechten tegen de bierkaai? Wat kerkelijke werkgroepen kunnen doen aan alkohol en drugsproblemen,' Interkerkelijk Beraad Verslaving Rotterdam, Rotterdam.

Iliffe, J. (1979) *A Modern History of Tanganyika*, Cambridge: Cambridge University Press.

Ismail, Q. (1997) 'Nation, country, community: the logics of Sri Lankan Tamil nationalism,' in *Community/Gender/Violence: Essays on the Subaltern Condition*, Chatterjee Partha and Jeganathan Pradeep, eds, Delhi: Oxford University Press.

Jameson, F. (1984) 'Postmodernism, or the cultural logic of late capitalism,' *New Left Review* 146: 53–92.

Janssen, O. and Swierstra, K. (1982) 'Heroinegebruikers in Nederland, een typologie van leefstijlen,' Criminological Institute, Groningen.

Jayawardena, K. (1986) *Class and Ethnic Conflict in Sri Lanka*, Colombo: Centre for Social Analysis.

Jeganathan, P. (1997a) 'A space for violence: politics, anthropology and the location of a Sinhala practice of masculinity,' in *Community/Gender/Violence: Essays on the Subaltern Condition*, Chatterjee, P. and Jeganathan, P., eds, Delhi: Oxford University Press.

——(1997b) 'All the Lords men?: ethnicity, and inequality in the space of a riot,' in *Collective Identities, Nationalisms and Protest in Sri Lanka*, Second edn, Vol. 2, Roberts, M. , ed., Colombo: Marga Institute.

Jones, E. and Grupp, F. W. (1992) 'Modernization and traditionality in a multi-ethnic society: the Soviet case,' in *The Nationality Question in the Soviet Union*, G. Lapidus, ed., New York and London: Garland.

Jones, F. (1981) 'Kwakoe en Cristus Brussel,' unpublished Ph.D. dissertation, Theologische Faculteit, Amsterdam.

Jones, J. (1991) 'Farmer perspective on the economics and sociology of coca production in the Chapare,' IDA Working Paper No. 77, Institute for Development Anthropology, Clark University.

Kanapathipillai, V. (1990) 'July 1983: the survivor's experience,' in *Mirrors of Violence: Communities, Riots and Survivors in South Asia*, Das Veena, ed., Delhi: Oxford University Press.

——(1993) 'The survivor ten years after the riots,' paper presented at the International Workshop, International Centre for Ethnic Studies, Colombo.

Kapferer, B. (1988) *Legends of People, Myths of State: Violence, Intolerance, and Political Culture in Sri Lanka and Australia*, Washington: Smithsonian Institution Press.

Kearney, M. (1991) 'Borders and boundaries of state and self at the end of empire,' *Journal of Historical Sociology* 4(1): 52–74.

——(1996)*Reconceptualizing the Peasantry: Anthropology in Global Perspective*, Boulder, Col.: Westview Press.

King, A.-D. (1989) *The Bungalow: The Production of Global Culture*, London and New York: Routledge.

King, E. and Anthony, D. (1976) *Colonial Urban Development: Culture, Social Power and Environment*, London and New York: Routledge.

Kjekshus, H. (1977) *Ecological Control and Economic Development in East African History: The Case of Tanganyika 1850–1950*, London: Heinemann.

Klugh, A. B. (1922) 'The plunger-ipette – a new instrument for isolating minute organisms,' *Journal of the Royal Microscopal Society*.

Kumari, J. (1986) 'Ethnic and class conflicts in Sri Lanka,' Centre for Social Analysis, Colombo.

Laclau, E., ed. (1994) *The Making of Political Identities*, London: Verso.

Lane, C. (1981) *The Rites of Rulers*, Cambridge: Cambridge University Press.

Lanza, G. (1995) *La Coca Prohibida*, Cochabamba: Dutch Co-operation Service for Development and CEDIB.

Laserna, R. (1985) 'Coca cultivation, drug traffic and regional development in Cochabamba, Bolivia,' unpublished Ph.D. dissertation, University of California at Berkeley.

Latour, B. (1984) *Les Microbes, Guerre et Paix, followed by Irréductions*, Paris: Anne-Marie Metailie.

——(1987) *Science in Action: How to Follow Scientists and Engineers Through Society*, Cambridge, Mass.: Harvard University Press.

——(1988) *The Pasteurization of France*, A. Sheridan trans. and J. Law, ed., Harvard: Harvard University Press.

——(1993) *We Have Never Been Modern*, Cambridge, Mass.: Harvard University Press.

——(1994) 'On technical mediation-philosophy, sociology, geneaology,' *Common Knowledge* 34: 29–64.

Law, J. (1994) *Ordering Modernity*, Oxford, UK, Cambridge, USA: Blackwell.

Law, J. and Mol, A. (1994) 'Regions, network and fluids: anaemia and social topology,' *Social Studies of Science* 24: 641–71.

Leach, E. (1958) 'What the rioting in Ceylon means,' in *The Listener*, June: 926.

Leach, M. and Mearns, R., eds (1996) *The Lie of the Land: Challenging Received Wisdom on the African Environment*, The International African Institute in association with James Curry (Oxford) and Heinemann (Portsmouth).

Leach, M., Mearns, R. and Scoones, I. (1997) 'Environmental entitlements: a framework for understanding the institutional dynamics of environmental change,' IDS Discussion Paper 359. Brighton: Institute of Development Studies, The University of Sussex.

Lee, M. E. (1997) 'From enlightenment to chaos: toward non-modern social theory,' in *Chaos, Complexity, and Sociology: Myth, Models and Theories*, R. A. Eve, S. Horsfall, and M. E. Lee, eds, London and New Delhi: Sage Publications, 15–29.

Leeuwis, K. (1993) *Of Computers, Myths and Modelling: the Social Construction of Diversity, Knowledge, Information and Communication Technologies in Dutch Horticulture and Agricultural Extension*, Vol. 36, Wageningen: Wageningen Studies in Sociology.

Lefebre, H. (1991) *The Production of Space*, Second edn, Oxford: Blackwell Publishers.

Lefwich, A. (1994) 'Governance, the state and the politics of development,' *Development and Change* 25(2): 363–86.

Lenders, M. and Rhoer, M. van der (1984) *Mija God hoe ga ik doen? Creoolse allenstaande moeders in Amsterdam*, Amsterdam: SUA.

Leons, B. M. and Sanabria, H., eds (1997) *Coca, Cocaine, and the Bolivian Reality*, New York: State University of New York Press.

Lewis, W. A. (1954) 'Economic development with unlimited supplies of labour,' *Manchester School* 22: 139–91.

Ligeon, I. A. van Roekel, R. and Wijngaart, G. van de (1990) 'Surinaamse vrouwen en harddrugs,' Preventieproject Alcohol en Drugs van de Rijksuniversiteit, Utrecht.

Lockie, S. (1996) 'Sociocultural dynamics and the development of the landcare movement in Australia,' unpublished Ph.D. dissertation, Charles Stuart University.

Lohman, M., ed. (1992) *Coca-Cronologia: Bolivia 1986–1992, Cien Documentos sobre la Problematica de la Coca y la lucha contra las drogas*, Cochabamba: ILDIS-CEDIB.

Long, A. (1998) 'Contested values: livelihoods and wildlife management intervention in the Central Luangwa Valley of Zambia,' unpublished paper, London School of Economics.

Long, N. (1984) 'Creating space for change: a perspective on the sociology of development,' Inaugural lecture, Wageningen, Agricultural University.

——(1988) 'Sociological perspectives on agrarian development and state intervention,' in *Development Policies: Sociological Perspectives*, A. Hall and J. Midgley, eds, Manchester: Manchester University Press.

——(1989) 'Conclusion: theoretical reflections on actor, structure and interface,' in *Encounters at the Interface. A Perspective on Social Discontinuities in Rural Development*, Long, N. ed., Wageningen, The Netherlands: Wageningen Agricultural University.

——ed.(1989) *Encounters at the Interface: a Perspective on Social Discontinuities in Rural Development*, Wageningen: Wageningen Agricultural University.

——(1994) 'Globalization and localization: new challenges for rural research,' Paper presented in the Seminario Internacional: Nuevos Procesos Rurales en Mexico, Teorias, Estudios de Caso y Perspectivas, Taxco, Guerrero, Mexico.

——(1996) 'Globalization and localization: new challenges to rural research,' in *The Future of Anthropological Knowledge*, H. L., Moore, ed., London and New York: Routledge.

——(1997) 'Agency and constraint, perceptions and practice. a theoretical position,' in *Images and Realities of Rural Life: Wageningen Perspectives on Rural Transformation*, H. de Haan and N. Long, eds, Assen, The Netherlands: Van Gorcum.

Long, N. and Long, A., eds (1992) *Battlefields of Knowledge: The Interlocking of Theory and Practice in Social Research and Development*, London and New York: Routledge.

Long, N. and Ploeg, van der J. D. (1989) 'Demythologizing planned intervention: an actor perspective,' *Sociologia Ruralis* XXIX 3/4, 226–49.

——(1994) 'Heterogenity, actor and structure: towards a reconstitution of the concept of structure,' in *Rethinking Social Development: Theory, Research and Practice*, D. Booth, ed., London: Longman.

——(1995) 'Reflections on agency, ordering the future and planning,' in *In search of the middle ground: essays on the sociology of planned development*, G. E. Frerks and den J. H. B. Ouden, eds, Wageningen: Wageningen Agricultural University.

Long, S.A. (1998) 'The Skeletal Man', unpublished paper.

Lovell, W.-G. (1990) *Conquista y Cambio Cultural. La Sierra de los Cuchumatanes de Guatemala, 1500–1821*. Antigua, Guatemala: CIRMA.

Lubin, N. (1984) *Labour and Nationality in Soviet Central Asia*, London: Macmillan.

Lynch, M. (1993) *Scientific Practice and Ordinary Action: Ethnomethodology and Social Studies of Science*, Cambridge: Cambridge University Press.

——(1996) 'DeKanting agency: comments on Bruno Latour's "On Interobjectivity",' *Mind, Culture, and Activity* 3(4): 246–51.

Lynn, D. R. (1996) 'The double-writing of statecraft: exploring state responses to illegal immigration,' *Alternatives* 21: 171–89.

Lyons, M. (1992) *The Colonial Disease: A Social History of Sleeping Sickness in Northern Zaire, 1900–1940*. Cambridge: Cambridge University Press.

Lyotard, J.-F. (1986) *The Post-modern Condition: A Report on Knowledge*, Manchester: Manchester University Press.

——(1993) 'Defining the postmodern,' in *The Cultural Studies Reader*, S. During, ed., London and New York: Routledge.

Macdonell, D. (1986) *Theories of Discourse*, Oxford: Basil Blackwell.

Macintrye, E. (1993) *Rasanayagam's Last Riot*, Sydney: Wordlink.

MacKenzie, M. J. (1990) 'Experts and amateurs: Tsetse flies, Nagana and sleeping sickness in East and Central Africa,' in *Imperialism and the Natural World*, J. M. MacKenzie, ed., Manchester: Manchester University Press, 187–212.

Maclean, G. (1926) 'History of an outbreak of Rhodesian sleeping sickness in the Ufipa district of Tanganyika Territory with short notes on cases and treatment,' *Annals of Tropical Medicine and Parasitology* 20: 329–39.

——(1927, 1928, 1929) 'Tanganyika Territory annual medical and sanitary report,' *Tropical Diseases Bulletin*.

——(1929) 'The relationship between economic development and Rhodesian sleeping sickness in Tanganyika Territory,' *Annals of Tropical Medicine and Parasitology* xxiii: 37–46.

——(1930) 'Sleeping sickness measures in Tanganyika Territory,' *Kenya and East Africa Medical Journal* 3: 120–6.

——(1933) 'Memorandum on sleeping sickness measures,' Government Printer, Dar es Salaam.

Malashenko, A. V. (1993) 'Islam versus Communism: the experience of co-existence,' in *Russia's Muslim Frontiers*, D. Eickelman, ed., Bloomington: Indiana University Press.

Malkki, L. (1992) 'National Geographic: the rooting of people and the territorialization of national identity among scholars and refugees,' *Cultural Anthropology* 7(1): 24–44.

——(1997) *Purity and Exile: Violence, Memory, and National Cosmology Among Hutu Refugees in Tanzania*, Chicago: University of Chicago Press.

Mallock, A. (1923) 'Note on the resolving power and definitions of optical instruments,' *Journal of the Royal Microscopal Society*.

Mallon, F. (1992) *Peasant and Nation. The Making of Postcolonial Mexico and Peru*, Berkeley: University of California Press.

Manor, J. (1982) 'Self-inflicted wound: inter-communal violence in Ceylon, 1958,' in The Collected Seminar Papers of the Institute of Commonwealth Studies, Vol. 30: 15–26, University of London.

Marchand, M. and Parpart, J.-L., eds (1995) *Feminism, Postmodernism, Development*, London and New York: Routledge.

Marcus, G. (1995) 'Ethnography in/of the world system: the emergence of multi-sited ethnography,' *Annual Review of Anthropology* 24: 95–117.

Marcus, G. and Fischer, M. (1986) *Anthropology as Cultural Critique: An Experimental Moment in the Human Sciences*, Chicago and London: University of Chicago Press.

Marglin, F. and Marglin, S., eds (1990) *Dominating Knowledge: Development, Culture and Resistance*, Oxford: Clarendon Press.

Markham, R. H. and Babbedge, A. J. (1979) 'Soil and vegetation catenas on the forest-savanna boundary in Ghana,' *Biotropica* 11(3): 224–34.

Marsden, T. K. and Arce, A. (1993) 'Constructing quality: globalization, the state and food circuits,' Globalization of Agriculture and Food, Working Paper No. 1, University of Hull and Wageningen Agricultural University.

——(1995) 'Constructing quality: emerging food networks in the rural transition,' *Environment and Planning A* 27: 1261–79.

Mbilinyi, M. (1988) 'Runaway wives in colonial Tanganyika: forced labour and forced marriage in Rungwe District,' *International Journal of the Sociology of Law* 16: 1–29.

Mead, M. (1956) *New Lives for Old: Cultural Transformations-Manus 1918–1953*, London.

Menaut, J. C. and Cesar, J. (1979) 'Structure and primary productivity of Lamto savannas, Ivory Coast', *Ecology* 60(6): 1197–210.

Miller, D. (1987) *Material Culture and Mass Consumption*, Oxford: Blackwell.

Mitchell, J. C. (1957) *The Kalela Dance: Aspects of Social Relationships Among Urban Africans in Northern Rhodesia*, Manchester: Manchester University Press.

Mitja, D. and Puig, H. (1991) 'Essartage, culture itinerante et reconstitution de la végétation dans les jachères en savanne humide de Cote d'Ivoire (Booro-Borotu, Touba),' in *La jachère en Africa de l'Ouest*, C. Floret and G. Serpantie, eds, Montpellier: Orstom.

Moloney, A. (1887) *Sketch of the Forestry of West Africa, with Particular Reference to its Present Principal Commercial Products*, London: Sampson Low.

Mongbo, R. (1995) 'The appropriation and dismembering of development intervention: policy, discourse and practice in the field of rural development in Benin,' unpublished Ph.D. dissertation, Wageningen, Agricultural University, The Netherlands.

Moore, H. (1996) 'An introduction,' in *The Future of Anthropology Knowledge*, H. L. Moore, ed., London: Routledge.

Moore, S. F. (1973) 'Law and social change: the semi-autonomous social field as an appropriate subject of study,' *Law and Society Review* Summer: 719–46.

——(1986) *Social Facts and Fabrications: 'Customary' Law on Kilimanjaro, 1880–1980*, Cambridge: Cambridge University Press.

Morgan, G. (1986) *Images of Organisation*, Beverley Hills, Newbury Park, London, New Delhi: Sage.

Nash, J. (1979) *We Eat the Mine and the Mines Eat Us: Dependency and Exploitation in Bolivian Tin Mines*, New York: Columbia University Press.

Naumkin, V., ed. (1993) *State, Religion and Society in Central Asia*, Reading, New York: Ithaca Press.

Nordstrom, C. and Martin, J.-A., eds (1992) *The Paths to Domination, Resistance and Terror*, Berkeley and Los Angeles: University of California Press.

Obeyesekere, G. (1977) 'Social change and the deities: rise of the Kataragama cult in modern Sri Lanka,' *Man* 12: 377–96.

——(1978) 'The fire walkers of Kataragama: the rise of Bhakti religiosity in Buddhist Sri Lanka,' *Journal of Asian Studies* 37(3): 457–76.

Okali, C., Sumberg, J. and Farrington, J. (1994) *Farmer Participatory Research: Rhetoric and Reality*, Exeter: Intermediate Technology Publications (ODI).

Olcott, M. B. (1987) *The Kazakhs*, Stanford, Cal.: Hoover Institution Press.

Olivier de Sardan, J. P. (1995) *Anthropologie et developpement: essai en socio-anthropologie du changement social*, Paris: Karthala.

Oppenheimer, A. (1996) *Bordering on Chaos: Guerrillas, Stockbrokers, Politicians, and Mexico's Road to Prosperity*, New York and London: Little, Brown and Co.

Panarin, S. (1993) 'The Soviet East as a new subject of oriental studies,' in Naumkin.

Pandey, G. (1992) 'In defense of the fragment: writing about Hindu-Muslim riots in India today,' *Representations* 37: 48–60.

——(1994) 'The prose of otherness,' in *Essays in Honour of Ranajit Guha: Subaltern Studies*, D. Arnold and D. Hardiman, eds, Delhi: Oxford University Press.

Panditharatne, B. (1961) 'The functional zones of the Colombo City,' *The University of Ceylon Review* 19(2): 138–66.

Parkin, D. (1995) 'Latticed knowledge: eradication and dispersal of the unpalatable in Islam, medicine and anthropological theory,' in *Counterworks: Managing the Diversity of Knowledge*, R. Fardon, ed., London and New York: Routledge, 143–63.

Parsons, T. (1966) *Societies: Evolutionary and Comparative Perspectives*, Engelwood Cliffs, NJ: Prentice Hall.

Peet, R. and Watts, M. (1993) 'Introduction: development theory and environment in an age of market triumphalism,' *Economic Geography* 69(3): 227–54.

Ploeg, van der, J. D. (1992) 'The reconstitution of locality: technology and labour in modern agriculture,' in *Labour and Locality: Critical Perspectives on Rural Change*, Vol. 4, T. K. Marsden *et al.*, eds, London: Fulton.

Poivre, P. (1768) *Voyages d'un philosophe; ou observations sur les moeurs et les arts des peuples de l'Afrique, de l'Asie et de l'Amerique*, Paris: Yverdon.

Poliakov, S. (1992) *Everyday Islam: Religion and Tradition in Rural Central Asia*, New York and London: M.E. Sharpe.

——(1993) 'Modern Soviet Central Asian countryside: traditional forms of property in a quasi-industrial system,' in Naumkin.

Poole, D. (1988) 'Landscapes of power in a cattle-rustling culture of Southern Andean Peru,' *Dialectical Anthropology* 12: 367–98.

——(1994) *Unruly Order – Violence, Power and Cultural Identity in the High Provinces of Southern Peru*, Boulder, Col.: Westview Press.

Porter, A. W. (1929) 'The formation of images and the resolving power of microscopes,' *Journal of the Royal Microscopal Society*.

Pottier, J. (1993) *Practising Development: Social Science Perspectives*, London and New York: Routledge.

Pratt, J. S. (1921) 'Mr Fred Enoch's method of mounting heads of insects without pressure,' *Journal of the Royal Microscopal Society*.

Prescott, J. R. V. (1978) *Boundaries and Frontiers*, London: Croom Helm.

Qutb, S. (1981) *Milestones*, Delhi: Maktabi Markazi Islami.

Rahubadha, S. (1986) *Sura Asura*, Colombo: Kosala Prakashakay.

Ranger, T. O. (1969) 'The movement of ideas: 1850–1932,' in *A History of Tanganyika*, I. N. Kimambo and A. J. Temu, eds, Kenya: Heinemann.

Rapport (1973) 'Pastoraat en druggebruik,' Report by the Commission 'Pastorale handreiking druggebruikers en -verslaafden' of the 'National Protestants Centrum voor de Geestelijke Vol.ksgezondheid', Nijkerk: Callenbach.

Rasnake, R. and Painter, M. (1989) 'Rural development and crop substitution in Bolivia: USAID and the Chapare regional development project,' Institute for Development Anthropology and reports on work supported by Human Settlements and Natural Resources Systems Analysis (SARSA), Clark University.

Richard, A. I. (1939) *Land, Labour and Diet in Northern Rhodesia*, Oxford: Oxford University Press.

Richards, P. (1985) *Indigenous Agricultural Revolution*, London, Boulder and Colorado: Hutchinson and Westview Press.

——(1996) 'Agrarian creolization: the ethnobiology, history, culture and politics of West African rice' in *Redefining Nature: Ecology, Culture and Domestication,* R. Ellen and K. Fuki (eds), Oxford/Washington: Berg.

Riches, D. (1987) 'Power as a representational model,' in *Power and Knowledge: Anthropological and Sociological Approaches*, R. Fardon, ed., Edinburgh: Scottish Academic Press.

Rivera, A. (1991) *Que sabemos del Chapare?* Cochabamba: CERES-CLACSO.

Roberts, M. (1989) 'The two faces of the Port of Colombo,' in *Brides of the Sea: Port Cities of Asia from the 16th-20th Centuries*, Frank Broeze, ed., Honolulu: University of Hawaii Press.

——(1995) 'The agony and ecstasy of a pogrom: Southern Sri Lanka, July 1983,' in *Exploring Confrontations, Sri Lanka: Politics, Culture and History*, Geneva: Harwood Academic Publishers.

Robertson, R. (1990) 'Mapping the global condition: globalization as the central concept,' *Theory, Culture and Society* 7: 15–30.

Roe, E. (1995) 'Except-Africa: postscript to a special section on development narratives,' *World Development* 23(6): 1065–9.

Röling, N. G. (1994) 'Platforms for decision-making about ecosystems,' in *The Future of the Land: Mobilising and Integrating Knowledge for Land Use Options*, L. O. Fresco, L. Stroosnijder, J. Bouma and J. van Keulen, eds, London: John Wiley & Son, 385–93.

——(1996) 'Creating human platforms to manage natural resources: first results of a research programme,' in *Agricultural R&D at the Crossroads: Merging Systems Research and Social Actor Approaches*, A. Budelmann, ed., Amsterdam: Royal Tropical Institute.

Röling, N. G. and Wagenmakers, M. A. E. eds (1998) *Facilitating Sustainable Agriculture: Participatory Learning and Adaptive Management in Times of Environmental Uncertainty,* Cambridge: Cambridge University Press.

Ronsbo, H. (1997) 'State formation and property: reflections on the political technologies of space in Central America,' *Journal of Historical Sociology* 10(1).

Rosaldo, R. (1989) *Culture and Truth: the Remaking of Social Analysis,* Boston: Beacon Press.

Rostow, W. (1960) *The Stages of Economic Growth: A Non-Communist Manifesto,* Cambridge: Cambridge University Press.

Rouse, R. (1991) 'Mexican migration and the social space of post-modernism,' *Diaspora* 1(1): 8–23.

Roy, O. (1991–2) 'Ethnies et politiques en Asie Centrale,' *Revue du Monde Musulman et de la Mediterranée,* 59–60, 17–36.

——(1994) 'Violence ethnique et conflicts ideologiques en Asie centrale,' Dossiers du CEDEJ, Cairo, 113–20.

Rumer, B. Z. (1989) *Soviet Central Asia: A Tragic Experiment,* Boston: Unwin Hyman.

Sadomskaya, N. (1990) 'Soviet anthropology and contemporary rituals,' *Cahiers du Monde russe et sovietique* XXXI (2–3), 245–54.

Said, E. (1994) *Culture and Imperialism,* London: Vintage.

Salomon, L. M. and Engel, G. H. P. (1997) *Networking for Innovation: a Participatory Actor-Oriented Methodology,* Amsterdam: Royal Tropical Institute, The Netherlands.

Sansone, L. (1992) 'Scitteren in de schaduw,' Amsterdam: Het Spinhuis.

Sayer, D. (1991) *Capitalism & Modernity: An Excursus on Marx and Weber,* London and New York: Routledge.

Sayyid, B. (1994) 'Sign o'times: kaffirs and infidels fighting the Ninth Crusade,' in *The Making of Political Identities,* E. Laclau, ed., London: Verso.

Schaffer, B. (1984) 'Towards responsibility: public policy in concepts and practice,' in *Room for Manoeuvre: An Exploration of Public Policy in Agriculture and Rural Development,* E. Clay and B. Schaffer, eds, London: Heinemann Educational Books.

——(1985) 'Policy makers have their needs too: Irish itinerants and the culture of poverty,' in *Labelling in Development Policy,* G. Wood, ed., London: Sage.

Scheper-Hughes, N. (1992) *Death Without Weeping: the Violence of Everyday Life in Brazil,* Berkeley, Los Angeles, Oxford: University of California Press.

Schoonheym, P. (1980) 'Je geld of...je leven, een sociaal-economische benadering van de religie der Para-Creolen in Suriname,' Utrecht: Institute for Cultural Anthropology, ICAU-mededelingen.

Schoute, S. (1994) 'Cultivating illegality: the case of coca in Bolivia,' unpublished MSc dissertation, Wageningen University, The Netherlands.

Schuurman, J. F., ed. (1993) *Beyond The Impasse: New Directions in Development Theory,* London and New Jersey: Zed Books.

Scoones, I. and Thompson, J. (1992) 'Beyond farmers first: rural people's knowledge, agricultural research and extension practice: towards a theoretical framework,' Overview Paper prepared for IIED/IDS Beyond Farmers First: Rural People's Knowledge Agricultural Research and Extension Practice Workshop, Institute of Development Studies, University of Sussex, 27–9 October.

Scott, J. C. (1985) *Weapons of the Weak: Everyday Forms of Peasant Resistance,* New Haven, Conn.: Yale University Press.

Seur, H. (1992) 'Sowing the good seed: the interweaving of agricultural change, gender relations and religion in Serenje district, Zambia,' unpublished Ph.D. dissertation, Wageningen Agricultural University.

Seymour, G. L. (1860) 'The journal of the journey of George L. Seymour to the interior of Liberia 1858,' *New York Colonization Journal*: 105, 108, 109, 111, 112.

Shahrani, N. (1993) 'Soviet Central Asia and the challenge of the Soviet legacy,' *Central Asia Survey* 12(2): 123–35.

Shanin, T. (1989) 'Ethnicity in the Soviet Union: analytical perspectives and political strategies,' *Comparative Studies in Society and History* 31(3): 409–24.

Shapiro, M. (1996) 'Moral geographies and the ethics of post-sovereignty,' in *Perspectives on Third World Sovereignty. The Postmodern Paradox*, M.-E. Denham and M.-O. Lombardi, eds, Basingstoke and London: Macmillan Press.

Shaw, R. and Stewart, C. (1994) 'Introduction: problematizing syncretism,' in *Syncretism/Anti-Syncretism*, C. Stewart and R. Shaw, eds, London: Routledge.

Shore, C. and Wright, S., eds (1997) *Anthropology of Policy: Critical Perspectives on Governance and Power*, London and New York: Routledge.

Sider, G. (1993) *Lumbee Indian Histories: Race, Ethnicity and Indian Identity in Southern United States*, New York: Cambridge University Press.

——(1994) 'Identity as history: ethnohistory, ethnogenesis and ethnocide in the south eastern United States,' *Identities* 1(1): 109–22.

Silver, B. (1992) 'Social mobilization and the Russification of Soviet nationalities,' in *The Nationality Question in the Soviet Union*, G. Lapidus, ed., New York and London: Garland.

Skalnik, P. (1990) 'Soviet ethnografiia and the national(ities) question,' *Cahiers du Monde russe et sovietique* XXXI(2): 183–92.

Skar, S. L. (1994) *Lives Together – Worlds Apart: Quechua Colonization in Jungle and City*, Oslo: Scandinavian University Press.

Sklair, L. (1991) *Sociology of the Global System*, New York and London: Harvester Wheatsheaf.

Smart, B. (1992) *Modern Conditions, Postmodern Controversies*, London and New York: Routledge.

Smiles, J. (1924) 'The correction of dark-ground illuminators,' *Journal of the Royal Microscopal Society*.

Smith, F. G. (1994) *Three Cells of Honeycomb*, Australia: Format Print Productions (private publication).

Smith, G., ed. (1993) *The Nationalities Question in the Post-Soviet States*, London: Longman.

Smith, W. (1977) *The Fiesta System and Economic Change*, New York: Columbia University Press.

Snesarev, G. P. (1974) 'On some causes of the persistence of religio–customary survivals among the Khorezm Uzbeks,' in *Introduction to Soviet Ethnography*, S. P. Dunn and E. Dunn, eds, Berkeley, Cal.: Highgate Road Social Science Research Station.

Spencer, J. (1990) 'Collective violence and everyday practice in Sri Lanka,' *Modern Asian Studies* 24 (3).

Spichiger, R. and Blanc-Pamard, C. (1973) 'Recherches sur le contact fôret-savane en Cote d'Ivoire: étude du recru forestier sur des parcelles cultivées en lisière d'un ilot forestier dans le sud du pays baoule,' *Candolleas* 28: 21–37.

Spichiger, R. and Lassailly, V. (1981) 'Recherches sur le contact fôret-savane en Cote d'Ivoire: note sur l' evolution de la végétation dans la région de Beoumi (Cote d'Ivoire centrale),' *Candolleas* 36: 145–53.

Spoor, M. (1993) 'Transition to market economies in former Soviet Central Asia: dependency, cotton and water,' *The European Journal of Development Research* 5(2): 142–58.

Starn, O. (1995) 'To revolt against the revolution: war and resistance in Peru's Andes,' *Cultural Anthropology* 10(4): 547–80.

Stebbing, E. P. (1935) 'The encroaching Sahara: the threat to the West African Colonies,' *Geographical Journal* 85: 506–24.

Stephen, H. J. (1983) 'Winti,' Karnak, Amsterdam.

Stepputat, F. (1994) 'Repatriation and the politics of space: the case of the Mayan diaspora and return movement,' *Journal of Refugees Studies* 7/2–3, 175–85.

——(1996) 'Politics of displacement in Guatemala,' submitted to the *Journal of Historical Sociology*.

Stirrat, L. R. (1992) 'Good governance and the market,' in *Contesting Markets: Analyses of Ideology, Discourse and Practice*, Roy, Dilley, ed., Edinburgh: Edinburgh University Press.

Stoll, D. (1993) *Between Two Armies in the Ixil Towns of Guatemala*, New York: Columbia University Press.

Strathern, M. (1991) *Partial Connections*, Maryland, Balt.: Rowman & Littlefield Publishers, Inc.

Stratton, J. (1996) 'Serial killing and the transformation of the social,' *Theory, Culture and Society* 13: 77–98.

Stump, D. M. (1921) 'An application of polarised light to resolution with the compound microscope,' *Journal of the Royal Microscopal Society*.

Suarez, L. (1993) 'Narcotrafico y Subdesarrollo en America Latina y El Caribe: Algunas Reflexiones,' in *Economia Politica de las Drogas: Lecturas Latinoamericanas*, R. Laserna, ed., Cochabamba, Bolivia: CERES-CLACSO.

Suny, G. (1993) *The Revenge of the Past*, Stanford, Cal. : Stanford University Press.

Swierstra, K. O., Janssen, O. and Janseen, J. H. (1986) 'Heroinegebruikers in Nederland, deel II: De reproductie van het heroinegebruik onder nieuwe lichtingen,' Criminological Institute, Groningen.

Swynnerton, C. F. M. (1923–1924) 'A critical summary of the preliminary observation on the sleeping sickness outbreak near Mwanza,' *Transactions of the Royal Society of Tropical Medicine and Hygiene* xviv: 142–50.

——(1924–1925) 'An experiment in control of Tsetse flies at Shinyanga, Tanganyika Territory,' *Bulletin of Entomological Research* xv: 313–37.

Tambiah, S. (1986) *Ethnic Fratricide and the Dismantling of Democracy in Sri Lanka*, Chicago: University of Chicago Press.

Taussig, M. (1980) *The Devil and Commodity Fetishism in South America*, North Carolina: University of North Carolina Press.

——(1987) *Shamanism, Colonialism, and the Wild Man: A Study in Terror and Healing*, Chicago and London: University of Chicago Press.

——(1992) 'Terror as usual: Walter Benjamin's theory of history as state of siege,' in *The Nervous System*, London & New York: Routledge.

——(1995) 'The sun gives without receiving: an old story,' *Comparative Studies in Society and History*, 368–98.

Tett, G. (1994) 'Guardians of faith: women in Soviet Tajikistan,' in *Muslim Women's Choices*, C. El-Solh and J. Marbro, eds, London: Berg.

Tohidi, N. (1995) 'Soviet in public, Azeri in private: gender, Islam and nationalism in Soviet and post-Soviet Azarbaijan,' Working Papers in International Studies, I-95–99, Hoover Institution.

Torres, G. (1994) 'The force of irony: studying the everyday life of tomato workers in Western Mexico,' unpublished Ph.D. dissertation, Wageningen Agricultural University.

——(1997) *The Force of Irony: Power in the Everyday Life of Mexican Tomato Workers*, Oxford and New York: Berg.

Turner, V. W. (1957) *Schism and Continuity in an African Society. A Study of Ndembu Village Life*, Manchester: Manchester University Press.

——(1974) *Dramas, Fields and Metaphors: Symbolic Action in Human Society*, Ithaca and London: Cornell University Press.

Valentine, D. (1992) 'The nation in Sri Lankan Tamil gathering in Britain,' *Pravada* 2(6): 12–7.

Vandergeest, P. (1988) 'Commercialization and commoditization: a dialogue between perspectives,' *Sociologia Ruralis* XXVIII(1): 7–29.

Vasquez, L. (1989) 'La Nueva Estrategia Nacional,' en Coca: Hacia Una Estrategia Nacional, Comision de Narcoticos y Farmacodependencia, reporte al Honorable Senado Nacional, ILDIS-Senado, 65–88, La Paz-Bolivia.

Vaughan, M. (1991) *Curing Their Ills: Colonial Power and African Illness*, Oxford: Polity Press.

Veena, D. (1990) 'Our work to cry, your work to listen,' in *Mirrors of Violence: Communities, Riots and Survivors in South Asia*, Vol. D. Veena, Delhi: Oxford University Press.

——(1995) *Critical Events: An Anthropological Perspective on Contemporary India*, Delhi: Oxford University Press.

Verhagen, E. (1987) 'Van Bijlmermeerpolder tot Amsterdam Zuidoost,' SDU, Den Haag.

Verschoor, G. M. (1997) 'Tacos, Tiendas and Mezcal: an actor-network perspective on small-scale entrepreneurial projects in Western Mexico,' unpublished Ph.D. dissertation, Wageningen Agricultural University.

Vigne, C. (1937) 'Letter to editor,' *Empire Forestry Journal* 16: 93–4.

Vijfhuizen, C. (1998) 'The people you live with: gender identities and social practices, beliefs and power in the livelihoods of Ndau women and men in a village with an irrigation scheme in Zimbabwe,' unpublished Ph.D. dissertation, University of Wageningen.

Vittachi, T. (1958) *Emergency 58: The Story of the Ceylon Race Riots*, London: Andre Deutsch.

Vries, P. de (1992) 'Unruly clients: a case study of how bureaucrats try and fail to transform gatekeepers, communists and preachers into ideal beneficiaries,' unpublished Ph.D. dissertation, Wageningen Agricultural University.

——(1997) *Unruly Clients in the Atlantic Zone of Costa Rica: A Study of How Bureaucrats Try and Fail to Transform Gatekeepers, Communists and Preachers into Ideal Beneficiaries*, Vol.78, Amsterdam: CEDLA.

Wagner, M. (1996) 'Environment, community and history: nature in the mind,' in *Custodians of the Land*, G. Maddox, J. Giblin, and Kimambo, eds, London: James Currey, 175–99.

Wallman, S. and Associates (1982) *Living in South London: Perspectives on Battersea 1871–1981*, London: Gower/London School of Economics.

Walters, J. (1995) 'Multi-religion on the bus: beyond 'influence' and 'syncretism' in the study of religious meetings,' in *Unmaking the Nation: The Politics of Identity and History in Modern Sri Lanka*, P. Jeganathan and Q. Ismail, eds, Colombo: Social Scientists' Association.

Warren, K.-B. (1978) *The Symbolism of Subordination. Indian Identity in a Guatemalan Town*, Austin and London: University of Texas Press.

—— ed. (1993) *The Violence Within. Cultural and Political Opposition in Divided Nations*, Boulder and San Francisco: Westview Press.

——(1993(b)) 'Interpreting la violencia in Guatemala: shapes of Mayan silence and resistance,' manuscript.

Warren, M., Slikkerveer, and Brokensha, D., eds (1995) *The Cultural Dimension of Development: Indigenous Knowledge Systems*, Exeter: Intermediate Technology Publications.

Waters, M. (1995) *Globalization*, London and New York: Routledge.

Weiner, M. (1993) *International Migration and Security*, Boulder, Col.: Westview Press.

Werbner, P. (1997) 'Introduction: the dialectics of cultural hybridity,' in *Debating Cultural Hybridity: Multi-Cultural Identities and the Politics of Anti-Racism*, P. Werbner and T. Modood, eds, London and New Jersey: Zed Books.

Wertheim, W. (1965) 'Society as a composite of conflicting value systems,' in *East-West Parallels: Sociological Approaches to Modern Asia*, First edn 1964, Chicago: Quadrangle Books.

Wetering, W. van (1987) 'Informal supportive networks: quasi-kin groups, religion and social order among Suriname Creoles in the Netherlands,' *The Netherlands Journal of Sociology* 23(2): 92–101.

——(1988) 'Ritual laundering of black money among Surinamese Creoles in the Netherlands,' in *Religion and Development: Towards an Integrated Approach*, P. Quarles van Ufford and M. Schoffeleers, eds, Amsterdam: Free University Press.

——(1995) 'The transformation of slave experience: self and danger in the rituals of Creole migrant women in the Netherlands,' in *Slave Cultures and the Cultures of Slavery*, S. Palmie ed., Knoxville: Tennessee University Press.

Whatmore, S. and Thorne, L. (1997) 'Nourishing networks: alternative geographies of food,' in *Globalising Food: Agrarian Questions and Global Restructuring*, D. Goodman and M. Watts, eds, London and New York: Routledge.

White, L. (1993a) 'Cars out of place: vampires, technology, and labour in East and Central Africa,' *Representations* 43(27): 27–50.

——(1993b) 'Vampire priests of Central Africa: or African debates about labour and religion in colonial Northern Zambia,' *Comparative Studies in Society and History* 35: 746–72.

——(1995) 'Tsetse visions: narratives of blood and bugs in colonial northern Rhodesia 1931–1939,' *Journal of African History* 36: 219–45.

Wikan, U. (1990) *Managing Turbulent Hearts: A Balinese Formula for Living*, Chicago and London: University of Chicago Press.

Willans, R. H. K. (1909) 'The Konnoh people', *Journal of the Africa Society* 8: 130–44, 288–95.

Willis, R. G. (1968) 'Kamcape: an anti-sorcery movement in South-West Tanzania,' *Africa* xxxviii(1): 1–15.

Wood, G., ed. (1985) *Labelling in Development Policy: Essays in Honour of Bernard Schaffer*, London: Sage.

Wooding, Ch. J. (1973) 'Winti: een Afro-amerikaanse godsdienst in Suriname,' Meppel: Krips Reproductions.

Woods, D. (1992) *The Power of Maps*, London: Routledge.

Worboys, M. (1994) 'The comparative history of sleeping sickness in East and Central Africa 1900–1914,' *History of Science* 32: 89–102.

Wright, M. (1988) 'Policy community, policy network and comparative industrial policies,' *Political Studies* 36(4).

Young, R. (1990) *White Mythologies*, London: Routledge.

Zaag, P. van der (1992) *Chicanery at the Canal; Changing Practice in Irrigation Management in Western Mexico*, Amsterdam: CEDLA.

Zaslavsky, V. (1993) 'Success and collapse: traditional Soviet nationality policy,' in Bremmer and Taras 1993.

Index

Abdel Metaal, S. 70, 71
actor-network theory 28n5, 30n14
actor-oriented approach 8, 21, 23–7,
    31n18, 189–200; centrality of actors'
    perceptions and representations
    189–91; collective actors 194–6;
    constraints and boundaries 191–2;
    livelihoods, networks and social
    interface 196–8; social drama and
    critical event analysis 193–4;
    transnational migration 198–200
actors: collective 194–6; and counter-
    development 19–20; and language of
    development 32, 38, 48–50; network
    of interconnections in construction of
    modernity in Bolivia 172–8, 181–3; *see
    also* actor-oriented approach
Adams, R. 195
Adjanohoun, E. 108
Africa: environmental change 25,
    100–11; societies 11; *see also*
    Cameroon; Tanganyika; Tanzania
Afro-Surinamese culture 141–58
agency 172–8, 183
agrarian movements, Latin America
    187–8
agriculture, Bolivia 43–8, 162–78
agro-export production 13, 15–16, 40–3,
    178; *see also* agriculture
Ahmed, D. 143
Akodrey 141
Al-Afghani 70
Albrow, M. 185
Alem, J. 173
Al-Ghanoushi, R. 69–70, 71
Alonso, Ana Maria 130, 138, 139
Al-Qaradawi, Y. 69, 71

alternative development 187; Bolivia 43–4,
    45–6, 168, 170–2, 178, 180
Althusser, L. 142
Al-Turabi, H. 70, 71
ambiguity 3, 7, 8, 21, 32
ambivalence 3, 21
Amsterdam, drug addiction among
    Surinamese Creole migrants 141–58
ancestral spirits 150, 156
Anderson, Benedict 57, 199
Anderson, Benjamin 108
anthropology: contribution to new
    evolving agendas for development
    research 13, 21–7; critical review of
    literature on modernity 1–31;
    ethnographic repositioning 7–9; and
    language of development 47–8, 49;
    role in exploring local/global
    transformations 184–201; and social
    mutation 182–3; Soviet ethnography
    53, 55–60
anti-witchcraft movements, Tanganyika
    75, 87–92, 94
Appadurai, A. 15, 52, 127, 199
Apthorpe, R. 24, 50
Arce, Alberto 13, 25, 35, 39, 50, 187
arenas *see* social arenas
Argentina, migrant labour 163–4, 165
Aubreville, A. 104, 108
Azerbaijan 54, 62

Bacon, E. 60
bakru (sprite from the wilds) 151
Bali 11
Barth, F. 21
Basch, L. 199
Baudrillard, J. 100, 109